D0457281

Advance Praise for *The New HR Analytics*

"Dr. Jac Fitz-enz and his associates have done it again! As the architect of the human capital movement, he has now defined and shaped predictive analytics that define more clearly how today's metrics can predict and lead to tomorrow's successes. The book both synthesizes and extends the measurement movement with outstanding essays where ideas are turned into action. HCM:21 will be the standard for how to go about scanning, planning, producing, and predicting organization processes in a predictive and rigorous way. Those of us who care about the HR profession are grateful that people like Fitz-enz continue to apply their knowledge to problems we care about."

> —Dave Ulrich, Professor, Ross School of Business, University of Michigan, and Partner, The RBL Group

"Dr. Jac Fitz-enz is always out on the leading edge of HR thought leaders. He's done it again with *The New HR Analytics*. Anybody who aspires to advance an HR or total rewards career in the next decade should read this book!"

> —Anne Ruddy, CCP, CPCU, President, WorldatWork

"The concept of managing people as an asset has been around for decades, but until now no one has been able to translate that compelling idea into real-world practice. Both HR professionals and line managers struggle all the time with 'people management' issues. Balancing the realities of getting today's work done with the very real need to anticipate future needs has eluded managers since the beginning of time.

"This book changes all that. Dr. Jac Fitz-enz and an impressive group of practitioners and thought leaders have pulled together both a comprehensive Human Capital Management framework and a very practical set of action-oriented recommendations that together enable you to leverage the one thing that makes your organization truly unique: your human talent. HCM:21 is by far the most effective approach to strategic human resource management and human capital planning I've seen anywhere."

> —James P. Ware, Executive Producer, Work Design Collaborative LLC

"In a world where business intelligence as applied to human capital is on the verge of becoming as oxymoronic as 'military intelligence,' Dr. Jac Fitz-enz continues to provide the thought leadership businesses need now more than ever when it comes to human capital management. Too many businesses today confuse correlation with causation, and Dr. Jac's four-phase human capital management system is a true antidote and the injection of innovation that businesses need to apply. As Dr. Jac succinctly puts it, there is nothing more powerful for a business than 'managing tomorrow, today' by properly applying analytics to its human capital."

> —Shyam Patel, COO, People Report

"Once again, Dr. Jac has led the way with critical research that enables organizations to create sustainable value through people."

> —Kent Barnett, CEO, KnowledgeAdvisors

"Once again, Jac Fitz-enz, aka Dr. Jac, has brought enlightenment to the enlightened. He's evolved his body of work and the enormity of understanding of translating data, to information, to knowledge, to success.

"Jac's latest endeavor has placed the question squarely before all decision makers, 'How do we know what we know before we know it?'

"It's part analytics, it's part experience, it's part intuition, it's part good luck, and it's all commitment. Commitment to demonstrating to decision makers throughout the organization that a thoughtful process, not usually linear in nature, always dynamic at the core, and entirely logical, can empower all of us to answer the questions, with insight and meaning, in a language that can be understood. Jac's life's passion has been to translate the simple but imminently elegant tools into a language not only that we can understand, but also that we can execute from.

"Predictive analytics is what we've been waiting for because it's the next level of understanding in Dr. Jac's long and evolving journey to empower us with the core tools, terminology, and logic to make a difference. The journey lives on!"
> —Ed Kleinert, Administrator, HR Information Technology, Memorial Sloan-Kettering Cancer Center

"In *The New HR Analytics*, Jac Fitz-enz extends his decades of leadership in human capital measurement. It is a call to action that should inspire leaders to rethink their assumptions and improve their decisions."
> —John Boudreau, Professor, Management & Organization, and Research Director, Center for Effective Organizations, University of Southern California

"*The New HR Analytics* is the breakthrough people management playbook that will transform how CEOs manage their human capital and their human resource function going forward. The HCM:21 model introduces leading-edge predictive techniques that maximize return on human capital investments while energizing and engaging employees. Organizations that ignore *The New HR Analytics* and Dr. Jac's HCM:21 system for predictive HR management are doomed to fail in the resurging economy. Hucametrics has reached the tipping point."
> —Ken Scarlett, President, Scarlett Surveys International

"Everybody knows that Jac Fitz-enz is acknowledged as the father of human capital strategic analysis and human performance benchmarking. For me he is also much more. He is a powerful lighthouse who lights the long way from the old human resources department to the new human capital strategic partner. A book by Dr. Jac is always an important milestone in human capital history."
> —Luis María Cravino, Cofounder and Codirector, AO Consulting S.A., Buenos Aires

"Dr. Jac is the pinnacle of vision and leadership in human capital analytics. This book paves the way for the next wave in the field."
> —Kirk Smith, Founder, W. Kirk Smith & Associates

"Dr. Jac's landmark book contains leading-edge human capital thinking and tools that will enable organizations to maximize operational impact by optimizing their investment in human capital."
> —John Matone, Vice President, AlignMark

THE NEW

HR
ANALYTICS

Predicting the Economic Value of
Your Company's
Human Capital Investments

Jac Fitz-enz

AMACOM

American Management Association
New York • Atlanta • Brussels • Chicago • Mexico City • San Francisco
Shanghai • Tokyo • Toronto • Washington, D.C.

WITHDRAWN

Bulk discounts available. For details visit:
www.amacombooks.org/go/specialsales
Or contact special sales:
Phone: 800-250-5308
E-mail: specialsls@amanet.org
View all the AMACOM titles at: www.amacombooks.org

This publication is designed to provide accurate and authoritative information in regard to the subject matter covered. It is sold with the understanding that the publisher is not engaged in rendering legal, accounting, or other professional service. If legal advice or other expert assistance is required, the services of a competent professional person should be sought.

Library of Congress Cataloging-in-Publication Data

Fitz-enz, Jac.
    The new HR analytics : predicting the economic value of your company's human capital investments / Jac Fitz-enz.
        p. cm.
    Includes index.
    ISBN-13: 978-0-8144-1643-3 (hbk.)
    ISBN-10: 0-8144-1643-8 (hbk.)
    1. Personnel management.   2. Human capital—Management.   3. Human capital—Cost effectiveness.   I. Title.
    HF5549.F557   2010
    658.3—dc22
                                                            2009053581

© 2010 Jac Fitz-enz
All rights reserved.
Printed in the United States of America.

This publication may not be reproduced, stored in a retrieval system, or transmitted in whole or in part, in any form or by any means, electronic, mechanical, photocopying, recording, or otherwise, without the prior written permission of AMACOM, a division of American Management Association, 1601 Broadway, New York, NY 10019.

About AMA
American Management Association (www.amanet.org) is a world leader in talent development, advancing the skills of individuals to drive business success. Our mission is to support the goals of individuals and organizations through a complete range of products and services, including classroom and virtual seminars, webcasts, webinars, podcasts, conferences, corporate and government solutions, business books, and research. AMA's approach to improving performance combines experiential learning—learning through doing—with opportunities for ongoing professional growth at every step of one's career journey.

Printing number

10 9 8 7 6 5 4 3 2 1

To the two Lauras,
my wife and my mother-in-law,
who take such very good care of me.

Contents

Preface

This book was twenty-five years in the writing. It started in 1984, with the publication of my *How to Measure Human Resources Management;* it was augmented with *Human Value Management* six years later; and then the concept was updated ten years ago in *The ROI of Human Capital.* Those books chronicle the development of metrics in human resources from its inception in the 1970s to today. They have passed the test of time with second and third editions, and two were honored with Book of the Year Awards from the Society for Human Resource Management.

Now, *The New HR Analytics* is both the product of these endeavors and the look into the future. Although this book talks to human resources managers, it deals with the broader issue of human capital management processes. Hence, it is as applicable to the work of line managers as to that of the human resources department. Anyone who manages people can find value in the model we present here and the case studies that are offered in support of that model.

HR as an Expense

Having come into HR in 1969 from ten years in line jobs, I could not understand why any company would create a function that was only an expense. But then, too, at that time line management itself was not so sophisticated. Management models of the day were a patchwork quilt of fads that came and went, sometimes to reappear later. Others flashed across the sky like a meteor and burned out when they hit the atmosphere of managerial impatience. During that period, HR was simply a place where you put people "who couldn't do any harm," as a manager in my company said at the time.

I quickly discovered the problem behind the perception. It had two parts. One part was that HR people actually believed and accepted the idea that they were an expense center and nothing more. To be sure, there were a few who fought that perception, but they were overwhelmed by the accounting-driven belief system of the time. The second part of the problem was that HR didn't know, and never talked about, the value they were generating because they couldn't—they had no language for it. All their terms were qualitative, subjective, and equivocal. Anecdotes were their only way of responding when management asked for evidence of the value added by HR's services.

"How is employee morale?"

"It's good!"

"How good?"

"Very good."

Could you run any other function with such performance indicators? It is enough to make one despair.

The Introduction of Metrics

The solution was obvious. We in HR needed to learn to speak in *quantitative*, objective terms, using numbers to express our activity and value added. Business uses numbers to explain itself. Sales, operating expenses, time cycles, and production volumes are principal indices that express business activity. In the 1970s, productivity was the key issue. In the 1980s, the quality movement emphasized process quality as a competitive advantage. Both relied on numbers to express degrees of change.

At the time, I asked the HR director of a major corporation if he was involved in these initiatives. He answered that they were not human resources management issues. Here were the major initiatives of the day, and he could not see what they had to do with people. Is it any wonder that people write about nuking the HR function?

During the 1970s, we in HR began to experiment with simple cost, time, and quantity metrics to show that HR was at least managing expense and generating something of value. In the beginning it was largely a defensive maneuver. But by the 1980s, we were able to show that we were indeed adding measureable value. In 1984, I wrote the first book mentioned earlier. In 1985, at my consulting company, the Saratoga Institute, we published the first national benchmarks, and this led to publication of *Human Value Management*, which was a marketing model applied to the HR function. By 2000, we had advanced the methodology to a point where we were talking about return on investment. Basically, we shifted the paradigm from that of running the HR department to that of managing human capital in the organization. At that point we were still using primarily standard arithmetic functions. Later in the decade we began to apply simple statistical tools, and this opened up the era of human capital analytics—which brings us to today.

The Era of Analytics

We are on the threshold of the most exciting and promising phase of the evolution of human resources and human capital management. We've gone from the horse and buggy to the automobile to the airplane. Now it's time to mount the rocket and head for the stratosphere.

Like arithmetic, statistics are bias free and are applicable over a vast range of opportunities. They can be used in studies of single, localized problems or for supporting organization-wide makeovers. The secret sauce of statistics is just like the source code of computer programs—a buried logic that can go step-by-step or leap ahead, using macros to speed to the solution.

Today, we shift our attention to predictability. This book is about *predictive management*. We think of it as "managing today, tomorrow." Predictive management, or HCM:21®, is the outcome of our eighteen-month study called the Predictive Initiative. It is the first holistic, predictive management model and operating system for the human resources function. We launched it in the last quarter of 2008 and it has been successfully applied in industry and government, in the United States and overseas.

HCM:21 is a four-phase process that starts with scanning the marketplace and ends with an integrated measurement system. In the middle, it addresses workforce and succession planning in a new way and shows how to optimize and synchronize the delivery of HR services. It is detailed in the chapters that follow.

The Organization of This Book

This book has been divided into four parts. Part I is an introduction to predictive analytics; Part II presents the HCM:21 model; Part III provides case studies; and Part IV offers a look at future applications. Part I lays the foundation. Chapter One explains the reasoning behind predictive analytics. It points out that major advances and sustainable performance typically disrupt the status quo, and it argues that human resources badly needs a model change if it is to catch up in the marketplace. Chapter Two extends that reasoning to show the benefits of and need for predictive analytics. It describes the various levels of analytics and their uses and benefits, and shows the evolution of metrics into predictive analytics. Accompanying essays by experts in the field reinforce this point.

In Part II, each chapter breaks down into two sections. The first section is a discussion of one step in the predictive management model, with its underlying premise, a description of the process, and some examples. The second section includes how-to-do-it research essays by practitioners and thought leaders in the field of human resources and human capital measurement.

In this part of the book, Chapter Three presents the first phase of the HCM:21 process. It makes the point that we need to shed light on and understand the market forces and internal factors that affect human, structural, and relational capital. And it introduces risk assessment as a fundamental part of modern human capital management. Chapter Four presents a model for workforce planning that replaces the industrial-era, gap-analysis, structure-focused practice of filling positions as needed with the concept of generating human capability. It details how this concept is different and better, and it concludes with a surprising example of how succession planning can be designed to drive top-line revenue growth.

Chapter Five shows how to change HR service delivery into a value-generating process. Examples are provided on how to analyze HR processes such as staffing and development, as well as turnover. In applying an input-throughput-output model, you discover how to find the most cost-effective combination of inputs and throughputs to produce the best output at your organization. Chapter Six completes the presentation of the HCM:21 model by offering a comprehensive approach to performance measurement and reporting. It posits an integrated three-point system that links strategic, operational, and leading indicators. Then it recaps the topic of analytics with an overview of the evolution of metrics that ends with business intelligence and predictability.

Part III consists of five chapters that constitute a series of detailed case studies from government and private companies. These are real-world examples of how problems were solved using predictive analysis. For instance, the Chapter Seven example is a supply-chain case at Ingram Content Group, which applied analytics to attack a long-term turnover and productivity problem. The results clearly demonstrate the practical gains that can be achieved through the application of measurement and analysis.

Chapter Eight shows how Enterprise Rent-A-Car and Monster partnered in selecting a site for an Enterprise call center. Monster's market and demographic database helped Enterprise select the most cost-effective location. In Chapter Nine, we have a case from Asia. Descon Engineering, headquartered in Lahore, Pakistan, used the predictive management model to improve operations. The case study describes the rationale, the process, and the results.

Chapter Ten's case study is of a government agency that applied predictive analytics to the problem of a suboptimized mission-critical position. I describe the unique circumstances and the barriers to analytics that we were able to overcome. Chapter Eleven is a case from the healthcare industry that illustrates how analytics and technology were combined at UnitedHealth Group to improve staffing and retention, two of HR's major challenges.

Part IV of the book is but one chapter, but a critical one for your organization's success in the future. Chapter Twelve points out what we know and what we need to know to keep going forward. It makes the case again for a disruptive strike, and it concludes with short statements from many leading practitioners and thought leaders, including Tim Mack, president of World Future Society, on the future of human capital analytics.

The appendix contains a series of sample worksheets, which you can use to translate the model described in these chapters into spreadsheets. There are instructions and examples of how to operationalize these HCM:21 concepts for your particular situation.

Acknowledgments

Thank you, all. Over the past three decades, many people have supported the development of metrics. Starting three years ago, a small group of people saw the potential for analytics and invited me to speak on the topic in over a dozen countries in North America, Europe, and Asia. I thank you for helping me broadcast the message to the world.

People who have specifically encouraged me and helped me think through the process include Kent Barnett and Jeffrey Berk, at KnowledgeAdvisors; Karen Beaman, Erik Berggren, Deb Besemer, Carol DiPaolo, Nick Bontis, Ray Burch, Mary Kay Byers, Kevin Campbell, Jim Benton, and John Hindle at Accenture; Luis Maria Cravino and Cecilia Bastide at AO Consulting in Buenos Aires; Joni Doolin, Sal Faletta, Charlie Grantham, and Jim Ware at The Future of Work; Humair Ghauri, Kirk Hallowell, Nancy Hanna, Jesse Harriott, Row Henson, Annette Homan, Doug Hubbard, Steve Hunt, Paul Jamieson, Michael Kelly, Pat Leonard, Hugo Malan, Tahir Malik, Raul Navarro, and Rugenia Pomi of Sextante

Brasil in Sao Paolo; Sara Palmer, Ron Pilenzo, and Mike Losey past presidents of SHRM; Lori Riley, David Scarborough, Ken Scarlett, Denise Sinuk, Kirk Smith, Florence Stone, Tony Tasca, Dave Ulrich, Eleo Ventocillo . . . and with my sincere apologies to anyone I missed.

Christina Parisi was the editor who helped me corral this rambling account of analytics. I also was helped by the services of Carole Berglie, an exceptional copyeditor.

When you step off the deep end, it is nice to know that there are folks ready to throw you a life ring if you need it. Many years ago, when I was first going public with this crazy idea that we could show the business value of human resources services, a good friend told me to ignore the horde of naysayers because what I was doing was the right thing. I can't tell you how much that helped my shaky confidence. I'm here to help you beat back the rabble.

My special gratitude goes to Robert (Bob) Coon, my best friend and compatriot for nearly thirty years, up and down the human capital analysis trail and on the golf course. He keeps me focused whenever I want to ramble and reins me in when my euphoria gets the better of my common sense. Last, but certainly not least, and most important of all, I thank my wonderful wife, Laura Esperanza Sanchez (isn't that a beautiful name?) Fitz-enz for her undying support. She takes care of everything so that I can focus on having fun writing.

Contributors

Part I

Luis Maria Cravino, "Measuring What Is Important." I have worked with Luis Maria Cravino and his partner Cecilia Bastide at AO Consulting, in Buenos Aires, Argentina, for over ten years. Luis is the leading voice on human capital measurement in South America. His books *Un trabajo feliz* (2003) and *Medir lo importante* (2007) are best sellers across the continent.

◆ ◆ ◆ ◆

Stephen Gates and Pascal Langevin, "Strategic Human Capital Measures." Dr. Stephen Gates, CFA, is Professor of Strategy at Audencia Nantes School of Management in France. After receiving his doctorate at New York University's Stern School of Business, Dr. Gates worked as a securities analyst at JP MorganChase and Crédit Agricole, then as a business researcher at The Conference Board before returning to academia. His research interests include human capital measurement and strategic performance measurement systems. Reach him at sgates@audencia.com.

Dr. Pascal Langevin is Professor of Management Accounting & Control Systems at EM LYON Business School in France. He teaches graduate, MBA, and executive programs. He served as the Managing Director of a small industrial firm and as the Financial Director of an outplacement company. His primary interests in research are in performance measurement and evaluation systems and their effects on decision makers' motivation and performance. Reach him at langevin@em-lyon.com.

◆ ◆ ◆ ◆

Kirk Smith, "From Business Analytics to Rational Action." Kirk is a highly regarded consultant with a wide range of experience in performance measurement, project management, and group facilitation. He has worked for Kepner-Tregoe and taught at the university level. He is also a performance consultant and an adjunct faculty member for three universities. His primary practitioner focus is on measuring and evaluating the effectiveness of performance-improvement projects, human capital analytics, transfer of critical thinking skills in client organizations, and facilitation of issue resolution through systemic solutions. He is a Ph.D. candidate in technology management with a specialization in human resource development, and is a Project Management Professional (PMP), Certified Performance Technologist (CPT), and Certified ROI Professional. Kirk can be reached at kirk@wkirksmith.com.

Part II

Joni Thomas Doolin, Michael Harms, and Shyam Patel, "The Intersection of People and Profits." Joni Thomas Doolin is CEO and Founder of *People Report*. She is the "leading light" for human resources management in the foodservice industry and is widely acknowledged as the key producer in the field. Michael Harm is Human Capital Analyst at *People Report*, and Shyam Patel is COO and Senior Analyst there.

People Report is the foremost provider of human capital metrics for the foodservice industry. Its database includes information on hundreds of chains, hundreds of thousands of managers, and millions of employees. Its hallmark is dish room to boardroom business intelligence, providing industry-leading, benchmarked research for key human capital metrics; best-employment practices; total rewards; and compensation for chain operators, franchisees, and independent restaurants. In addition to its reports and publications, *People Report* offers first-rate speakers, newsletters, webinars, and acclaimed industry conferences throughout the year. For more information, go to www.peoplereport.com.

♦ ♦ ♦ ♦

Ryan M. Johnson, "More Than Compensation." Ryan Johnson has more than ten years' experience in public policy, public affairs, research, and consulting strategy work. He is a major thinker in the field of compensation, especially in new total-rewards systems. Ryan, a Certified Compensation Professional (CCP), is responsible for issues management, research, government affairs, and publishing at WorldatWork. Prior to joining WorldatWork, he was at Gerbig, Snell/Weisheimer of Columbus, Ohio, and the Morrison Institute for Public Policy at Arizona State University. Ryan started his career in Washington, D.C., on the staff of the U.S. House of Representatives' Committee on Small Business. He later worked as a research analyst for the Institute for Strategy Development, a private, financial institution–oriented think tank. Johnson has also authored articles on topics such as current legislative and regulatory developments, stock option expensing, executive compensation proxy disclosure, employee bonus programs, professional ethics, employee recognition, paid time off, outside director pay, consumerism in benefits, work life, sales compensation, flexible work schedules, telework, disaster recovery/continuity of operations, salary surveys, salary budget surveys, and total rewards.

WorldatWork (www.worldatwork.org) is a global human resources association focused on compensation, benefits, work life, and integrated total rewards to attract, motivate, and retain a talented workforce. Founded in 1955, it is a network of more than 30,000 members and professionals in seventy-five countries, with training, certification, research, conferences, and community. It has offices in Scottsdale, Arizona, and Washington, D.C.

❖ ❖ ❖ ❖

Rugenia Pomi, "Best in Brazil." Rugenia Pomi and her partner Raul Navarro have led the development of human resources metrics in Brazil since the early 1990s. They are rightly regarded as the pioneers in quantitative analysis in Brazil.

❖ ❖ ❖ ❖

James P. Ware, "Scenario Planning." Jim has over thirty years' experience in research, executive education, consulting, and management. For the past half-dozen years he and Charlie Grantham have been pioneering the field of future work structures through the Future of Work consortium. Jim Ware is also a cofounder of the Work Design Collaborative and has spent five years on the faculty of the Harvard Business School. His life's work has been focused on the changing nature of work and the impact of technology and workforce demographics on where, when, and how work gets done. His most recent book, *Corporate Agility*, co-authored with Charles Grantham and Cory Williamson, addresses the need for organizations to coordinate and integrate the HR, IT, and facilities management functions to develop new business capabilities for competing in a flat, global economy.

❖ ❖ ❖ ❖

Kenneth Scarlett, "Quality Employee Engagement Measurement." Kenneth joined Scarlett Surveys International, a world leader in employee engagement surveys, in 1984 and became its president in 1992. His experience prior to entering the family business was in manufacturing management, automotive marketing research, and new-product launch. Ken has published many articles pertaining to employee attitudes, engagement, and morale, and has worked directly with top leadership at hundreds of organizations to accurately measure and improve employee engagement and economic contribution. Currently, Ken is leading Scarlett Surveys to the forefront of the human capital management revolution by helping companies apply predictive employee engagement hucametrics within an updated and accountable people management structure.

Scarlett Surveys International has over forty-five years of experience in the employee attitude research field, having surveyed over 15 million employees in over twenty-two languages thus far. Scarlett Surveys is globally recognized for providing unique, high-value, employee engagement measurement surveys and Web-based survey metric management systems proven to improve business performance and employee work life.

◆ ◆ ◆ ◆

Erik Berggren, "Truly Paying for Performance." Erik is a native of Sweden, with experience in both Europe and the United States. He is a leading thinker and practitioner at SuccessFactors, concentrating on performance management and compensation. He was an active participant in the Predictive Initiative consortium. SuccessFactors Research group is a global leader in performance and talent management, with more than 2,200 customers and 4 million users of its software around the world. Erik has a strong background as a management and strategy consultant, and publishing credentials that include numerous papers on how talent management practices help companies increase competitiveness and improve financial results. He is a frequent speaker at conferences around the world. Currently, Erik is synthesizing his research into a book with the working title *Win Through People*. Erik can be contacted at eberggren@successfactors.com.

◆ ◆ ◆ ◆

F. Leigh Branham, "The Slippery Staircase." Leigh Branham is famous for his work on talent retention. Author of the best-selling *The 7 Hidden Reasons Employees Leave*, Leigh has a long history of leading-edge thinking and work on employee disengagement. He is Principal and Founder of Keeping the People, Inc., in Overland Park, Kansas. Since 1995, he has been researching the root causes and dynamics of employee disengagement and turnover. He helps organizations achieve their strategic objectives by implementing more effective employee engagement practices and by becoming better places to work. With his first book selected as one of the top thirty business books of 2005, he is now at work on a new book dealing with the secrets of the best places to work in America. His commentary on the challenges of keeping good people appeared in the June 2008 issue of the *Harvard Business Review*. He can be contacted at LB@keepingthepeople.com or through his Web site, www.keepingthep eople.com.

◆ ◆ ◆ ◆

Kirk Hallowell, "Roberta Versus the Inventory Control System." Kirk is Director of Learning and Development for Tegrant Corporation, in DeKalb, Illinois. Kirk is accountable for talent development, learning, and succession planning for Tegrant's corporate function and three strategic business units. He was previously a Senior Consultant for Personnel Decisions International, and has presented nationally on the topics of executive leadership development and return on investment in human capital.

◆ ◆ ◆ ◆

Robert Coon, "The Treasure Trove You Already Own." Bob recently retired after nearly forty years in human resources management in the automotive, computer, and supply chain industries. He worked with me at Four-Phase Systems in the 1970s, where he played a key role in developing the measurement processes later published at Saratoga Institute. He also served as President of Saratoga Institute. Most recently he was Vice President of Human Resources for Menlo Worldwide LLC, the leading logistics component of Con-Way Inc., the $5.4 billion global supply chain services company. His establishment of Menlo University won the national CUBIC Award in 2003 for the "Best New Corporate University in America." Prior to joining Menlo Worldwide, Bob served as President and COO of the Saratoga Institute. He also teaches "Measuring HR Effectiveness" for the University of California's HR Extension Program. In 2008, Bob was elected an Honored Member of the Bay Area Human Resource Executives Council and was a member of its board of directors for fourteen years.

◆ ◆ ◆ ◆

Lisa Disselkamp, "Waking the Sleeping Giant in Workforce Intelligence." Lisa is the author of *No Boundaries*, a breakthrough publication in workforce data management, as well as *Working the Clock;* these books represent the first and only comprehensive treatments on time and labor management systems. In them, she describes how to use time and labor management data in a predictive rather than a reactive manner. Lisa is president of Athena Enterprises, a management consulting firm specializing in time and attendance system implementations and workforce management business processes. Her clients range from companies of a few hundred employees to over 70,000. She is a frequent speaker at management conferences across North America. In 2008 she was recognized as "Woman of the Year Technology Star."

◆ ◆ ◆ ◆

Nico Peruzzi, "Predictive Analytics for Human Capital Management." Nico is a partner with Outsource Research (www.orconsulting.com), a full-service provider of quantitative research and high-end analytics. He prides himself on the ability to translate in-depth statistical analyses into actionable findings to help his clients make better business decisions. Conjoint analysis, segmentation analysis, and predictive modeling are some of his areas of expertise.

◆ ◆ ◆ ◆

Kent Barnett and Jeffrey Berk, "Using Human Capital Data for Performance Management During Economic Uncertainty." Kent Barnett is the Founder and CEO of KnowledgeAdvisors, and Jeff Berk is Chief Operating Officer there. Barnett and Berk co-authored the book *Human Capital Analytics: Measuring and Improving Learning and Talent Impact*. Kent was also a Founder and President of Productivity Point International. He speaks internationally on topics related to people and performance. Jeffrey led the Benchmarking Group at Andersen prior to joining KnowledgeAdvisors. He brings a deep level of expertise in measurement and analytics to the organization and is responsible for designing and implementing the suite of products and services for KnowledgeAdvisors.

KnowledgeAdvisors is a leading provider of learning and talent-measurement solutions. Its market-leading analytics system, Metrics that Matter®, is used by many of the largest, most successful organizations to measure learning and talent management programs. As a leader in human capital analytics, KnowledgeAdvisors combines measurement expertise, on-demand evaluation software, and integrated analytics solutions with benchmarking to help organizations gain the necessary insight on how best to develop their workforce. Its analytics solutions automate and template the data collection, storage, processing, and reporting on people processes in the human capital/talent management arena.

◆ ◆ ◆ ◆

Lee Elliott, Daniel Elliott, and Louis R. Forbringer, "Using HR Metrics to Make a Difference." Lee Elliott is Vice President for Human Resources and Fund Development at Saint Francis Medical Center in Grand Island, Nebraska. In addition to working in human resources, he is a professor at Doane College, where he teaches business, psychology, statistics, and experimental methods. His son, Daniel, is completing his Ph.D. in computer science at Colorado State University. Dan's areas of research interest include computer vision, statistical modeling of high dimensional data, neural networks, and application of machine learning techniques to real-world problems. Dr. Louis (Lou) R. Forbringer is Vice President of Strategic Talent Management for Catholic Health Initiatives (CHI), a national nonprofit health organization with headquarters in Denver, Colorado. Lou received his Ph.D. and MA in Industrial/Organizational Psychology from the University of Akron.

Part III

Wayne M. Keegan, "Impacting Productivity and the Bottom Line: Ingram Content Group." In my opinion, Wayne Keegan is one of the most effective human capital managers in the country. This case is a small example of the outstanding work he has done in developing and applying human resources metrics for over two decades. If you want practical solutions for human capital management, Wayne is your man.

Keegan's HR experience covers twenty-six years mostly at the vice-presidential level in several industries. He first used metrics extensively at the ERTL Company in 1991, when he participated in Dr. Fitz-enz's annual "HR Effectiveness Report." At Ingram, Wayne has tracked HR operating data annually since 1999, applying it to positively affect Ingram's profitability

♦ ♦ ♦ ♦

Jesse Harriott, Jeffrey Quinn, and Marie Artim, "Leveraging Human Capital Analytics for Site Selection: Monster and Enterprise Rent-A-Car." Jesse Harriott is Chief Knowledge Officer, SVP for Monster Worldwide. During his tenure, he has helped drive Monster's annual revenue from $300 million to over $1.3 billion. Dr. Harriott created Monster Intelligence, the research division at Monster focused on the human capital marketplace, and he has grown the division into Monster Insights, the company's international research arm. Monster Insights provides workforce planning analytics to help Monster customers make informed decisions about today's most pressing human capital issues. He is the author of the book *Finding Keepers*. In 2009, Dr. Harriott was named by *Boston Business Journal* as one of Boston's "Top 40 under 40."

As part of Monster's Strategic Thought Leadership initiatives, Jeff

Quinn is the Senior Director of the Monster Intelligence efforts. Monster Intelligence provides groundbreaking information and actionable insights, helping Monster's customers with strategic human capital planning. He focuses on developing research and data to foster a deep relationship with Monster customers. Jeff also played a key role in production of the Workforce Intelligence Reports. Jeff has been with Monster since 2004.

Marie Artim is the Assistant Vice President, Recruiting, for Enterprise Holdings, Inc. She is responsible for company-wide strategies and directives that involve advertising, marketing, interactive media, training, and tools for the 200+ Enterprise recruiters hiring across all brands, including more than 8,000 college graduates each year. Marie took over global recruiting responsibilities in 2000.

◆ ◆ ◆ ◆

Umair Majid and Ahmed Tahir, "Predictive Management at Descon Engineering." Umair Majid is currently managing the HR functions, as Incharge HRM, of two large-scale business areas (Infrastructure Projects Business Area and Plant Construction and Services Business Area) at Descon Engineering. He did his MBA work in human resources at Iqra University, Lahore, Pakistan. Ahmed Tahir is currently working as Team Leader, Organizational Development, at Descon Engineering. Ahmed received his master's degree in human resource management (MHRM) from the University of the Punjab, Lahore, Pakistan.

◆ ◆ ◆ ◆

Judy Sweeney, "UnitedHealth Group Leverages Predictive Analytics for Enhanced Staffing and Retention." Judy Sweeney is Vice President and Head of Taleo Research. She has more than thirty years of enterprise software development, marketing, and HCM research experience. Ms. Sweeney leads a team of researchers who provide primary and secondary research on the current and future state of talent management. Prior to joining Taleo, Ms. Sweeney was a Senior Vice President of AMR Research, where she led a team of analysts to study human capital management, enterprise applications and infrastructure, and the supply chain. Her specific research focus was on HCM and midmarket ERP. Ms. Sweeney holds a BS in Management from the University of Massachusetts.

Taleo (NASDAQ: TLEO) is the leader in on-demand unified talent-management solutions that empower organizations of all sizes to assess, acquire, develop, and align their workforces for improved business performance. More than 3,800 organizations use Taleo, including 47 of the

Fortune 100 and over 3,000 small and medium businesses, for talent acquisition and performance management, in 200 countries and territories. Taleo's Talent Grid harnesses the resources of the Taleo community of customers, candidates, and partners to power the talent needs of companies around the world.

PART 1

Introduction to Predictive Analytics

CHAPTER ONE

Disruptive Technology: The Power to Predict

What do Amazon, Sony, Swatch, the San Francisco 49ers, and McDonald's all have in common? The answer is that they are examples of what Harvard professor Clay Christensen has described as "disruptive technologies." That is, these companies were dramatically innovative ideas that transformed their industries. Amazon rewrote book selling, Sony revolutionized the music business, Swatch upset the watch industry forever, the 49ers brought an innovative strategy that changed professional football, and McDonald's added a totally new dimension to food service

Despite recent labor-market transformations brought on by global competitiveness, the liquidity crisis, management scandals, and federal government intervention, very little has changed within the "people game." There has been no seminal shift in the way we manage people during a time of fundamental renovations in organizational structures, cultures, and workforce compositions. One year we are worried about where we will find sufficient "talent" and the next we are worried about how we get rid of older workers to free up progression space for younger people. But beyond that, we still treat employees as expenses. Management's attitude about human behavior oscillates between totally predictable to absolutely indecipherable. Meanwhile, the latest advances in analytic tools are ignored. HR managers claim to be too busy to change the way they operate, thereby leaving themselves continually behind the curve, adding to operating expenses and claiming that their value is immeasurable.

For this and similar transgressions, the human resources department is distinct from and largely disconnected from other corporate functions. Although computer technology has made the job internally more efficient, HR has not delivered strategic value because it does not have a strategic management model. It continues to buy packaged products and apply them as patches to an obsolescent form. This is tantamount to repainting a clunker and expecting its miles per gallon performance to improve. Products—that is, software, survey instruments, training packages, and so forth—are tools, not solutions. If the organization's fundamentals are weak, new tools won't change them. In fact, they might even solidify the weakness. Today and tomorrow, organizations desperately need a disruptive human capital management technology based on analytics.

What Is Analytics?

To answer the question of what analytics actually is, I go to the meeting of art and science. The arts teach us how to look at the world. The sciences teach us how to do something. When you say analytics, people immediately think of statistics. That is incorrect. Analytics is a mental framework, a logical progression first and a set of statistical tools second (see Figure 1.1).

Various dictionaries define *analytics* as the science of analysis, from the Greek *analutika*, including the principles of mathematical analysis. That is, it is the process of dismantling or separating into constituents

Figure 1.1. The nature of analytics.

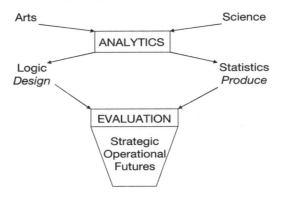

to study. So, simply stated, analysis is about taking something apart to understand it better. In answering complex physical or behavioral science questions, statistical methods are often utilized. For solving organizational problems, we need a logical structure to parse out the many variables that can affect human performance. Once we have identified those variables, we can employ statistics as necessary.

Introducing HCM:21®

For the first time, there is an opportunity to make a quantum leap in human capital management, a leap from obsolescence to innovation, through the application of analytics. It is our plan for predictive management, or HCM:21 (human capital management for the twenty-first century). This breakthrough program was developed over a period of eighteen months as part of our Predictive Initiative, a consortium of major organizations and thought leaders who were committed to transforming people management into a strategic function.[1]

HCM, or human capital management, is the framework of logic that is used to gather, organize, and interpret data, and subsequently also knowledge, for the purpose of assessing the probability of upcoming events. HCM takes the gambling out of decision making. It helps you overcome a reliance on past data and obsolete experience, and replace it with insights regarding the future and the tools for influencing it. This is called "Managing tomorrow, today."

The Value of Insight

Insight into the future is the greatest asset anyone can have. Consider how wealthy you would be if you had bought petroleum futures in 2006, or had accumulated a large amount of cash in August 2008, a month before the liquidity crisis slammed the global markets.

If you had made those moves at the right time, would you have been lucky or wise? Luck comes in two forms: dumb luck and true luck. Dumb luck is when you meant to bet on the number 6 horse but bet on the number 5 by mistake and won by accident. True luck seems to be a function of preparation, and there is a story from the golfing world that makes the point.

One day, Gary Player—one of only four professional golfers to win all four major tournaments, the U.S. and British Opens, the PGA, and the Masters—was practicing sand shots. A man watched as Player knocked most of the shots from the bunker into the cup. He said to Player, "Son, that is the luckiest thing I've ever seen." Player responded, "Sir, I find the more I practice, the luckier I get."

Most organizations do not rely on dumb luck to save them from market fluctuations. They prepare by buying commodity futures to protect themselves from shortages or cost increases; they buy advertising space a year at a time to obtain volume discounts. But what do they do in the human capital arena to offset future surprises? In most cases, the answer is nothing. Ask most staffing managers what their most cost-effective staffing strategy will be in the coming year or their most fruitful applicant sources. Or, ask the training manager what the most effective method is for bringing the salespeople up to speed on the new product line. They could not give you an answer based on anything other than anecdotal, obsolete experience. The chief administrative officer of a major bank once told me that he spends over $250 million annually on training, and yet had no idea if it was effective. No wonder he had to take TARP money. The human resources function applies a helter-skelter approach to service delivery. It does not have a management model or operating system with predictive capability—that is, until now.

The Plan

The remainder of this book focuses on a predictive management model that is driven by human capital analytics. Specifically, the HCM:21 system consists of four phases:

1. *Scanning.* All the external market forces and internal organizational factors are listed in terms of how they might affect the organization's human, structural, and relational capital. Additionally, the interdependencies and interactions across these three forms of capital are recognized and accounted for. This is the critical, often ignored, point.

2. *Planning.* Workforce planning is reconstituted as capability development. The industrial-era, gap-analysis, structure-focused model is replaced with an agile system focused on building sustainable human capability rather than filling positions; in fact, many of those older positions will be restructured or eliminated.

3. *Producing.* Human resources services are studied as processes with inputs, throughputs, and outputs. Statistical analysis is applied to uncover the most cost-effective combination of inputs and throughputs to drive desired outputs.

4. *Predicting*. A three-point measurement system is designed to include strategic, operational, and leading indicators. The causal and correlational aspects of the three points are used to tell a comprehensive story.

A number of cases and models from practitioners and thought leaders supplement each phase of the plan and show how basic metrics and predictive analytics are being applied across many different settings in the Americas, Europe, and Asia.

♦ ♦ ♦ ♦

In summary, HCM:21 is a model and a methodology for managing human capital, talent, or simply people. It is distinct and disruptive in that "people management" has always been a loosely connected, out-of-synch batch of processes for hiring, paying, training, and sustaining talent. This is why people claim to "hate" HR. As a result, the function is being dismantled through outsourcing and parceling out to finance and operations. The time clearly is *now* for HR professionals to face these realities and adopt a future-focused, integrated management model. The rest of this book shows you how to do this, beginning with Chapter Two, on the promise of analytics and predictive management.

Note

1. The Predictive Initiative sponsors and contributors are as follows: organizations—American Management Association, Accenture, Blue Shield-CA, Ceridian, Fidelity, Future of Work, KnowledgeAdvisors, Lehman Brothers, Monster, National Reconnaissance Organization, Oracle, Scarlett Surveys, SuccessFactors, and Target stores; individuals—Karen Beaman, Nick Bontis, Robert Coon, Sal Faletta, Douglas Hubbard, Paul Jamison, Denise Sinuk.

CHAPTER TWO

Toward Analytics and Prediction

"The world is full of people whose notion of a satisfactory future is, in fact, a return to the idealized past."

—**ROBERTSON DAVIES,** *A Voice from the Attic*, **1960**

I introduced human resources metrics in 1978, with a series of public workshops based on my experience running a human resources department for a bank and later a computer company. Since then metrics have experienced a long, slow, and somewhat unsteady evolution. With every economic downturn we seem to retreat to the old familiar, if ineffective but comfortable, ways. As the market reopens, so do our minds and we try once again to make progress. In my view, human capital metrics passed through several evolutionary steps and continues to evolve. These are shown in Figure 2.1.

The Language of Metrics and Analytics

If HR professionals truly want to be part of the business, metrics—and especially predictive analytics—will open the door to that citizenship. Metrics are the language of organizational management. If you do not speak the same language as your audience, you cannot make an impression. Conversely, when people share an idiom, and more important, a mindset, they have the basis for a relationship. The research reported in Workforce Intelligence Reports 2007 and 2008 revealed the rationale for

Figure 2.1. Evolution of human capital metrics.

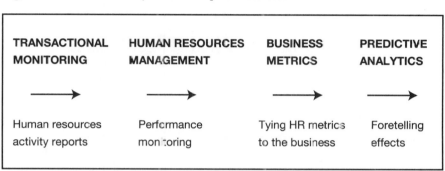

a management model that promises to help establish better communications between line managers and human resources professionals.[1]

Human resources analytics is a communications tool, first and foremost. It brings together data from disparate sources, such as surveys and operations of different units or levels, to paint a cohesive, actionable picture of current conditions and likely futures. As in most cases, human capital measurement began with simply recording inputs and outputs of the workforce. This is the province of accounting. Accountants monitor income and expense to tell management what ensues as a result of past decisions and investments. HCM takes us beyond that. It positions management with a view of tomorrow.

First Steps

There are five ways to measure anything in business. They are cost, time, quantity, quality, and human reaction. The central question is: Which is most important to track? The answer is: It depends. If we accept that measurement is an activity and activity is expense, it follows that we don't want to waste our time on metrics of little value. Value comes from knowledge of things that matter. And what matters is a business question, not an HR question: what matters at what points in time and for what organizational purpose.

This takes us to the five steps of analytics.

Step 1: *Recording our work (i.e., hiring, paying, training, supporting, and retaining).* If we learn through measurement how efficient our processes are, we can improve them, thus creating value for the organization indirectly by saving money or time, or by increasing the ratio of output to input, or by making an employee or customer happier as the result of a less intrusive process or a better result.

Step 2: *Relating to our organization's goals (i.e., quality, innovation, productivity, service [QIPS])*. QIPS encompasses the fundamental goals of any organization. Targets are set periodically by senior management across these process outcomes and are reviewed on a regular basis. We want to link the results of our work to its impact on QIPS goals. This shows there is value in our work.

Step 3: *Comparing our results to others (i.e., benchmarking)*. To be effective, benchmarking requires knowledge of the organizations to which we will be compared. Broad data about a comparative group in an industry or a region have only marginal value because of their great variance within that population. The more detail we can find, the more the value of the benchmarks.

Step 4: *Understanding past behavior and outcomes (i.e., descriptive analytics)*. This is the first level of true analysis. It looks for and describes relationships among data without giving meaning to the patterns. It is exploratory rather than predictive. From it, we begin to see trends from the past; yet, it is risky to extrapolate from the past into the future, considering the volatile, rapidly changing markets of today and likely tomorrow.

Step 5: *Predicting future likelihoods (i.e., prescriptive analytics)*. This form of analysis relates what we know to what we don't know. It compares what happened yesterday to what will probably happen tomorrow. Predictive analytics ascribes meaning to the patterns observed in descriptive analysis. Banks use this method to predict the creditworthiness of borrowers. Insurers use it to predict patterns of illness and mortality. Human resources can apply it to decisions about the expected return on human capital investments in hiring, training, and planning.

Ascending the Value Ladder

As we move from understanding the efficiency of our processes to being able to predict the organizational outcomes for a given human capital investment, we ascend the value ladder. Figure 2.2 shows the relative value of each step.

In almost every case, organizations start at Step 1, collecting basic data on cost, time, and quantity. This is where we began human resources measurement in 1978 and is described in detail in my earlier books. Up to that point, we had only vague notions of what had resulted from the

Figure 2.2. Measurement's ascending values.

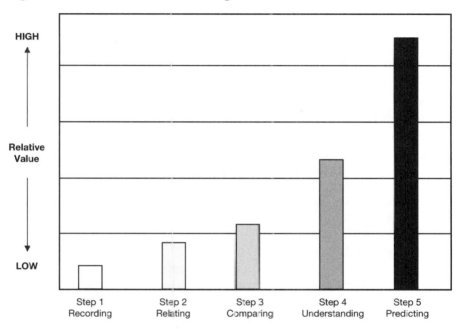

work of the personnel and training functions. When HR is operating in a commercial business, or even a nonprofit organization, it needs to know and be able to explain why, what, and how it is doing what it does. It is only reasonable that when we ask for resources, we explain what we are going to do with them and the value that we intend to produce as a result. In a sense, it is not much different from asking our children what they are going to do with their allowance. When we learn from collecting cost, time, and quantity data, eventually we will ask ourselves what the quality of this work is and how it affects others. For example, we upgrade from cost per hire and time to fill requisitions to quality of hires. If we spend money on training, the questions are: How relevant is the training? Are the trainees doing a better job as a result of this experience?

To assume that our work has value without offering any supporting data is arrogant and a dereliction of duty. It is also dangerous. Why do you think every economic downturn decimates functions such as training? No reported value!

Eventually, some will come along with data that purports to show the greater value of their services. If we cannot provide contrasting data, management is obliged to shift resources from "we" to "them." This is happening more and more as business becomes increasingly competitive—and that is reasonable. Management is charged with making the best use of the resources provided by shareholder investments.

Descriptive Analytics

There is a tendency within management for oversimplification. At the C-level, the workforce is seen as a mass, a monolith, when in actuality it is made up of many subsets. Descriptive analytics allows us to drill down into the workforce to uncover subgroups around given sets of characteristics. This type of analytics reveals and describes relationships and differences between the groups. It can also show past and current behaviors or interests among the groups, but it is limited to exploration rather than prescription.

There are many ways to use descriptive models to understand the workforce in detail. Practically any group characteristics can be carved out for consideration; all that is required are the variables that make up the characteristics (age, education, family status, benefits selections, skills, interests, potential ratings, etc.). Basically, this is workforce segmentation, just as marketing does customer segmentation. Why do this? Obviously, the purpose is to improve the return on investment (ROI) of subsequent HR services. This is what it means to be a business partner.

As an example, in Chapter 4 we deal with capability planning, and we segment the workforce into four groups for investment purposes. These groups are:

1. Mission-critical—the small group that has the largest effect on performance and revenues

2. Differentiators—the group with unique skill sets that help to generate competitive advantage

3. Important—the operatives who keep the organization functioning day to day

4. Movable—those with capabilities that can be outsourced, retrained, transferred, or terminated

From this categorization, we can make cost-effective investment decisions regarding development, retention, and recognition. By this segmentation, the organization optimizes its resources that are committed to the workforce.

Prescriptive Analytics

This form of analysis relates what we know currently to what we want to know about the future. Whereas descriptive analytics reveals current data patterns, predictive analytics gives meaning to those patterns for the future. With practice, one can look at historical data and foretell, to some degree, the likelihood of a future occurrence. The key phrase is "to some degree." If we believe we can assess and mitigate risks with estimates based on the past, we are on dangerous ground. In the interconnected, unpredictable, explosive global market, that is a most difficult, if not impossible, task. It is true that simple behaviors such as years of perfect past attendance probably predict near-perfect future attendance. However, complex behaviors such as leadership and engagement require some rigor in forecasting.

Predictive analytics expresses the future in terms of probabilities. It helps management make decisions that minimize risks and increase ROIs. No analytic application can predict the future with absolute certainty; but, in my experience, when properly applied it will substantially reduce variability. And as casinos know, winning is only a few percentage points different from losing.

Models are an example of a predictive application. When we build a success model based on traits, skills, and experiences, we increase the probability of selecting the right people to hire, train, and promote. For instance, I used the model of a field-engineering manager at a computer company to prioritize engineers for management training. We found that there were a few key unforeseen differences between effective and ineffective managers. For example, effective managers had taken nonengineering courses when they had an option less effective managers stayed strictly within the engineering curriculum. From this and other discriminating data, we developed an algorithm that ranked all engineers. Those persons who most closely matched the model were the first to receive training. Thus, the trick is to let go of biases (i.e., one's alma mater) in favor of behaviors that are better predictors of the performance required. There is no way other than through analytics that management can come to realize the complex drivers of success.

Causation

I have left the highest and most sophisticated level of human capital analysis until now. It is the combination of descriptive and prescriptive analytics that we call *causal analysis*. Professor Nick Bontis, at McMaster University in Hamilton, Ontario, Canada, is one of the earlier and most effective practitioners of human capital causal analysis, sometimes called causal modeling. With causal modeling we can find the hidden root cause of a problem or make a business proposition for a human capital investment.

In Bontis's learning-impact model he points out that the success of training is not a function only of the courseware and trainer delivery. It is very much the result of the perceived value of the training by the trainee. One way to find and express training's business value is to survey the trainees, asking them to score their perceived value on a scale of 1 to 100 percent; the courseware, from 1 to 5 points; and the delivery, 1 to 5 points. Then you put these factors into an equation such as the one below:

Perceived Value		Courseware		Delivery		Cumulative Score
.80	x	4	x	5	=	16

(maximum possible is 25: 1.0 x 5 x 5)

As any of the ratings change, the cumulative score changes as well.

The various uses for this simple causal model are broad indeed, including how people are chosen for the training, how the perceived value of the training changes from before to after, how the training department's performance can be tracked, and on and on.

When causal analysis is combined with predictive management, the power is truly remarkable. Predictive management is the model and mind-set that was developed by the Predictive Initiative. (It is described in Chapter 10 of the second edition of my book *The ROI of Human Capital*).[2] Bontis was a key contributor to the initiative and has published several examples of his work on causal modeling over the past decade. They can be seen on his Web site, www.bontis.com.

The Power of Analytics

High-risk decisions have to be made under circumstances that are seldom completely clear. For example, what actions are necessary to retain mission-critical talent under certain market conditions? Would we select incentive compensation, challenging assignments, work-life balance, or rapid promotions? What data do we have to support such a critical future decision? If the mission-critical population is large, geographically dispersed, and its technology or customers are changing, who can say which action will have the highest success rate? Certainly, relying on the past to predict the future is the summit of stupidity.

Knowledge is the base from which prediction emerges. Without knowledge there would be no tools and no structure. If knowledge is power, then foresight is the lever to take advantage of that knowledge. This is where predictive management enters.

Being able to foretell what is likely to happen with a high degree of probability depends on four things:

1. Comprehension of past and current events

2. Understanding not only trends but also the drivers behind them

3. Being able to see patterns of consistency as well as change

4. Having tools to describe the probability of something in the future

Human Resources Analytics

Until now the missing piece within business intelligence (BI) has been data on human capital and especially *predictive* human resources analytics (HRA). HRA is an outgrowth of and marriage between human resources metrics and general business analysis. HRA brings to life the logic within HCM:21. Previously, human resources metrics has been confined almost exclusively to labor issues as they relate to the business plan. HRA has opened the door to a much broader and more useful view of the metrics. It can draw on any or all BI data to both support the delivery of human resources services and influence the behavior of all levels of employees, up to and including executives. HRA turns human resources metrics toward the future. It takes past and current strategic and operational data and adds leading indicators. Data on retention, readiness, leadership, and engagement speak to what is likely to come tomorrow. Indeed, this is the newest lever in the business intelligence machine.

The Model for Predictive Management

Today, organizations are huge pools of objective data, as well as subjective knowledge, attitudes, and beliefs. Electronic and behavioral science technologies—the tools to manipulate and make sense of that data—are available to almost everyone at reasonable cost. The only questionable element is the will to take advantage of these great resources.

HCM:21 is the broad strategy that provides the framework for analyzing an organization's data. It takes brainstorming lists, interview and survey data, and market research and organizes these elements around human, structural, and relational capital phenomena. By applying HRA tools, predictive management uncovers the connections and interdependencies among organizational activities. Study of the outcomes at the strategic, operational, and leading-indicator levels yields insights into the future. It tells not only what, how, and why something happened yesterday, but, most importantly, also what is the likelihood of something happening tomorrow. Figure 2.3 outlines the four phases of HCM:21 and the arrows indicate how predictive analytics link the phases.

Within any population there is a range of skill, knowledge, attitudes, values, and interests. Many people say they are interested in doing something, but only a relatively small number have the skill or drive to do it, with or without training. If you are truly interested in learning how to conduct human capital analytics, and you have the stamina to see it through, you will have a competitive advantage over 95 percent of the population.

Figure 2.3. The HCM:21® model.

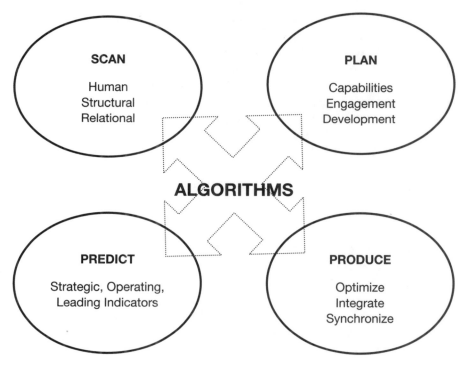

Notes

1. Workforce Intelligence Reports, 2007–2008, Workforce Intelligence Institute, San Jose, California.
2. Jac Fitz-enz, *The ROI of Human Capital* (New York: AMACOM, 2000), 160–85.

WHY ANALYTICS IS IMPORTANT

The three essays that follow deal with why measurement is important, what strategic metrics are, and how to translate analytics into action.

MEASURING WHAT IS IMPORTANT

Luis Maria Cravino

"Everything that can be counted does not necessarily count and everything that counts cannot necessarily be counted."

—ALBERT EINSTEIN

This is an opportunity to summarize my personal connection with the measurement approach of human capital management in the last twelve years. I hereby state certain contradictions, uncertainties, discordant perspectives, or just starting points to begin reflecting about assumptions that are automatically or mechanically applied and that, in many cases, cause serious problems. First, I deal with what is *not* working right in the field of measuring human capital management, which I have called "measuring system crises." Then, I introduce my version of which indicators we should bear in mind and what constitutes what we could call "measuring what is important."

The Crises in Measuring Systems

The current situation in human resources measurement is a series of crises.

The Excess Indicator Crisis

Research published in the magazine *Psychological Review*, quoted in the book *The Knowing-Doing Gap* by Jeffrey Pfeffer and Robert I. Sutton, states that human beings can generally manage seven things at the same time, plus or minus two. That seems reasonable.[1]

In my work as a consultant, many times I have come across performance management systems that aim at focusing people's efforts by limiting the number of objectives that can be set per year. The usual number is five, although in certain cases I have seen seven or eight, at the most. The purpose is to prevent dispersion, keep people focused, and so on. However, I have seen (and I'm not exaggerating) management systems with more than 500 indicators to monitor aspects of human capital management, even in medium-size, not very sophisticated companies. Too many indicators? Certainly. All this measurement can only create more confusion. In addition, so much effort expended in measuring takes time and energy away from the management process itself.

For a long time I have tried to work out what the actual cause is for such confusion. This confusion might occur because many managers are obsessed with measuring everything, with knowing everything that is going on, and with imagining that if they have many numbers, everything will be under control. Also, many managers have a simple way of thinking, based on the fact that people do things with the idea that they are being measured for what they do. Although it is true that there is a certain relationship between measurement and behavior, this connection is not 100 percent linear and direct. But if we believe that we can assess behavior by means of measurement, there is a possibility of believing that "the more indicators, the more control."

The Crisis in Understanding What Measurements and Parameters Mean

I have no doubt that measurement is an important task in managing any process or function. Measurement gives us information, which in many cases is crucial to solving problems, making effective decisions, improving results, and the like. But when I think in detail what measurement means in itself, I can end up with serious problems. This lack of detailed thought is probably, from my point of view, one of the main sources of wrong decisions in company management.

In many organizations, there is an assumption, a very deeply rooted one, that cost reduction is essentially good, or else that increasing productivity levels is essentially good. The problem is that these two assumptions are not always true in every case. For instance, let's consider the number of people who work in the human capital management function in a certain company, and let's relate that to the number of people who work in that company. Based on those two figures we can establish a classical productivity indicator:

$$\frac{\text{Number of employees of human capital management}}{\text{Total staff}}$$

At first, this indicator may imply that if we want to improve productivity, in terms of what a collaborator of the human capital management area can "address," we should reduce the number of collaborators in the human capital management area. Simple—but it may be wrong.

Another aspect of this crisis occurs when we obsessively study comparative data, when sources of comparison are inappropriate or inconvenient, or when they are not correctly understood. Using such data is more harmful than good. For example, when we do benchmarking in human capital management, we need to think that the companies that provide information have unique characteristics. Their implicit uniqueness does not invalidate the comparison process, but we need to remember that every detail the companies provide for a benchmarking sample has a history behind it. That is why we should think of a parameter as a piece of overall information (although calculated with great effort and level of precision) that provides overall information to serve as a reference point, to begin a reflection process.

The Crisis of Extremes

Benchmarking to prevent the "self-centeredness disease" is well known. Self-centeredness is thinking that the world around you, or the company, is "more or less" the world you see. Over time I have observed, in both large and medium organizations, such dysfunctional behavior that comes from self-centeredness.

For example, some managers make decisions always based on the background they themselves have generated to make such decisions. Their written procedure manuals or their informal culture is their major source of information and consultation, so when a problem arises the question they ask is: Where inside is the solution to this problem? In many cases, internal growth started when the company was unable "to go beyond its boundaries" and keep within its life limits. Consequently, their view of the world comes down to the view of the world that their company has: that their colleagues are their co-workers (although they are thousands of miles away and speak different languages), that their trips abroad are intracooperative, and that their literature is the newsletters that the company itself publishes.

On the other hand, corporate life has expanded in recent decades, so if there still is an openly self-centered manager, he or she would be a living dinosaur. Yes, we can say that self-centered people, in their several categories, are dying off; replacing them are "externalists" or "extreme benchmarkers," who overuse the external view. They are always asking, searching, or in other ways trying to get to know what others are doing.

Nobody questions the importance of knowing what happens outside, but such knowledge should be preceded by knowing what happens inside. Generally, benchmarking will not help resolve incorrectly formulated questions or questions that are misdirected. Externalism can harm human capital management as much as self-centeredness can. An appropriate balance between looking outside and knowing the inside seems to be the obvious solution to this crisis.

The Crisis of Putting Process Measurement Ahead of Results Measurement

Is it surprising that most indicators of human capital management are more closely related to processes than to results? Cost accounting quickly tells us how much has been spent on any item. After all, counting money is easier than measuring happiness. Counting hours is easier than analyzing competence. Counting days is easier than estimating potential. Also, most process measurements can be analyzed without exceeding the limits of the function itself.

In many organizations, the administrative cost of paying salaries is a clearer indicator than staff performance levels and how much the cost of salary administration affects the company's overall profitability. As far as I know, the latter is only a few dollars per employee; however, how much does the level of staff performance affect the operative and financial results? Unquestionably, it is much more when that performance is functioning at a level it should be.

The reasoning seems obvious. If we analyze how much every measurement contributes, we could say that the former (knowing the administrative cost of paying salaries) is a measurement of little added value, but that the latter (measuring the staff performance) can provide valuable information with a very significant impact. The explanation for why the processes are measured more frequently than the results is probably accounting convenience. It is easier to measure and fewer people are bothered. For many managers, measuring processes makes them feel in control. In some extreme cases, they come to think that their work is about managing processes, forgetting that their function is to deliver results that lead to the accomplishment of higher results.

The Crisis in Thinking That Everything Measured Equals Everything Existing and That Everything That Is Measured Can Be Managed

Obviously, this is not a crisis exclusive to human capital management. On the contrary, it is an existential crisis when certain organizations reduce, sometimes grotesquely, their own nature to their own measurements.

It is sad, and even difficult, to understand that this assumption has spread to human capital management, where participants are supposed to be aware that a significant and relevant part of reality exists even when it cannot be measured, and that the most important things have value but not an estimated price or cost. Indeed, we must be aware that time and cost measurements can be objective, but that other measurements are subjective or relative, and that some factors simply are impossible to measure. For instance, staff satisfaction exists and it is crucial for performance, even if it is not measured. Likewise, I have also found that sometimes certain measurements are viewed as if they were objective, when actually they are not.

This crisis can be resolved with an extra dash of common sense. Measurement is important for those situations where measurement is essential for management. For that reason, though, we should not assume that every management skill can be measured in objective terms. Management can be based on certain hypotheses, and it is not necessary to prove them all in order to know if management has been successful. For example, a handshake and a smile from a collaborator tell more about his or her "engagement" than an opinion poll. A sincere pat on the shoulder can do more to motivate than a bonus calculated with a rigorous algorithm. With interpersonal relationships, common sense is a key we should not forget.

The Crisis of Rearview-Mirror Vision

The most traditional and mostly noted crisis in control systems in the corporate field is what I term *rearview-mirror vision*. Most measurements are based on the past—an unchanged past. Information about the past is important as long as it helps us understand the present and enables us to make decisions about the future.

I have been in South Florida many times during the hurricane season. It is interesting to see forecasters showing a hurricane or storm path in three time dimensions—where it has been, where it is now, and where it will be. Of course, the first two are true and the latter is just a probability. The past is represented by a line that starts across the Atlantic Ocean from Africa, the midsection (the present) by a twirling storm icon, and the third (the future) by two or more lines that show the most likely paths. It is true that, in many cases, the hurricane does not respect the probable path signaled by forecasters and diverts in another direction, making a left or right turn unexpectedly.

In the measurement of human capital management, there are many more beginnings and middles, and probably infinitely more possible final paths. Trying to predict the future with certainty is always beyond our intellectual possibilities, even with wide and accurate measurements. Yet trying to predict the future and proactively attempting to make it favorable are two of the key elements of success in corporate activity.

Measuring What Is Important

Based on the crises mentioned previously, I provide a model for their solutions, founded on the following assumptions:

* That which is measured should possess obvious consistency. In other words, two or more people should be able to interpret the information provided by the measurement in the same way.

* That which is measured should be important and should provide added value. For example, measuring staff satisfaction is important and valuable, as there is huge empiric demonstration that this aspect significantly affects results.

* The factors measured should be limited to a few, which allows focusing, and should be associated with the company's strategic concerns. The model is based on the results and consequences of human capital management—that is, a company may invest in staff selection (process), and the consequence or result is how many people were hired. Most indicators to measure human capital management (standardized indicators) are based on processes.

A value chain, shown in Figure 2.4, summarizes the model. This value chain has three stages. The basement, or "Past," represents the consequences of previous actions or decisions like the financial information you can get from a balance sheet. The ground floor, or "Present," represents the current reality. The first floor, or "Future," represents the levers that build the next times. The figure illustrates what the important fields

Figure 2.4. Value chain for HCM model.

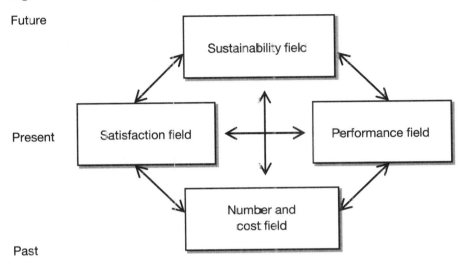

Future

Sustainability field

Present   Satisfaction field   Performance field

Number and
cost field

Past

are and where the impact of human capital management on organizations can be observed. It also makes obvious the need to use very flexible criteria to develop the measurement indicators.

First, there is a *number and cost field* The company's staff and working costs are figures that generally refer to the past. Human resources management generates the impacts that can be seen in this field. This chart's specificity depends on the nature of the business, on the strategic concerns, or on the form that added value takes. But it is clear that people responsible for the area cannot ignore the variables, such as how many people work in the company or how much was paid for salaries.

The second is the *performance field*. It shows what is currently being achieved and how it is being achieved. Most human resources management actions and initiatives should be aimed at improving performance. What is human capital or human resources management for? It is to help working people accomplish what they set out to do. That is why performance management is by far the most important operating tool and assessment is just part of that. Human capital management works, or is supposed to work, so that every person, every group, and the organization as a whole can reach the objectives that have been set. Here, management by competence—generic as well as technical—is a crucial aspect, as it is practically impossible to meet objectives without the knowledge, abilities, attitudes, and values required for successful performance.

The third element, which also belongs to the present, is the *satisfac-*

tion field. Here, I disclose my personal obsession—that everybody should have "a happy job." Without a doubt, there is an extraordinary relationship between performance and satisfaction, a virtuous circle. People who work well are satisfied, and when they are satisfied, they work better. To achieve this satisfaction, people's "engagement," or commitment, should be developed. An important aspect of this is the boss-collaborator relationship, measured with 360-degree feedback—it is engagement's alpha and omega. Also, among the best evidence of satisfaction is retention rate, which is calculated at 100 percent minus the voluntary turnover index.

But there is a fourth field, which is related to the future, and I call this the *sustainability field*. Here, I use two elements and two concepts for its analysis. The elements are talent and organizational knowledge; the analysis concepts are flow and stock. For example, the water in a container is stock, but if the glass is cracked and there is leakage, or if it is placed under the tap and is filling up, that is flow. What mainly assesses a company's money flow and stock in the future is the stock and flow of talent and knowledge. For instance, the percentage of key positions that have an identified successor, or the percentage of promotions granted, is directly related to the positive flow and accrual of talent. Similarly, the number of patents, technical documents, papers, databases, or manuals produced by a company increases its intellectual capital.

The model takes us to the next point. In the past months, I have discussed with hundreds of colleagues and students from our profession the following questions:

1. What is the important thing that human resources management should do?
2. What should we measure?

The second question is the natural consequence of the first, so we begin by defining what to do, and then we measure. Figure 2.5 shows a command board developed from the result-field model shown in Figure 2.4.

For that reason, I suggest a debate. In the past months, I have discussed with hundreds of colleagues and students from our profession two critical questions: (1) What is the important thing that human resources management should do? (2) What should we measure? The second answer is the result of the first question. Therefore, we should define what to do, and then we should measure. However, the conclusions arrived at after these meetings have been really surprising to me, since many people admit to not having ever asked themselves the first question, despite their having tried to answer the second question.

Figure 2.5. Command board for result-field model.

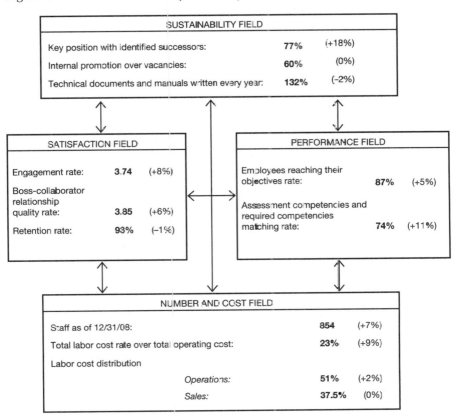

This change of natural order, whereby we place the "what to do" ahead of the "what to measure," may be one of the reasons human resources management has been so slow, uncertain, and sinuous about changing its destiny from a support area to a strategic partner. I encourage this debate; human capital management is the approach that deals with "making people work better to achieve their objectives, be happier, and provide a better future for all of us."

Note

1. G. A. Miller, "The Magical Number Seven, Plus or Minus Two: Some Limits on Our Capacity for Processing Information," *Psychological Review*, 63 (1956), 81–97, quoting Jeffrey Pfeffer and Robert I. Sutton, *The Knowing-Doing Gap* (Buenos Aires: Editorial Granica, 2005), 192.

STRATEGIC HUMAN CAPITAL MEASURES: USING LEADING HCM TO IMPLEMENT STRATEGY

Stephen Gates and Pascal Langevin

While the field of human capital measurement has been gaining ground over the past twenty years, it still remains largely disconnected from business strategy. In a recent report published by The Conference Board, only 12 percent of respondents reported making significant use of leading human capital measures (HCMs) to meet their strategic targets or key performance indicators (KPIs).[1] Nevertheless, 84 percent of the same respondents predicted that their use of HCMs to meet these goals will increase over the next three years. In this essay, we explore how HR professionals can align leading HCMs with strategy and use these measurement tools to enhance the implementation of human capital strategy through greater accountability and communication. We first provide results of a study showing that performance is indeed related to the implementation of HCMs, but also that few companies have yet to reach an advanced stage. We address the role that the HR function plays in the definition and implementation of strategy and HCMs. We then explore the leading HCMs that may predict the achievement of strategic goals. Finally, we present results regarding how HCMs are reported in scorecards to increase managers' information as well as accountability.

Implementation of HCMs and Performance

In many companies, benchmarking HR practices with rivals or "aspirational peers" has developed as a way of testing whether HR efforts and HCMs add value. Becker and Huselid warn, however, that a company should track HR practices against its own strategy: "Strategies are successful when they create a unique value proposition. . . . [T]hat means the measure of HR's *strategic* performance must be focused internally on those unique, strategically relevant contributions—not externally on non-strategic measures such as cost per hire or benefits as a percent of revenue."[2]

Since human capital plays a fundamental role in the creation of value, the use of relevant HCMs can contribute greatly to achieving the company's strategic goals. First, managers can use HCMs to identify and pay attention to key competencies, which can thus be used to build a competitive advantage. Second, HCMs can improve the evaluation of strategy execution. Instead of using *lagging* indicators that measure performance after the fact, practitioners have developed approaches that aim at using *leading* indicators to measure drivers of performance.

Satisfactory performance at the human capital level increases the predictability of a good performance at the company level. Strategy maps in their various forms, such as the Balanced Scorecard with its "learning and growth" quadrant,[3] and Skandia's Value Scheme[4] and its formulation into the Navigator, are striking examples of models where HCMs are considered to contribute in a fundamental way to achieving strategic objectives. We can expect that the more advanced a company is in the implementation of HCMs, the higher its performance will be.

Yet, implementing HCMs is a difficult process that can stretch out over a long period, especially if the resources allocated to the project are inadequate and subject to cuts. Typically, the first step is to determine an accurate headcount, which can be a formidable task in itself, especially in large, global companies. Next, tracking the cost of HR activities with HCM efficiency measures of time and cost—more operational metrics—comes into play. Later, monitoring investments in workforce capability, with HCMs measuring effectiveness and impact, are created and implemented. Accordingly, Boudreau and Ramstad[5] propose three categories of HCMs corresponding to the stage of advancement of HCM implementation: (1) efficiency measures that focus on cost and report the financial efficiency of human resources operations; (2) effectiveness measures that reflect the effectiveness of human resources programs on the competence, motivation, and attitude of the workforce; and (3) impact indicators that measure the impact of human resources programs and processes on business performance.

To analyze the predictability of HCM implementation on performance, we designed a study that relies on a quantitative analysis of survey questionnaires collected from 104 HR executives as well as on a qualitative investigation using six interviews. Our results show that performance is positively associated with the stage of implementation of HCMs.[5] The development of HCM systems—as well as, in a general way, the implementation of performance measurement systems—enables an organization to measure and, it is hoped, to better manage its performance.

Quotes from our interviews confirm that measuring human capital helps decision making. For example:

* "The new director intends to use human capital metrics in a dashboard to open each monthly meeting with the HR managers in the businesses. This dashboard will be used as a diagnostic tool to help information-driven decision making."

* "Once they were in managers' performance scorecard, human capital metrics entered into their line of sight and results improved."

However, most companies in our survey have not reached an advanced stage of HCM implementation. Table 2.1 indicates that only 43 percent of the sample respondents have reached the last two stages, where the greater benefits of linking HCMs to strategy could be realized.

In this sample, fewer than half of the respondent companies would even be able to align with strategy. Until companies achieve this last phase, the value of the HCM measurement effort is often unclear, which can slow progress even more. HCM implementation can also depend on HR managers' involvement in developing the company's strategy.

The Role and Perspective of the HR Function

HR professionals can enhance the role that the human resources function plays in strategy formulation and implementation. Our results show that the more HR managers participate in the definition of strategy, the more advanced the company is in the implementation of its HCMs.[7] HR managers who participate in the development of strategy seem to be aware of the importance of using HCMs to align human resources with the strategy. Furthermore, our study shows that HR managers would like to develop HCMs that are consistent with strategy.[8] In companies following a differentiation strategy, they are interested in HCMs measuring employees' innovative capacities,[9] whereas in cost-leader companies, HR managers prefer HCMs measuring employees' ability to manage costs.[10] This confirms the "fit" (or alignment) literature that maintains that performance measurement systems that are aligned with strategy can be extended more specifically to HCMs.

This result was confirmed in interviews. For example, one respondent stated:

Table 2.1. *Stage of HCM implementation (% of respondents).*

HCM Implementations	Percentage Response
Our company does not measure human capital.	98.0
We are working on defining HC measures and beginning to collect data.	27.7
We have efficiency (time and cost) HC measures in place.	27.7
We have efficiency and effectiveness (ability, motivation, performance) HC measures in place.	35.7
We have efficiency, effectiveness, and impact (on business process and strategic outcome) HC measures in place.	6.9

> We are trying to develop a three-level human capital scorecard.
> The first level will consist of company-wide basic core key per-
> formance indicators for all [of] the workforce. The second level
> will be more strategic, linking human capital metrics to next
> year's business units' development plans. The third level will be a
> top-down human capital measurement effort focused on talent
> and performance management for a selected group of employees.
> So this requires that we develop a high degree of strategic align-
> ment for the second and third level of human capital measures.

Thus, HR professionals can create or customize strategic HCMs and
implement them within the company's strategic performance measurement system to enhance performance. The more knowledge that HR professionals have about which human capital enablers help implement
strategy, the more they can focus on customizing HCMs aligned with
strategy.

However, Figure 2.6 indicates that only 22 percent of respondents
claim that HR is a full partner in developing and implementing business
strategy. Less than half (47 percent) claim that HR does more than simply
help implement business strategy once it has been developed.

Figure 2.6. HR's role in strategy formulation.

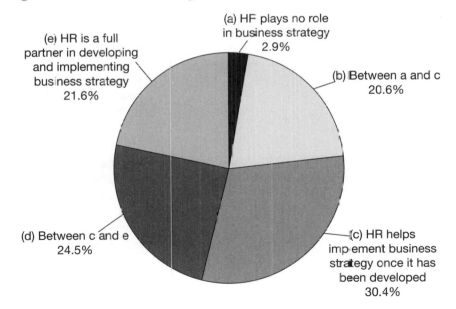

HR's lack of involvement in formulating or actively implementing strategy could limit HR partners' ability to understand their managers' business KPIs, and to help them deliver these KPIs with the help of HCMs. It could also explain why so few companies do create HCMs to measure the capacity to innovate or to identify new business opportunities. In our sample, the low involvement of the HR function in the strategy formulation could explain the low stage of HCM implementation.

One solution can be found with Huselid, Becker, and Beatty,[11] who advocate a new, supplementary scorecard for executives to manage and measure their workforce in conjunction with HR. They argue that a "workforce scorecard" should be the means to execute their people strategy, in addition to the overall balanced scorecard and the specific HR scorecard for the activities of the HR department. The authors encourage senior executives to take greater responsibility for setting measures and targets for people. In this way, HR's lack of involvement in setting strategy would not hinder the execution of the company's people strategy through selecting the best-aligned HCMs.

The Quest for Predictive HCMs

While human capital measurement could vary according to the company's strategy, HR's involvement in strategy formulation, and the stage of HCM implementation, the search for *predictive* metrics continues. The performance indicators that human resources people monitor and the tasks they undertake are directly linked to financial performance. Success in recruitment increases productivity through increasing revenue per person or decreasing cost per unit produced. Success in training has similar effects, *provided the lessons are remembered and used*. But as with other human capital metrics, establishing direct causal relationships and translating these truisms into a system for controlling action is tricky. Identifying which create leverage is trickier still.

But how can a company determine which HCMs are the most effective leading indicators? By comparing the rankings for the most frequently used measures to the measures that survey participants found to be leading metrics, we can make a number of observations (see Table 2.2).

First, the percentages indicate that there is a low level of consensus on what constitutes a leading HCM. Only a third of respondents consider that leadership or readiness measures are leading. Second, of the four main leading HCMs, only one—employee engagement—is frequently used (more than 50 percent of cases). The results raise two questions:

Table 2.2. Leading HCM and frequency of use.

Human Capital Measures (HCMs)	Leading HCM*	Frequency of use†
Employee engagement	69.2%	77.9%
Leadership	38.5	47.1
Employee commitment	36.5	40.4
Readiness level	33.7	44.2
Turnover (voluntary)	28.8	94.2
Employee satisfaction	28.8	64.4
Competence level	27.9	36.5
Workforce diversity	24.0	78.8
Training	21.2	57.7
Promotion rate	17.3	44.2
Executive stability (or churn)	17.3	31.7
Workforce age	16.3	65.4
Health and safety	14.4	48.1
Span of control	8.7	39.4
Depletion cost	5.8	14.4
Other	4.8	8.7

* = % of HR professionals naming these HCMs as being leading indicators; † = % of HR professionals naming these HCMs as being in use in their company.

1. Why is there so little agreement on what is considered to be a leading HCM?
2. Why are the most frequently used HCMs lagging, not leading, measures?

One would expect that for HCMs to align with strategic KPIs and help managers achieve them, leading, rather than lagging, HCMs would be more appropriate. However, other studies have shown that some HCMs seemed to be adequate in many situations. For example, Dr. Jac Fitz-enz's work with companies since the 1980s suggests that eight predictive HCMs have wide validity in a large number of circumstances:[12]

1. *Professional/Managerial Ratio:* The number of professionals and managers expressed as a percentage of the total number of full-time equivalents in the workforce. In general, the higher the ratio, the greater the prospect for future growth and profitability.

2. *Readiness Ratio:* The percentage of key jobs with at least one person ready to take over. This measure suggests the resilience of the organization against disruption. The closer to 1, the better.

3. *Commitment Ratio:* The percentage of staff committed to the company's vision. Measured by employee survey, the higher, the better.

4. *Leadership Rating:* Performance rating of current leaders, as measured by the staff, again through a survey.

5. *Climate-Culture Rating:* The percentage of staff giving top scores about whether the company is a good place to work. Measured by survey, this is predictive of the employee retention rates, and therefore retained knowledge.

6, *Training Rating:* Scores from current programs. But what's important is developing skills to get the job done now, not necessarily those needed for prospective future requirements. Having skills you don't use and don't need subtracts from corporate value, rather than adding to it.

7. *Accession Ratio:* The ratio of new and replacement hires as the percentage of total employment. In most organizations a high number indicates hidden costs and delays, which damage productivity.

8. *Depletion Ratio:* Annual percentage of top talent lost. This is a negative indicator. The higher the number, the worse your future prospects.

Other experts suggest additional formulations of predictive HCMs. Although Michael Bokina, former manager at Saratoga/PwC, stressed that every organization is different, making it difficult to offer "typical" leading indicators, generic correlation analysis shows that three HCMs are leading indicators.[13]

1. *Executive Stability Ratio and Separation Rate:* Corporations with executives having more than three years' executive experience lowers voluntary turnover.

2. *Management Ratio and Promotion Rate:* The number of employees that each manager supports impacts the number of promotions. Span of control is important in developing employees professionally: A manager supervising fewer employees has a lower number of promotions available.

3. *Training Investment Factor and Promotion Rate:* More dollars allocated to training will increase professional employee development.

Mark Graham Brown suggests using as a starting point a simple human capital index made up of four submetrics: number of years in the business or field, level in the company by job grade or organizational chart, performance rating, and number of positions or assignments held. The index would then assign a percentage to each of these. Brown also suggests a more complex index involving one component in which experience and performance measures are grouped together and a second that groups competencies and skills.[14]

As a major company ERP software provider, SAP reported on its own effort, starting in 2003, to link human capital practices with performance improvements.[15] When the business was struggling a few years earlier, management also became dissatisfied with its efforts to track investments in human capital. It knew these investments were growing in importance, but the systems it had in place to measure them weren't adequate. Working with Accenture, it developed a model involving measuring thirteen human capital processes that fed into seven HC capabilities. One year into its turnaround efforts it found that many initiatives seemed to be paying off in relatively high process and capability scores.

Nevertheless, many HCMs get reported only at quite a high level of aggregation, which may be sufficient for understanding what's happening in functions with a large number of largely undifferentiated workers. But Huselid and colleagues make the point that "companies simply can't afford to have 'A players' in all positions. Rather, businesses need to adopt a portfolio approach to workforce management, systematically identifying their strategically important A positions, supporting B positions, and surplus C positions, then focusing disproportionate resources on making sure A players hold A positions."[16] The risk associated with having the wrong person in a job is high, as is the opportunity cost of keeping an A person in a C job. The implication is that human capital measurement needs to be quite granular: "We all know that effective business strategy requires differentiating a firm's products and services in ways that create value for customers. Accomplishing this requires a differentiated workforce strategy, as well."[17]

Moreover, even when well focused on a differentiated workforce, leading HCMs can backfire if not properly integrated with the complex system of the organization. John Boudreau and Peter Ramstad say that attempts to link HR practices to strategic ones are often crude and not really integrated.[18] An organization might have the strategic goal of increasing sales of solutions, and then set an HR measure to increase bonuses for solutions-selling activities. But without business integration to ensure that products themselves integrate into solutions or that the right talent pools are in place, the bonuses won't work.

Increasing Accountability and Communication with HCMs

Use of HCMs in Scorecards

In order to learn more about how widespread these techniques are for increasing HCM accountability, our questionnaire asked about the use of HCMs in scorecards and in managers' bonus plans.

In Figure 2.7, 69 percent of our survey respondents acknowledged that HCMs are being used in a scorecard. Logically, this would increase the chance for a regular review of key HCM metrics. However, 69 percent of respondents also rated the effectiveness of the HCMs in their scorecard as moderate or less than moderate. Clearly, even when HCMs are found in a regular reporting tool such as a scorecard, this does not necessarily guarantee that they are successfully applied.

One method to sharpen managers' focus on HCM metrics and targets is to embed the metrics in bonus plans. While they might not agree with the construction of the metrics or the measures as targets, managers will become more aware of the company's people goals. Survey data also suggest that putting people measures in bonus plans correlates with successful links between business strategies and certain people measures (turnover, leadership, and health and safety).[19] In our study, 56.7 percent of respondent firms reward managers based on people measures; 47.8 percent of respondents also reported that HCMs receive over 15 percent weighting in bonus plans. At this level of weighting, managers have a strong interest in taking HCMs and people activities more seriously.

Nevertheless, when asked if the HCMs are aligned with company strategy, 63.8 percent admit that they are less than moderately or only moderately aligned in bonus plans. This lack of alignment does not bode well for the role of HCMs in helping managers achieve their strategic business goals or KPIs.

HCMs as Communication Tools

Human capital measures are communication tools that can convey important information to HR and business leaders. Figure 2.8 shows that 78 percent of respondents to our survey indicated that their companies

Figure 2.7. Use and effectiveness of HCMs in a scorecard.

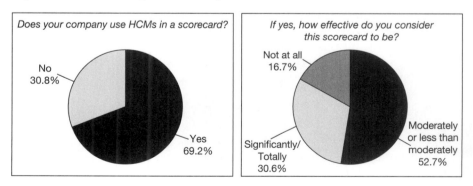

Figure 2.8. Frequency of reporting HCMs to top management.

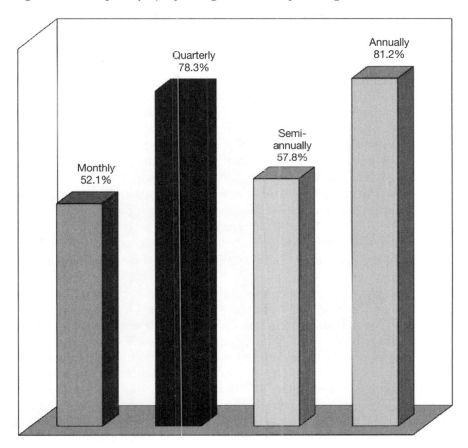

release their HCM results to senior leaders on a quarterly basis, perhaps reflecting a desire to align the perspectives of HR professionals with those of business managers, who also report on a quarterly schedule. But it should also be noted that 52 percent of participating companies present HCM results on a monthly basis, allowing the measures to be of greater help in identifying where corrective action is needed at an earlier stage.

Not only does the timing of the reporting vary from company to company, there are wide differences in the number of measures presented to top management: 23 percent of companies report one to three HCMs; 34 percent report four to six HCMs; 10 percent report seven to nine HCMs; and 33 percent report ten or more. The majority of respondent companies offer between four and ten HCMs, reflecting the belief of performance management experts that managers may have difficulty focusing on more than seven measures at a time.[20]

The number of HCMs may also be influenced by the fact that the distribution of people metrics reports in surveyed companies is limited primarily to top management. That is, 43 percent of respondents distribute HCMs to selected business managers, while only 19 percent of firms circulate HCM results to all business managers. One HR professional spoke from experience in saying that when the people measures spread good news, then the report is widely distributed; if they do not reflect a positive picture, then circulation is limited. She explained that broad distribution of results without a clear understanding of what the people measures mean and how they are linked to business strategy could lead to misinterpretation. While this may be true, the relatively small distribution of results also means that the findings are seldom broken down to the appropriate level for action planning.[21] A potential solution for both problems would be to provide both HR generalists and managers with systematic training in the use and interpretation of people measures.

Making HCMs Deliver on the Promise

Developing a strategic human capital orientation and applying human capital metrics to implement it remain high on the list of HR directors' priorities in many companies. While human capital strategy should derive from the company's overall strategy, which by definition should be unique and inimitable, many HCMs are standardized and often benchmarked against competitors. Nevertheless, our results demonstrate that HR managers do align their interests in choosing and/or creating leading HCMs with their companies' strategy.

While there was little consensus about which HCMs are leading, employee engagement seems to be one likely candidate for most survey participants. Experts are proposing a number of creative HCMs that could fit company strategy. Moreover, HR professionals are experimenting with leading HCMs that are applied to specific elements of the workforce—notably, those identified as strategic talent groups.

Accountability for human capital measurement could be enhanced by first convincing business managers that HCMs will help them to manage their workforce better, not just to manage HR activities better. To equip managers with the necessary knowledge to use HCMs, HR should also invest in training not only HR partners but also the business managers themselves. Training could show managers how human capital targets link to their strategic plan KPIs, and help them meet the HC targets set in their bonus plans.

Even when they are not used to set targets in bonus plans, HCMs can improve communication about the impact of human capital activities for workforce performance and results. The frequency of reporting HCMs could be greater and the breadth of distribution of HCM reporting could be widened. If monthly HCM reporting were done throughout the management ranks, HCMs could play a more important role as leading indicators of human capital performance and so allow managers to take more timely corrective actions.

Notes

1. *Measuring More Than Efficiency: The New Role of Human Capital Metrics*, R-1356-04, p. 7. The authors appreciate the contribution of The Conference Board, a not-for-profit organization that works as a global, independent membership organization in the public interest, with offices in New York, Brussels, Hong Kong, and Beijing. It conducts research, convenes conferences, makes forecasts, assesses trends, publishes information and analyses, and brings executives together to learn from one another.
2. B. Becker and M. Huselid, "Measuring HR? Benchmarking Is Not the Answer," *HR Magazine*, December (2003), 57–61.
3. R. S. Kaplan and D. P. Norton, *The Balanced Scorecard: Translating Strategy into Action* (Boston: Harvard Business School Press, 1996).
4. L. Edvinsson, "Developing Intellectual Capital at Skandia," *Long Range Planning* 30, no. 3 (1997), 366–73.
5. J. Boudreau and P. Ramstad, "Strategic HRM Measurement in the 21st Century: From Justifying HR to Strategic Talent Leadership," in *HRM in the 21st Century*, eds. M. Goldsmith, R. Gandossy, and M. Efron (New York: John Wiley, 2003), 79–90.
6. $R^2 = 0.280$, $p < 0.01$. We used Boudreau and Ramstad's categories to measure HCM stage of implementation. We measured performance with an eight-item question designed by T. C. Huang, "The Effects of Linkage Between Business and Human Resource Management Strategies," *Personnel Review* 30, no. 2 (2001), 132–51.
7. $R^2 = 0.251$, $p < 0.01$. We measured HR involvement in the definition of strategy by using the items given in Figure 2.5.
8. We measured strategy by asking respondents to indicate the percentage of their sales accounted for by products representing use of a low-cost or differentiation strategy, the total amounting to 100 percent. We also measured their interest in HCMs by designing a question listing eight categories of HCMs reflecting innovation or cost reduction. Two types of HCMs were derived: One factor measured employees' work efficiency and cost-consciousness (efficiency indicators), whereas the second factor measured employees' entrepreneurial and innovative capabilities (innovation indicators) We then analyzed the association between these two variables.

9. $R^2 = 0.297$, $p < 0.01$.

10. $R^2 = -0.193$, $p < 0.05$.

11. M. Huselid, B. Becker, and R. Beatty, *The Workforce Scorecard, Managing Human Capital to Execute Strategy* (Boston: Harvard Business School Press, 2005).

12. J. Fitz-Enz, Webcast presentation to The Conference Board's working group on human capital measurement, May 4, 2006, New York.

13. M. Bokina, presentation to The Conference Board's working group on human capital measurement, Washington, D.C., June 6, 2006.

14. M. G. Brown, "Human Capital's Measure for Measure," *Journal for Quality and Participation* 22, no. 5 (September–October 1999), 28–31.

15. S. Cantrell, J. M. Benton, T. Laudal, and R. J. Thomas, "Measuring the Value of Human Capital Investments: The SAP Case," *Strategy & Leadership* 34, no. 2 (2006), 45.

16. M. Huselid, R. W. Beatty, and B. E. Becker, "'A Players' or 'A Positions'? The Strategic Logic of Workforce Management," *Harvard Business Review* 83, no. 12 (December 2005), 110–17.

17. Ibid., 117.

18. J. Boudreau and P. M. Ramstad, "Strategic HRM Measurement in the 21st Century: From Justifying HR to Strategic Talent Leadership," a Cornell University working paper, 2002.

19. *Linking People Measures to Strategy: From Top Management Support to Line Management Buy-in*, The Conference Board, 1342-03-RR, p. 26.

20. A. Davila, R. Kaplan, and R. Simons, *Performance Measurement and Control Systems for Implementing Strategy* (Upper Saddle River, N.J.: Prentice Hall, 2000), 239–40.

21. A. Yeung and B. Berman, "Adding Value Through Human Resources: Reorienting Human Resources Measurement to Drive Business Performance," *Human Resource Management* 36, no. 3 (Fall 1997), 334.

FROM BUSINESS ANALYTICS TO RATIONAL ACTION

Kirk Smith

Now that organizations have fine-tuned human performance, supply chain, operations, processes, cycle time, and other targeted areas, how can they continue to improve performance? In their book *Competing on Analytics*, Thomas Davenport and Jeanne Harris identify business analytics as the key to gaining competitive advantage. According to the authors, it is this "extensive use of data, statistical and quantitative analysis, explanatory and predictive models, and fact-based management" that can drive the decisions and actions that will yield performance improvements and opportunities for innovation. When metrics were introduced to human resources in 1978, the purpose was to give HR the tools to understand and communicate the value of its services. Today, it is no longer a choice. This essay describes how and why analytics must become part of HR's tool kit.

Getting Started

Beginning with the business intelligence and decision support systems movements of the 1960s, and the ubiquitous enterprise-wide technology systems such as Enterprise Resource Planning (ERP) and Customer Relations Management (CRM) of recent decades, the data for business analytics have become available. While many companies, overwhelmed by all these data, cry "data, data everywhere but not a drop to drink," others are what Davenport and Harris call "analytic competitors"—the companies with the skills and support needed to use data effectively. But both groups struggle with the same endgame, or how to use the data to make good business decisions that lead to effective action and provide positive business results.

The gap between data and action is bridged by good decision making. The business analytics literature uses the term *decision making* a lot—I mean, a heck of a lot. But decision making is usually portrayed as a given. It assumes that people know how to make good, rational decisions as long as they have data and the chops to take action. It assumes that if you can find hidden gems in data, the decisions are automatically made. Maybe they are; but are they good, rational decisions that have a positive impact on business results? The literature tells us what needs to be done, but not how to do it. It's like the first step of the old Steve Martin comedy routine on how to get rich: "Okay, first you get a million dollars, then you . . ."

One roadblock people often encounter with decision making is knowing where to start. I recommend starting with a decision statement—a short statement describing what you need to decide or recommend. This helps keep your attention focused on the purpose of the decision. An example of a decision statement is: "Select high potentials to be included in the leadership development program." Keeping the statement visible to all involved in the decision helps keep everyone focused on what you are trying to accomplish. You may have to refer back to it often. Simply agreeing on a decision statement will often bring a group much closer to making a decision.

The next step is to develop objectives. These are the criteria that will influence the choice and help you define success. The reason you do this is to help evaluate your alternatives fairly. Without these objectives, how will you know when the goal—your decision—is met? Another common mistake in decision making is to look at your alternatives before developing your objectives, allowing pet alternatives to influence your objectives and bias your decision process. For example, in the leadership development program stated previously, the objectives taken from correlative data of existing successful leaders could be as follows:

* At least two years of service
* Managed at least one high-profile project
* Team lead or higher
* At least some graduate-level education
* Good communication skills as assessed by the manager

Next, you classify the objectives into "musts" and "wants" to help determine the role that these objectives will play in the decision; that way you can be clear about what is mandatory and what is desired. To qualify as a "must," the objective has to have a yes answer to these three questions:

1. Is it mandatory?
2. Is it measurable (with a limit)?
3. Is it realistic?

Once you have determined your "musts," everything else is a "want." It should be noted that a "must" is not necessarily your most important objective—just a minimum standard for screening. The biggest mistake people make here is having too many "musts." If you follow the above criteria, there should be very few. For our example, let's say that "At least two years of service" is our only "must." This process sometimes requires patience on the part of the decision-making group. Next, you weigh the "wants" by assigning relative values to them to show how much each "want" will influence the choice. The most important "wants" get a value of 10. These are the benchmarks. All others are given weights based on their relative importance to the benchmarks. There can be more than one benchmark; leading this discussion in the group can sometimes require a modicum of facilitation skills and patience.

After you have classified your objectives into "musts" and "wants," now and only now do you generate alternatives by identifying or creating possible choices to expand the number of choices and increase the chances of picking winners. Continuing with our example, querying your data warehouse with your criteria should give you alternatives.

But suppose you generate twenty alternatives and have only ten slots available? The next step is to screen the alternatives through the "musts" to determine if any alternatives meet the "musts." This eliminates choices that do not meet minimum requirements. Gather and record factual data, determine if alternatives are a "go" or "no go," and eliminate any "no go" alternatives. With the remaining alternatives, compare them against the "wants," evaluating their relative importance to determine which alternatives create the most benefit. You do this by:

* Recording factual, accurate supporting data
* Scoring the best performer for each objective with a 10
* Comparing the relative performance of other alternatives (0–10)
* Multiplying the objective weight by the performance score
* Totaling the weighted scores

In our example, you would consider the top ten scores, but you have not made your decision yet. You have to consider risks. In the risk-management step, you try to identify potential adverse consequences by identifying future threats for the best performers. This helps you understand the risk of choosing the alternative. In our example, you would take the top ten performing alternatives and ask questions such as:

* What could go wrong, short and long term, if this alternative were chosen?
* What disadvantages are associated with this alternative?
* Where might information about this alternative be invalid or wrong?
* What are the implications?

An example of a risk in our example might be "If we choose John, he would have to be taken off the ABC Project and that would jeopardize its success." For each risk, ask if you are willing to accept the risk to gain the benefits of the choice. If yes, pick it. If no, repeat for the next alternative until you have your ten candidates for the program.

The Rewards of a Decision-Making Process

Having a common, fact-based decision-making process requires commitment, critical thinking, and rational thought. It is not easy to implement in an organization that is used to shooting from the hip, going with the gut, or winging it, but the benefits are plentiful. It consistently brings logic and clarity to the way decisions are made. When a structured, evidence-based decision process is used, the following are likely to occur:

* Focus is maintained.
* Objectives are identified and weighted.
* Facts and not politics play a larger role.
* Facts are more fully shared.
* Biases are minimized.
* Common language facilitates communication.
* Less information is overlooked.
* Experience and judgment are used more effectively.

The point is that sound, systematic decision making complements the skilled use of business analytics, creating a powerful performance-improvement tool. Figure 2.9 summarizes the decision analysis process.

For those organizations interested in reaping the benefits of a fact-based decision culture, a good measurement system is a necessity. You should have a good measurement system, but you need to be careful that you are not just setting up a measurement bureaucracy. It is tempting to fall into the trap of measuring what is easy or just measuring for its own sake—but neither of those does any good. To be able to make sound decisions, you need to measure the right things. Start at the top. What metrics does the organization value most? Is it net profit, EBITDA, operating profit, cash flow? Find out and make sure what you measure is linked to the most important organizational measures. What are the drivers in human capital management? Whatever you choose, it should support the organization being managed as an adaptive system.

An Example

This powerful decision-making tool can be demonstrated in the way we at Kepner-Tregoe (KT) use a specialized human capital analytics system to collect, store, retrieve, and report on the effectiveness of our skills-transfer programs. The data mart helps us uncover gaps, patterns, and trends that allow us to make process-improvement decisions for our clients that are based on relevant data. The system uses a participant survey to gather data in seven categories—instructor, environment, courseware, learning, job impact, business results, and ROI. Sixty days later, a follow-up survey is sent to true-up the job impact and business results data and to gather information from participants about the barriers to and

Figure 2.9. The decision analysis process.

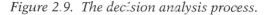

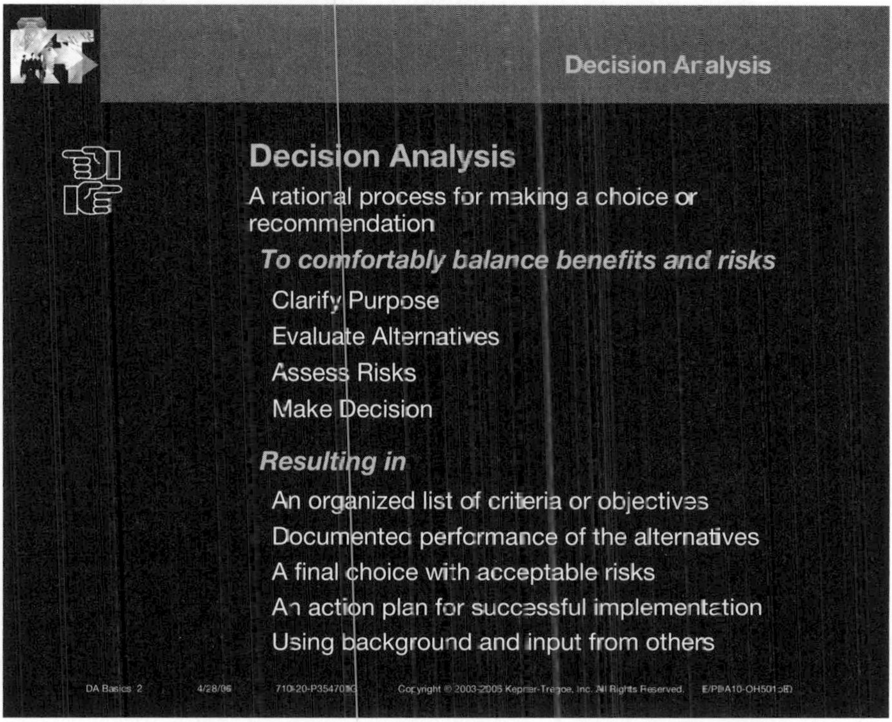

DA Basics 2   4/28/06   710-20-P354700   Copyright © 2003-2005 Kepner-Tregoe, Inc. All Rights Reserved.   E/PBA10-OH501-0ID

enablers for using their new skills. We then analyze these data to find correlations, patterns. and gaps. From here, we can make decisions and take actions that remove barriers, encourage enabling factors, improve processes, and optimize the effectiveness of future interventions.

For example, in a recent study, we sent a customized follow-up survey to determine the overall effectiveness of a large-scale KT training program and the key variables that contributed to its effectiveness. The highest correlation with improved productivity was with participants who had met with their managers before and immediately after the training to discuss expectations and intended actions for using new skills. While this result is hardly a surprise, a significant portion of the managers did not bother to conduct this key step. There was also a strong association between confidence in using the new skills and awareness of when to use them—that is, the triggers or signals to perform. Similarly, those with the most confidence in using their skills tended to demonstrate the greatest performance improvement.

We worked with the client to use these and other data to make informed decisions for future training. More sophisticated statistical analyses are planned to determine causal links between variables that will help us build predictive models and optimum profiles of participants, as well as discover leading indicators to predict trends.

Business analytics and decision analysis are powerful tools in the performance-improvement toolbox. With annual spending on learning and development alone estimated to be as high as $100 billion in the United States, human capital analytics, as a subset of business analytics, and systematic decision making have great potential for uncovering untapped opportunities for improvements in human performance through good decision making about future required resources, plans, policies, schedules, or structures.

PART 2

The HCM:21® Model

CHAPTER THREE

Scan the Market, Manage the Risk

"It is remarkable how far some people will go to avoid thought."
—THOMAS ALVA EDISON

Every endeavor, from sports to warfare to business operations, demands preparation if you expect to succeed. In a business enterprise, or even a not-for-profit organization, preparation starts with an environmental scan. An environmental scan studies all forces external to an organization that are relevant to its operation. HCM:21 also looks internally at situations that may need reconfiguring in the new term. The key question a scan answers is: What is going on outside and inside that might affect future operations?

There are scans and there are scans. Many scans are little peeks into the future as a preparation for budgeting Often, there is no intent to change anything. The scan is seen as a perfunctory act, which must be done to satisfy someone. Of course, someone looks at the market, but how broadly or deeply does the person study it? A true scan, however, is both wide and deep. It is not confined to one aspect of the external environment, such as labor demographics or economic trends. The intent is to find something useful, not just collect information that confirms current or past beliefs. True scans cover every potentially relevant variable outside the organization, as well as inside. In the process, this intent acknowledges that there are factors inside an organization that could benefit from an in-depth review, and these include, but are not limited to, the CEO's vision, brand, culture, leadership, financial viability, and employee capabilities.

The other aspect of a true scan is that it looks for connections between and among the external and internal forces at work in the organization's environment. This is where the "value door" opens. Because an organization is so complex, the variables constantly connect, collide, separate, and frustrate each other. They can both reinforce and create chaos. This interplay is often unrecognized because most organizations operate as a set of silos. Each function can become so myopic that it doesn't see, know, or care about the others. Indeed, this is a perennial misalignment problem that many organizations struggle with, and it is a barrier to their sustainable success.

The Big Picture

Predictive management, or the essence of HCM:21, executes a strategic scan of the external forces and internal factors that can affect the three fundamentals of an organization: human, structural, and relational capital. *Human capital* is your employees. *Structural capital* is the things you own, ranging from patents and copyrights, to software programs and codified processes, to physical facilities and equipment. *Relational capital* is the knowledge and contacts you have with external stakeholders, which includes everyone who is touched by your organization—the list can be quite long.

Externally, the forces can include at least the following:

Industry trends
Competitors
Brand reputation
Technological advancements
Regulations and laws
Regional, national, and global economic situation
Globalization demands
Customer demands and interests
Supplier capacity
Materials quality, prices, and availability
Labor supply
Job applicants
Educational institutions
Stockholders

There are also internal matters that might affect the organization's ability to manage effectively. The inside list includes factors that need to be reviewed in light of recent market trends The list can include:

Vision
Values
Culture
Leadership
Management wisdom
Mission-critical retention rates
Engagement levels
Facilities and equipment
Product life cycles
Employee brand awareness
General turnover levels
Skills and capability levels
Financial capability
Ability to enter new markets
Quality, innovation, productivity, service (QIPS) levels

Figure 3.1 is an outline or template, in the form of a matrix, for a strategic scan of an organization's environment. It is not all-inclusive; in practice, the list of forces and factors that management generates can be much larger. Still, this matrix shows the range of effects likely to be relevant to your organization. By using this matrix, you can see the connections and influences across various cells. Management acknowledges superficially that everything in an organization is tied together; however, the interrelationships are often downplayed. Focusing on these interdependencies is the first place where our model brings in the critical concept of *integration*.

Look at the template. Do you see how people and facilities interact? How obvious is it that technology affects both employees and customers? Only after you take this initial step can you begin to plan for the future. Otherwise, you are operating like Lewis and Clark, exploring an unknown territory. Every morning, you will wake up wondering what danger will be lurking over the next hill.

You might have noticed that, among the items listed as "internal factors," is brand. Although brand is a separate factor, in actuality, a CEO's vision, culture, and brand must overlap and function in a single, integrated manner. Obviously, a CEO's vision drives the corporate culture; in turn, culture and brand correlate. If your brand stands for high quality, great service, or precision, then your culture must personify that. A loose

Figure 3.1. Template for a strategic scan.

Organizational Capital	Human	Structural	Relational
External Forces			
Labor supply	Acquire and retain	Remodel workspaces	Find new contacts
Economy	Incent service	Sell off real estate	Retain customers
Globalization	Find new people	Reorganize	Expand suppliers
Regulations	Modify benefits	Go green	Lobby government
New technology	Train staff	Invest in equipment	Update customers
Competitors	Research new knowledge	Design new products	Speed to market
Internal Factors			
CEO's vision	Translate for employees	Make new signs/forms	Advertise in market
Culture	Employee branding	Protocol review	Talk to customers
Brand	Describe to employees	Design facilities	Marketing materials
Capabilities	Facilitate/support	Upgrade processes	Sell competence
Leadership	Survey employees	Review span of control	Visit customers
Finances	Control new hires	Manage expenses	Curtail travel

culture cannot provide great service or high-quality products. Additionally, culture and brand are made visible in the way you design and maintain work spaces (structural capital). Product quality is certainly dependent on good tools, well-maintained facilities, and efficient processes.

The more you examine the matrix, the more you will understand how interdependent everything is within an organization. Ironically, companies work against that concept as they set up separate silos for functions and reward departments for their performance—performance that may or may not support the overall effectiveness of the organization.

Disruptive Technologies Bring Change

Consider the health-care debate in America today. All parties, from providers to insurers to the government, have a stake in any changes to be made in our health-care delivery system, especially how to curb the steadily rising costs while expanding health care to all people. Providers want to do the best job they can, while limiting their liability for errors.

Insurers want to provide coverage as long as they can raise premiums fast enough to maintain profits. Government's goal is to expand coverage to the uninsured without raising taxes. In all the arguments, the basic point is not being addressed. How do we contain costs and still provide service when 70 percent of the money goes to pay health-care professionals? The answer is disruptive technology.

We have to think differently. The old model doesn't work because it is inherently inefficient. Hospitals have always run on a cost-plus model. That is no longer feasible, for several well-known reasons. So, how do we disrupt the model? Disruption seldom comes from inside, where all the vested interests lie. It intrudes from outside, where fresh visions are born. In this case, we need a vision from outside of new ways to manage inside costs.

Think of the just-in-time (JIT) inventory control and process optimization that were adopted in the 1970s. America adopted the inventory-maintenance ideas from the Japanese system for reducing costs. And it is not only the material cost that is saved; in a JIT inventory system a company also doesn't have to pay for a large warehouse. Inventory does not become obsolete as it sits waiting to be used; hence, waste is eliminated. Also, there doesn't have to be a large staff to manage masses of material.

Applying the idea to health care, we find isolated cases in America where hospital managers use JIT and have cut some material costs by over 50 percent. Process optimization also has cut costs by reducing the time that health-care providers spend on administrative procedures. Streamlining the time it takes to get supplies and to discharge patients has helped hospitals shift nursing staff to providing care in lieu of filling out forms. Additionally, this shift in work cuts down on nursing errors, which often add to a patient's time in the hospital. Open-minded, in-depth scanning can reveal relationships among forces and factors, and that marketplace data can be turned into management intelligence.

Another Case of Missed Opportunity

The value of scanning comes through in another example. In this one a major retailer had been gradually introducing nonperishable food items into its general operation. Although the food was processed and packaged, it required special handling that the retailer's regular shoe boxes and sweaters didn't. Yet, this situation was not immediately appreciated by management. But the scan revealed new problems involving structural capital. Now, warehouses had to be cleaner and more sensitive goods had to be handled differently. The scan showed management that heating and air-conditioning, plus refrigeration, were now mission-critical issues.

Additionally, the scan pointed out that within America's vastly diverse populations, there were significant differences in food consumption. If the retail stores and warehouses were in Los Angeles or Miami, they needed to stock Mexican and Latin American foods—and this meant more than tortillas and jalapeños. Other cities had large Indian, Greek, and Middle Eastern populations to be considered. Before the scan, some stores in those ethnic enclaves lost sales and market share because they didn't consider the needs and desires of their customers. For managers accustomed to offering clothing and furnishings, meeting this new need was a challenge.

This example is not offered here to suggest that the managers were stupid. What it showed was that people tend to rely on past experience and so they miss seeing opportunities. The past is not a precursor to the future anymore. When the philosopher George Santayana said that "those who cannot remember the past are condemned to repeat it," he meant the lessons learned from the past, not past methods per se.

The Value of Statistical Analysis

We work to develop algorithms with our clients so as to statistically analyze and weight the connections between their external forces and internal factors, as well as the issues that come later, such as process optimization, service delivery, and performance measurement. To reveal those connections, clients collect operating data and format it in a way that allows us to carry out the statistical analyses. This leads to predictability.

The value of analysis is in the patterns in data that it uncovers. These patterns are not readily apparent in standard reviews and reports. Hence, analytics is more about structure and logic than about statistical procedures. Statistics are useful only if they are applied to the right issues. Large organizations are so complex and their operations so far-flung that it is virtually impossible for management to see some of the vital connections and influences. But using computing power and analytic tools to mine the data can yield vast and varied phenomena. There is a natural reluctance among managers to accept that statistical methods are more accurate than their judgment. Yet, the experience of managers is contaminated by common human traits of bias, misperception, and faulty memory. In 136 studies of the judgment accuracy of experienced managers, only 8 studies showed that manager predictions were more accurate than simple regression equations applied to the same problems. In a post-study review, the analysts believed that random-sampling errors accounted for the mistakes in the predictive power of statistics and that actually regression beat manager memory every time.[1]

The Importance of Risk Assessment

Risk is a central element in any kind of planning. A statement about the future carries with it the risk of being somewhat to totally wrong. Even grand financial models miss some aspect, which can lead to disastrous investments. Today, there are many more external forces driving companies now than in the past, and that involves recognizing risk. Stability is gone for good; it has been replaced by volatility, extending far into the future. And, unquestionably, human capital management is a high-risk game in this uncertain market. More than ever, human capital planning must now include risk assessment.

Risk assessment has three steps. First, the scan lists every factor that can potentially have an impact on the organization. For human capital management, those factors are edited to those that could have the biggest negative or positive effect on the organization's people, operations, structure, and external relations in the foreseeable future. Then, the question is asked: What will be the impact if these occur? See Figure 3.2 for a sample.

At the corporate level, examples of potential risks could be immediate

Figure 3.2. Sample HR risk assessment.

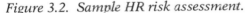
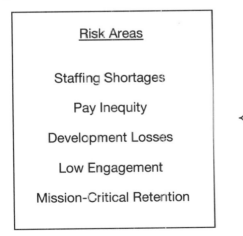
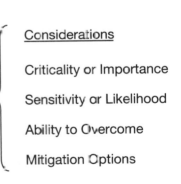

Risk Areas	Considerations
Staffing Shortages	Criticality or Importance
Pay Inequity	Sensitivity or Likelihood
Development Losses	Ability to Overcome
Low Engagement	Mitigation Options
Mission-Critical Retention	

loss of revenue, inability to deliver competitively, harm to the organization's reputation, legal penalties, and loss of future revenue. On the positive side, if a new product release exceeds expectations, great—but will the company be prepared to service that increased level of uptake?

Second, each risk is rated on a scale of, say, 1 to 3 with regard to its likelihood of occurring. How do you decide the likelihood something is going to happen? You have to look beyond the experience of people in the organization and research current media reports. That is where the threat lies—so listen to the maniac fringe. Visionaries and others operating at the outskirts often see ahead more clearly than do those in the establishment, who have something to protect.

Remember, almost every disruptive change has come from outside the current leaders in a business or industry. Consider the personal computer, the mini steel mill, the digital watch, Internet book sales, and overnight package delivery. Each idea came from an outsider. Managers have some control over internal factors but they have little or no control over those outside the organization. If one of these threats or opportunities materializes, what might be the extent of the disruption? How long will it take the organization to respond? And do you have the ability to implement effective risk-mitigation measures?

The third step involves applying the optional responses. From importance and likelihood, you decide how to mitigate the effects of those risks. For example, how will you handle the following?

* Avoid the risk by postponing or not implementing something—or just wait?

* Transfer the risk to a third party—in which case, who could do it better?

* Reduce risk by introducing controls, but how and what controls? Accept the risk if the cost outweighs the benefit—but how to balance the situation?

* Capitalize on an unexpected positive result—or how best to stay agile?

Your task is to develop a risk-mitigation plan that prepares you ahead of any problem's arrival. It is similar to a disaster-recovery plan. That is, if the worst happens, you are ready to clean up in the most expeditious manner. This approach reduces damage and confusion, and helps you move on with a minimum of distraction. In short, while the unprepared flail about in the bushes, trying to get back on the trail, you distance yourself from the pack.

One of the most effective ways to prepare for the unexpected is to develop a playbook, much as is done in the game of football. The playbook lists the defensive and offensive plays that are ready to be used, given certain circumstances. Jim Ware's essay "Scenario Planning," in Chapter Four, describes how to use a playbook.

The Data Speak for Predictive Management

In 2007, The Hackett Group published the results of its research on the effects of managing human assets. It studied 125 human resources/ human capital benchmarks over a three-year period. The metrics were chosen to reflect a balance between talent management and corporate efficiency and effectiveness, and the purpose was to zero in on the effect of human capital planning and management on productivity, customer satisfaction, and employee commitment, and by extension, on sales, profits, and shareholder value.[2]

Hackett's research found a strong correlation between improved financial performance and top-quartile performance in four key talent-management areas:

1. Strategic workforce planning, which involves identifying the skills critical to a company's operation and how these needs match up against those of the existing workforce

2. Staffing services, including recruitment, staffing, and exit management; and workforce development services such as training and career planning

3. Overall organizational effectiveness, including labor and employee relations, and performance management

4. Organizational design and measurement

Companies with top-quartile talent management, which includes planning, outperformed typical companies across four standard financial metrics. They generated EBITDA (earnings before interest, taxes, depreciation, and amortization) of 16.2 percent versus 14.1 percent for typical companies. This gap netted a typical Fortune 500 company (based on $19 billion revenue) an additional $399 million annually in improved EBITDA. How much more do you have to sell to net $400 million?

The most interesting point in the findings correlated with another study, which reported that top talent-management performers operate very differently from their peers.[3] According to the report, top performers are 57 percent more likely than their peers to have a formal HR strategic plan in place, more than twice as likely to facilitate strategic workforce planning discussions with senior management, and 50 percent more likely to link their learning and development strategy to their company's strategic plan.

Ready, Aim, Begin

The environmental scan of external forces and internal factors discussed in this chapter produces a picture of what is likely to happen, what you have to compete with, and how these things will affect your human, structural, and relational capital. Risk assessment prepares you for possible major problems and rates the types of risks you might expect. It gives you a framework for identifying and mitigating that risk. From this you have a foundation for an advanced capability and succession-planning program.

Now, you are enabled to make plans to build management and leadership capabilities across mission-critical functions. Rather than continuing to apply an industrial model of filling holes with interchangeable bodies (gap analysis), you think in terms of building capability for the intelligence age. These are the issues in this chapter.

Notes

1. Ian Ayres, *Super Crunchers* (New York: Bantam Dell), 120–21.
2. "Companies Can Improve Earnings Nearly 15% by Improving Talent Management Function," The Hackett Group Research Alert, 2007.
3. Workforce Intelligence Report, Human Capital Source, 2008.

HOW TO IMPROVE HR PROCESSES

The essays that follow discuss issues of how people and profits fit together, how a new view of compensation can be used as a total-rewards process, and what the best-practices companies do to earn that title.

THE INTERSECTION OF PEOPLE AND PROFITS: THE EMPLOYEE VALUE PROPOSITION

Joni Thomas Doolin, Michael Harms, and Shyam Patel

Any study of human capital management is ultimately about one thing: eliciting results. It's an age-old question—How do you turn a disparate group of individuals into a high-performing team that drives the bottom line? *People Report* has spent over a decade exploring the connection between people and profits. What we have found is that, now more than ever, people matter.

Human capital is the defining component of any successful business. Between every great business plan and every consumer exist the people who will implement the steps necessary to ensure the plan's ultimate success or failure. It is at this pivot point that hard and soft sciences collide, and for this very reason, human capital remains enigmatic to many in the business world. It is the human element that makes it so explicitly fascinating—and unpredictable.

While the variability of human behavior can be a source of frustration, any predictability you can garner becomes a key competitive advantage. This is where metrics and the use of measured human capital intelligence become mission critical. *People Report* is highly regarded as the foremost provider of human capital and business intelligence for the foodservice industry, the largest employer in the United States other than the government. While measuring the people practices of an organization is not always easy, measuring the results is. What we have found is that highly engaged, motivated teams outperform their peers, time and time again. The first step is hiring the right people; the second step is keeping them. As we have known for years in the marketing department, the key to attracting and keeping new consumers is in understanding your value proposition. We have likewise identified and defined the key inside the organization: knowing your company's *employee value proposition*.

Exploring the Employee Value Proposition

It is crystal clear to most operators that recruiting and retaining quality employees is as difficult as ever. As one industry CEO recently lamented, "Everything works about half as well as it used to." But before we simply concede defeat and accept the fact that shifting labor market conditions have made recruitment and retention perilous, consider this: The U.S.

Army and Marine Corps continually meet and exceed their recruitment and retention goals. And this comes in the midst of a two-pronged offensive in the Middle East with the prospect of extended tours and mortal danger for new enlistees. This is a clear demonstration of what can be done.

So how does the armed forces do it? It started by adjusting the value propositions it offered new enlistees, from offering sign-on bonuses to changing its internal culture to a kinder, gentler army. We understand the importance of creating a value proposition for our guests—one that will get them to come to you again and again, talk about you to their friends, and use you for different meals and occasions. It's all about building raving fans. But how many of us think the same way about our employees? What about their value proposition? If we want to attract "raving" employees, how do you do it? How do you convince people they can't miss the opportunity of working for your company?

What Is Your Employee Value Proposition?

As employee needs and values have transformed and the workforce has diversified, we have started to think about the employee value proposition as the connection between people and profitability: The critical link between employee and guest is the key to organizational performance. Although a lot of lip service is paid to the idea that people are an organization's greatest asset, they often are treated as disposable assets.

American psychologist Abraham Maslow developed the idea that certain basic needs must be met in each of our lives, and once these needs have been met, it frees us to increase our engagement and continue our development. Maslow's hierarchy of needs has five levels:

1. Self-actualization: personal growth and fulfillment
2. Self-esteem: achievement, status, responsibility, reputation
3. Belonging and love: family affection, work group
4. Safety: protection, security, order, law, stability
5. Survival: basic life needs—food, shelter, sleep

For most people, work plays a huge role in their lives, and just as individuals have needs, so too employees have needs. While many employers take every available step to separate their employees' work lives from their "real" lives, making work life more like real life will help attract and retain a talented workforce. This starts with meeting the basic needs of your employees by providing them with necessary compensation and benefits, as well as an environment designed for professional growth.

If employers can satisfy the basic needs of their workers, the result will be an engaged group of employees who drive profitability, as Figure 3.3 shows.

If a company wants to succeed—today and in the future—it must attract and retain great employees. As most business gurus contend, "In the long run the most profitable companies are those that take care of their people. . . . Without qualified people who are happy and productive, the company's long-term prospects are mediocre at best."[1]

Engines of Revenue Growth

The impact of good people on an organization cannot be underestimated. While many in the business community would likely categorize employees as "necessary expenses," they should be more willing to think of their employees as "engines of revenue growth." This language may resonate already with chief people officers and human resources depart-

Figure 3.3. The employee value proposition.

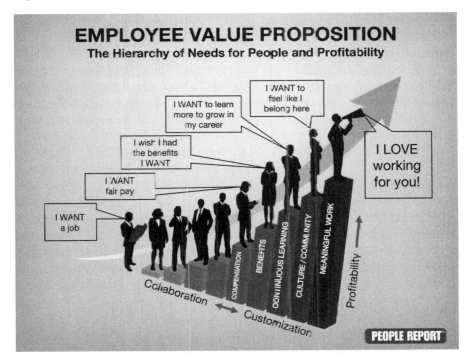

Source: People Report, 2009.

ments, but it should sound the loudest in boardrooms and financial departments across the industry.

When we look at the financial performance of those companies that have won *People Report* Best Practices Awards—that is, companies with recruitment and retention numbers that are best in class—the results are astounding. Those companies whose people practices exceed those of their peers' exhibit markedly stronger total restaurant sales growth and comparable restaurant sales growth.[2]

Compensation

The concept of a people-driven enterprise means that you must make a strong case for actively recruiting and retaining your best employees. The question is: How do we accomplish this? If we return to the needs hierarchy shown in Figure 3.3, we find it no surprise that the most basic employee need to be satisfied is an individual's compensation and benefits. Typically, the obvious tool for organizations to meet those needs is periodic compensation increases. However, even in the current recessionary period, a paycheck is easily replicated by competitors; remember—"If people come for money, they will leave for money."[3]

That is not to say that a competitive compensation offering is unimportant. But when we look more closely at the compensation practices of the foodservice industry compared to other industries, we find that average starting salaries are exactly that: average. The industry responded by adding bonus and incentive programs, under the assumption that it would attract productive employees who would be paid to perform.

Unfortunately, foodservice industry bonuses have become more of an entitlement than an incentive, and the industry is learning a lesson that professional baseball's New York Yankees picked up during the past decade: high compensation does not guarantee high performance. In fact, when reviewing the relationship between comparable restaurant sales and general manager bonuses as a percentage of base salary, we see as many companies paying an identical bonus as a percentage of base salary for negative comparable sales results as positive results (see Figure 3.4). Note that the compensation packages offered to Group 1 and Group 2 are strikingly similar, even though their performances are not.

This is not a critique of the industry's variable pay plans; we understand the complexity of incentivizing thousands of operating managers. Rather, it illustrates how difficult it is to differentiate yourself from your competitors using these practices. That is, underperforming companies are paying as well as high-performing companies.

Figure 3.4. Comparative results of base salary and sales.

Pay Doesn't Always Equal Performance

	Group 1	Group 2
Base Salary	$60,980	$60,283
Average Quarterly Bonus	$4,059	$4,901
% General Managers Bonused	82%	81%
Average Comp Sales	−2.64%	2.44%

Source: People Report, Casual Dining, January–June 2007.

Similarly, it is difficult to stand out from the crowd because of the standard benefits packages your company might offer. Benefits matter—they are often very important to employees—but 85 to 90 percent of our *People Report* consortium members offer the same benefits; see Figure 3.5 on page 62. They do not differentiate you from your nearest competitor, and your employees have no incentive to stay longer because their next employer is offering basically the same package.

Benefits have become to employees what shelves at the market have become to consumers—a commodity that you must offer but that is less frequently a reason to come or to buy. That said, while a quality, standard benefits package has become commonplace in the industry, companies have been able to differentiate themselves by customizing their packages to best meet individual needs of employees. People want to feel as if they are taken care of and appreciated as individuals. Simply offering a more flexible package can make or break a decision to stay. So, if you have determined that compensation and benefits are not necessarily creating an incentive for your employees to stay with you, where do you look next?

Figure 3.5. Comparative benefits packages in the foodservice industry.

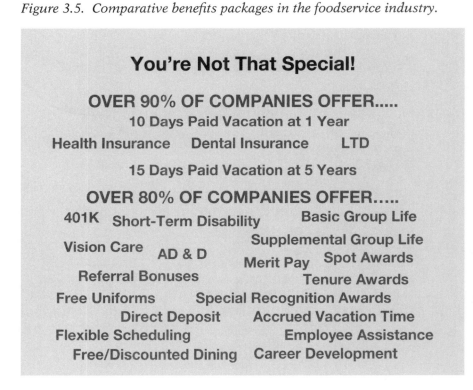

Source: *People Report*, 2009.

A Paycheck and More

We find it everywhere else in the workplace. As best-selling author and business consultant Chester Elton notes, "While a paycheck gets them to show up every day, it doesn't buy long-term engagement."[4] As a look at the needs hierarchy shows, people do not want just a paycheck—they want a paycheck and more.

Part of the "more" most employees want can be seen in the higher steps up the hierarchy. They want to grow in their role and have a chance to move up within the organization, and they want to feel that they are appreciated and that they belong. Developing this sense of community and a culture of continuous learning starts with finding the right people.

Nearly all restaurants struggle to find and retain hourly employees. But data reveal that much of the industry's recruitment efforts seem based on a strategy of hope, as in you hope someone walks in the door, an employee refers a friend, or a candidate reads an advertisement in the paper. Even in this extremely upside-down employment market, there are still open jobs, and the rate of employee turnover means that the search for enough of the "right" workers continues.

Many proactive operators have turned to data mining, as "data mining shows that these personality traits are better predictors of worker productivity (especially turnover) than more traditional ability testing."[5] Data mining and predictive analytics help match employees who are most compatible with particular jobs. Talent assessment and screening firms specialize in helping match applicants to job requirements, assisting companies in streamlining the process. They help find the best fit that leads to hiring employees with a much longer tenure. And while technology is a great way to improve the odds of recruiting and hiring good employees, the operators must also turn to new, diverse pools to find the top talent. Years of research have validated the advantages of both data mining and hiring and retaining a diverse workforce. Both lead to improved retention of managers and employees.

Retention Drives Sales

Retaining quality employees really is like finding that bottle of fine wine that improves with age and increases in value over time. This is especially true in the case of selecting general managers. In reviewing our data, we found that companies that reported the lowest comparable (comp) unit sales also employed general managers with the shortest average tenure. Not surprisingly, those companies whose comparable sales were the highest had hired general managers with the longest average tenure. In short, retention pays off, as shown in Figure 3.6.

If increased sales are not enough to get your attention, here's something else that will win you over. The tenure of general managers impacts the retention of managers and employees as well. As the length of employment for general managers increases, line-level management and hourly employee turnover plummets. Among *People Report* member companies, those that rank in the top third for management tenure—whose managers stay the longest—have almost 20 percent less management and 50 percent lower hourly turnover numbers. This calculates to a massive savings in comparison to the direct competition. Not only do companies with longer tenured general managers see increased comp sales, but they also see significantly reduced rates of management and hourly turnover, as shown in Figure 3.7.

What does all this equate to in dollars? Based on the overall cost of turnover, for every point a 100-unit company saves in hourly turnover, it recoups $205,000 annually in costs. Likewise, for every point saved in management turnover, it recoups $140,000 in annual costs.[6]

Figure 3.6. Comparative tenure results for general managers.

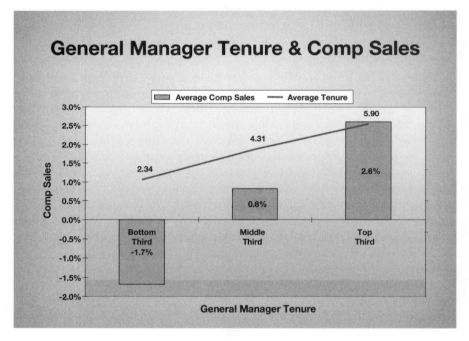

Source: *People Report*, 2009.

Now, translate that into what could happen for you. What if your initiative helped you reduce your organization's hourly turnover by 10 percent and management turnover by 3 percent? That would result in an estimated cost savings in excess of $2.5 million annually for a company with 100 units. We have consistently been able to validate the value of recruiting and retaining quality employees. This is a winning investment; or, authors Bill Catlette and Richard Hadden note in their book *Contented Cows Give Better Milk*, "In the final analysis, 'people factors' are frequently *the* key source of competitive advantage—the factor least visible to the naked eye and most difficult to emulate. Sooner or later, we must come to grips with the fact that most businesses aren't so much capital- or expertise- or even product-driven as they are PEOPLE-driven."[7]

A Place They Belong

Creating a workforce where people feel included is important, for this reason: People don't work where they *have* to; they work where they *want* to. Even in this economy, the best people will not stay forever where they

Figure 3.7. Impact of general manager tenure.

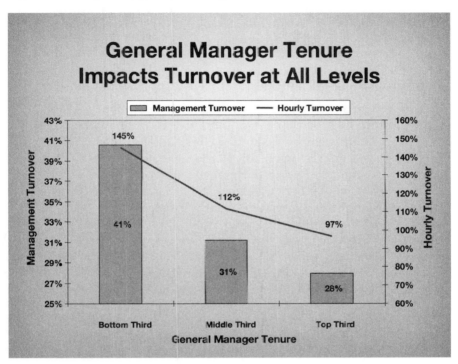

Source: People Report, 2009.

are not appreciated. Turnover is frequently driven by emotion; feeling overlooked, underutilized, and unappreciated leads people to move on. Chester Elton has dubbed this workplace phenomenon "presenteeism." While job abandonment continues to plague our industry, how many of us also battle presenteeism? As Elton points out, "Absenteeism is easy to spot, but presenteeism describes workers who show up every day, but aren't really there."[8]

Indeed, there's an undoubtedly human element in retention and performance in all industries, particularly those as labor-intensive as foodservice. "Human beings are uniquely capable of regulating their involvement in and commitment to a given task or endeavor. . . . The extent to which we do or do not fully contribute is governed more by *attitude* than by necessity, fear, or economic influence."[9] Much of this attitude stems from the culture of the work environment. Do employees feel like members of the work community? Do they feel as if they have a chance to increase their role in the organization or do they simply feel viewed as "replaceable cogs in a machine?"[10] One thing is certain: When the work environment begins to sour, the best employees are often the first ones out the door because they have the most options.

One Size No Longer Fits All

Customized experiences are an increasingly popular concept in all aspects of life. Not that long ago, three television networks dominated the national landscape, commanding huge audiences on a nightly basis. Now, they are awash in competition. The same goes for most large daily newspapers, which have seen declining circulation and advertising revenue for years as new, more targeted mediums have become prevalent. We are rapidly progressing toward a "what-we-want-when-we-want-it" society—the music you want at the click of a button, on-demand television, self-designed clothing. You can even customize your M&Ms. Who was *Time* magazine's person of the year in 2007? You. It's a customized world. People are not only comfortable with this level of customization in their lives, they expect it. Why should work be any different?

When attempting to satisfy worker needs, it is increasingly clear that you must first identify worker *wants*. Not all workers want the same things. For example, the employee value proposition that might appeal to college students may not be as attractive to baby boomers. Instead of trying to appeal to everyone, and in the process satisfying no one, successful companies are taking a novel approach to recruiting and providing for their employees. They carefully identify their target worker audience and then appeal directly to that crowd. As Mark Penn, political strategist and co-author of *Microtrends*, writes, "The power of individual choice has never been greater, and the reasons and patterns for those choices never harder to understand and analyze. The skill of microtargeting—identifying small, intense subgroups and communicating with them about their individual needs and wants—has never been more critical. . . . The one-size-fits-all approach to the world is dead."[11]

Many examples can be found of successful companies that attract and keep great employees because they are successful in following a niche strategy. For example, Figure 3.8 on the facing page lists several highly successful programs.

These companies have discovered underserved and untapped sources to recruit, satisfy, and retain managers and employees. There's a recognition that different groups of people have different needs, as shown in Figure 3.9. By identifying and satisfying these groups individually, companies can create a pool of happy, loyal, and satisfied employees.

Figure 3.8. Companies that have customized employee programs.

Source: People Report, 2009.

The foodservice industry is, at its core, just that—an industry founded on service. When the employees serve the guests, and the employer serves the employees, everyone's needs have been met and the foundation is laid for continued growth and success.

Conclusion

Our research indicates that leading companies have long since moved past relying on traditional compensation and benefits offerings to attract and retain a quality workforce. Instead, they operate with a focus on "total rewards," offering a combination of competitive compensation and benefits, flexible schedules, lifestyle rewards, switched-on training programs, an inclusive workplace, and a commitment to lifelong learning. These same companies think creatively about how they recruit new employees to join them. They cast wide nets that encompass women, minorities, students, retirees, and candidates from other industries. They

Figure 3.9. Employee niche needs.

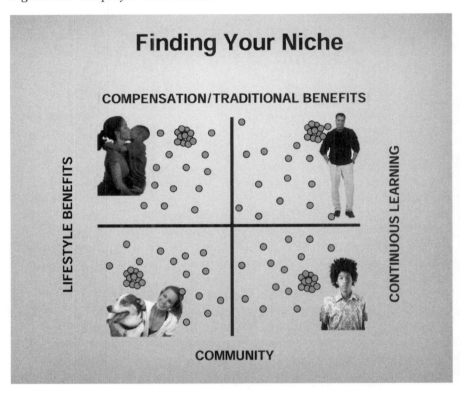

Source: *People Report*, 2009.

count on referrals and recognition as a great place to work to attract candidates to their doors. These approaches enable proactive operators to meet the challenge of the times. Change is imperative, and in both the near and longer term, human capital excellence will be a textbook advantage for the winners in this marketplace.

Notes

1. Roger Herman et al., *Impending Crisis: Too Many Jobs Too Few People* (Winchester, Va.: Oakhill Press, 2003), 2.
2. Comparable Store Sales. Year over year sales increase/decrease in units operating for a full twelve months.
3. Jeffrey Pfeffer and Robert I. Sutton, *Hard Facts, Dangerous Half-Truths & Total Nonsense: Profiting From Evidence-Based Management* (Boston: Harvard Business School Press, 2006), 123.

4. Adrian Gostick and Chester Elton, *The Invisible Employee: Realizing the Hidden Potential in Everyone* (Hoboken, N.J.: John Wiley & Sons, 2006), 24.

5. Ian Ayres, *Super Crunchers: Why Thinking-by-Numbers Is the New Way to Be Smart* (New York: Bantam Books, 2007), 28.

6. *People Report* Survey of Unit Level Practices, Dallas, 2007.

7. Bill Catlette and Richard Hadden, *Contented Cows Give Better Milk: The Plain Truth About Employee Relation and Your Bottom Line* (Germantown, Tenn.: Saltillo Press, 2001), 7.

8. Gostick and Elton, *The Invisible Employee*, xv.

9. Catlette and Hadden, *Contented Cows*, xiv.

10. Pfeffer and Sutton, *Hard Facts*, 68.

11. Mark J. Penn and E. Kinney-Zalesne, *Microtrends: The Small Forces Behind Tomorrow's Big Changes* (New York: Grand Central Publishing, 2007), xi.

MORE THAN COMPENSATION: ATTRACTING, MOTIVATING, AND RETAINING EMPLOYEES, NOW AND IN THE FUTURE

Ryan M. Johnson

It has become clear that today's battle for employee talent involves much more than well-designed or competitively generous compensation and benefits programs. While these programs can undoubtedly be critical, the most successful companies have realized that they must take a broader, more holistic look at the factors involved in attraction, motivation, and retention. Further, they know they must deploy all of these elements—compensation, benefits, work life, performance management, recognition, employee development, and career opportunities—in unison with their strategic advantage. Indeed, the organizations that integrate these traditionally disparate elements into a "total rewards" philosophy will be the most competitive organizations in the coming decades.

Total rewards: All of the tools available to an employer that may be used to attract, motivate, and retain employees. Total rewards can include anything the employee perceives to be of value resulting from the employment relationship.

Some Historical Context

For centuries, the basic premise of the employer-employee relationship has been the same: An individual (the employee) provides his or her time, talent, and/or effort to an organization and, in exchange, the organization (the employer) reciprocates with compensation or pay. Despite the long-term stability of this exchange relationship, many employers have struggled in recent decades with a core question: Is pay by itself adequate to effectively attract, motivate, and retain employees?

Fifty years ago, when the fields of compensation and benefits were emerging, the prevailing practices in most companies were based on simple formulas that served the entire employee population. Pay or salary "structures" were just that—rigid and highly controlled—and benefits programs were designed as a one-size-fits-all for a mostly homogeneous workforce. In the 1970s and 1980s, however, the workforce began to change in fundamental ways, and employers began to face a new competitive landscape. As households began shifting away from the sole-breadwinner model that had been prevalent in the 1950s and '60s, new government mandates related to employee benefits were becoming law, and huge multinational firms were emerging in an increasingly global competitive environment.

Collectively, these forces and others caused business leaders to seek new ways to improve their talent and labor practices. Personnel or HR professionals—particularly those specializing in compensation and benefits—were challenged to contain costs and contribute to improved business results. It did not take long for many to realize that incremental improvement of one-size-fits-all pay and benefits programs would simply not be enough. New vehicles for delivering compensation, like variable pay and equity—most often limited to the most senior executives—were introduced.

By the 1980s, forward-looking professionals were recognizing that bringing together compensation and benefits, and thinking holistically about them, could create advantages in recruiting. Soon, some organizations were talking about their "total compensation" package in an effort to provide a competitive advantage in attracting and retaining talent. Certainly, increased efficiencies and cost controls were the mandate for survival, but many organizations recognized that an integrated and enriched "value exchange" between employer and employees could accelerate business success.

By the mid-1990s, the holistic concept had evolved again, in response to an ever-changing business environment. The first notions of "total rewards" were advanced as a new way of thinking about combining both the tangible and intangible levers that employers could use to successfully attract, motivate, and retain employees.

The Evolution of Pay to Total Rewards

Since the late 1990s, a handful of different total-rewards models have been published by consulting firms, thought leaders, and the nonprofit association for total-rewards professionals (WorldatWork). While each approach presents a unique point of view, all of the models recognize the importance of thinking holistically and of leveraging multiple programs, practices, and cultural dynamics to satisfy and engage the best employees and, ultimately, to contribute to improved business performance and bottom-line results, as shown in Figure 3.10.

The Role of a Global Association

As the global association representing the various professions that make up the field of total rewards, WorldatWork has served as a focal point for intellectual-capital development and dialogue about this topic. In 2000, after facilitating a discussion with leading thinkers in the field, WorldatWork introduced its first total-rewards framework intended to advance the concept and help practitioners think and execute in new ways. The model focused on three elements:

1. Compensation

2. Benefits

3. The work experience: acknowledgment, balance (of work and life), culture, development (career/professional), and environment (workplace)

Figure 3.10. The concept of total rewards.

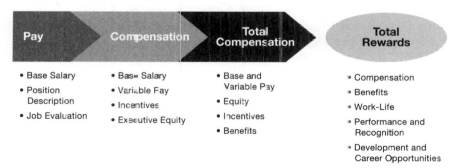

Until the late 1990s, this association of professionals had focused solely on compensation and benefits. Yet, specialists and generalists alike agreed that compensation and benefits—while foundational and representing the lion's share of human capital costs—could not be fully effective unless they were part of an integrated strategy of other programs and practices to attract, motivate, and retain top talent.

Thus, the "work experience" aspect of the association's first total-rewards model included aspects of employment that could have been either programmatic or part of the overall workplace experience. For instance, recognition or acknowledgment could come in the form of a formal rewards program or be as simple as a verbal "thank you" from the boss or co-worker. Similarly, workplace flexibility could manifest itself as a formal telework program with policies and procedures or be simply an organizational culture and practices that embrace concepts of a balanced work-life relationship.

The Association's First Total-Rewards Model (2000)

During the early 2000s, as companies became exposed to the total-rewards concept, understanding of the concept advanced and more organizations began to adopt the philosophy. By mid-decade, survey data from WorldatWork members revealed that professionals were primarily using the terms *total rewards, total compensation,* or *compensation and benefits* to describe the collective strategies deployed by their companies to attract, motivate, and retain talent, as shown in Figure 3.11.

But a study by Deloitte in the same year showed the concept still in growth mode in terms of its adoption in the corporate world.[1] In response to a survey question about how "employee total rewards" was being defined in their companies, a 56 percent majority viewed it somewhat narrowly, as "compensation, long-term incentives, and all other cash-based items." Only 11 percent of Deloitte respondents defined "total rewards" as "all possible financial and nonfinancial factors affecting an employee's experience, including corporate communications, deployment, job training, etc."

In response to another question, almost two-thirds of respondents said they were exploring the possibility of managing rewards components in an integrated fashion or at least were interested in the concept.

Taking Total Rewards Further

During the past decade, while the concept of total rewards was gradually being adopted by leading organizations, practitioners were beginning to experience the power of leveraging multiple factors to attract, moti-

Figure 3.11. First total-rewards model.

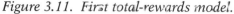

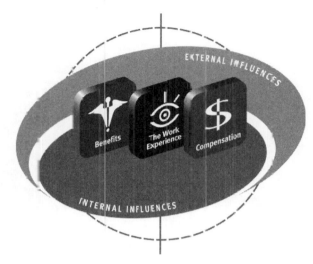

vate, and retain talent—high-performing companies were able to watch the concepts in action. At the same time, human resources professionals, consulting firms, service providers, and academic institutions made steps toward the notion of total rewards.

After more than a year of research and input, WorldatWork published an updated integrated total-rewards model in 2006, which reflected the next generation of thinking about total rewards. As with the first model, the second model placed total rewards in a context, presented a perspective to the profession, and championed the delicate art and science of combining five elements to achieve optimum business results, as shown in Figure 3.12.

The new model contained five total-rewards elements, each of which included programs, practices, elements, and dimensions that collectively defined an organization's strategy to attract, motivate, and retain employees. The five elements were: compensation, benefits, work life, performance and recognition, and development and career opportunities.

On a practical level, the five elements represented a toolbox from which an organization could select to offer an employee value proposition that created value for both the organization and the employee.

The five elements were not mutually exclusive. Nor were they intended to represent the ways companies organize or deploy programs and the functions within them. For instance, performance management may be driven by a compensation function or may be decentralized in

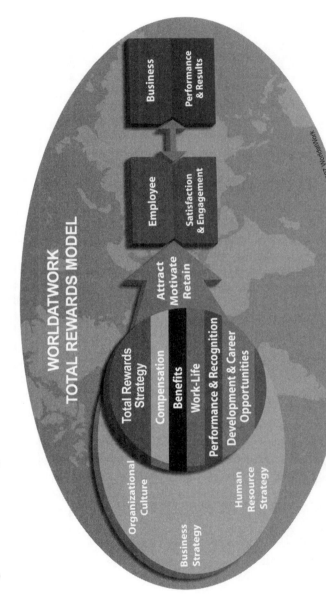

Figure 3.12. Second-generation total-rewards model.

line organizations; it can be managed formally or informally. Likewise, recognition can be considered an aspect of compensation, benefits, and work life.

In the six years between 2000 and 2006, both the thinking and practice of aspects that had constituted the work experience evolved considerably. It was important to recognize this evolution in the 2006 model and categorize its work-life element. Other portions of what was formerly considered the work experience became the context in this new model.

The Second Total-Rewards Model (2006)

The second-generation model recognized that total rewards operate in the context of overall business strategy, organizational culture, and HR strategy. Indeed, a company's unique culture or exceptional brand value may be a critical component of the total employment value proposition. The backdrop of the model is a globe, representing two concepts: (1) that the model's conceptual framework is applicable on a global basis; and (2) that there are external influences on a business, such as legal and regulatory issues, cultural factors and practices, and global competition.

An important dimension of the model is its "exchange relationship" between the employer and employee (the two-way arrow). As noted at the outset, successful companies realize that productive employees create value for their organizations in return for tangible and intangible value that enriches their lives. That has always been the essence of the exchange between employer and employee, and the model predicts that it will continue to be the case.

Compensation: Includes fixed (base) pay and variable pay (pay at risk). Also includes several forms of variable pay, such as short- and long-term incentives. The most traditional element in total rewards and a key to business success.

Benefits: Programs that protect employees and their families from financial risks. Includes traditional programs such as medical, dental, and retirement, as well as newer, nontraditional programs such as identity theft and pet insurance. During the past decade, this element of total rewards has been challenging for U.S. companies, owing to ever-rising health-care premiums and seemingly shrinking health-care benefits. For at least a decade, businesses have been trying to redefine the traditional benefits program.

Work Life: Any programs that help employees do their job effectively, such as flexible scheduling, telecommuting, and child-care programs. Has become one of the most talked-about areas of total rewards, garnering substantial media attention. Some organizations have indicated that work life is the "secret sauce" to their success in attracting, motivating, and retaining talent.

Performance and Recognition: The alignment of organizational and individual goals toward business success. Recognition is a way for employers to pay special attention to workers for their accomplishments, behaviors, and successes. It reinforces the value of performance improvement and fosters positive communication and feedback. Recognition can be programmatic or cultural in its execution.

Development and Career Opportunities: The concept of motivating and engaging the workforce through planning for the advancement and/or change in responsibilities to best suit individual skills, talents, and desires. Tuition assistance, professional development, sabbaticals, coaching and mentoring opportunities, succession planning, and apprenticeships are all examples of career-enhancement programs.

The Key to Success: Attract, Motivate, Retain

In aggregate, the five elements—or however many elements are represented in another total-rewards model—represent the levers that organizations (and total-rewards professionals) can pull and push to successfully attract, motivate, and retain employees. They are the items the employer exchanges in the exchange relationship.

Obtaining an adequate (and perpetual) supply of qualified talent is obviously essential for an organization's survival. In many cases, attracting the right employees is a key plank of the business strategy. One way an organization can accomplish this is to determine which "attractors" within the various total-rewards categories bring the kind of talent that will drive organizational success. Attraction strategies can vary widely among industries and companies, and can be substantially different owing to workforce demographics. For instance, older, retired Americans might be lured back into the workforce if the company offers strong health-care or prescription-drug benefits, rather than generous cash compensation. On the other hand, software or gaming companies might offer more cash and relatively light health-care benefits to attract a younger, generally more healthy demographic.

Regarding retention, an organization's long-term success can hinge on keeping employees who are valued contributors for as long as is mutually beneficial. Desired talent can be retained by using a dynamic blend of elements from the total-rewards package that reflects employees' needs and lifestyles as they move through their career. However, not all retention is desirable, which is why development of a formal retention strategy is essential.

Finally, the concept of total rewards strives to cause employees to behave in a way that achieves the highest performance levels. Motivation comprises two types:

1. *Intrinsic Motivation.* Linked to factors that include an employee's sense of achievement, respect for the whole person, trust, and appropriate advancement opportunities, intrinsic motivation consistently results in higher performance levels.

2. *Extrinsic Motivation.* Most frequently associated with tangible rewards such as pay, working conditions, co-worker relations, benefits, and such.

Applying a Total-Rewards Model

How can total-rewards professionals apply these concepts to their everyday business practices? Using a fictional Fortune 500 company as an example, I show how attracting, motivating, and retaining talent can—and should—take many forms.

For example, if the company is a high-tech software manufacturer, teleworking may be necessary to the overall business environment. In fact, with knowledge workers, the absence of a telework program could mean an inability to attract future talent, which certainly affects the bottom line. In addition, surveys, conversations with individuals, and analysis of employee demographics may lead total-rewards professionals to realize that those high-tech knowledge workers could be far better motivated by stock options than by substantial health insurance benefits. Thereby, the company measures and molds its total-rewards strategy to fit both workers and organizational needs.

In tailoring a total-rewards program, the savvy human resources professional will need input from both line managers and colleagues before defining a strategy, implementing it, and measuring its success. For example, work life may be viewed as a separate function in some organizations, while other organizations may consider it a component of the benefits strategy.

Where Is Total Rewards Headed?

The membership database of WorldatWork has yielded information on the evolution of job titles, as explained earlier, but there is also anecdotal evidence that some companies are beginning to brand their own versions of total rewards—a type of "internal branding" that seems the next move in this field.

While Notre Dame University promotes total rewards to its employees, the pizza company Dominos encourages employees to get their "piece of the pie," referring to its variety of rewards programs. Reportedly, the company extends the pizza analogy to its employee collateral materials, showing how various elements of its programs can be combined to customize a "benefits pizza." Starbucks has branded its total-rewards concept as "your special blend," again, making an obvious play on its coffee products. "Your special blend" indicates the ability that employees have to customize their total-rewards offering.

In the battle for employee talent that will dominate tomorrow, companies like Starbucks and Dominos are well positioned to compete because they have removed some of the organizational procedures that, in the past, might have led the organization simply to throw more money into the compensation silo, hoping that would solve the retention issue. Branding their own total-rewards programs gives them the flexibility to adapt, thereby meeting the needs of the four generations of workers who will be their future talent pool. But whether it's a branded program or not, organizations that integrate flexibility into their benefits programs, combining the traditionally disparate elements into a total-rewards philosophy, will be the most competitive organizations in the coming decades.

Note

1. 2006 *Employee Rewards Survey: The Next Generation*, 5.

"BEST IN BRAZIL": HUMAN CAPITAL AND BUSINESS MANAGEMENT FOR SUSTAINABILITY

Rugenia Pomi

For the past fourteen years, Sextante Brasil has published the *Brazilian Human Capital Management Survey*, aimed at understanding the discriminators on people management among the best companies in Brazil. This survey has come to be regarded as the prime source of quantitative and qualitative data on strategic positioning of human resources in Brazil. Based on the data, in 2007 Sextante Brasil created the Best in Brazil Seals for Human Capital and for Business Management for Sustainability to acknowledge and recognize companies that presented the best results in these areas. The companies' scores in the Brazilian survey are based on the following pillars:

* Business value creation
* Safety and health
* Labor and union relationships
* Retention
* Equity and internal income distribution
* Learning, training, and development
* HR professionals and HR team

These seven pillars are detailed in seventeen specifics themes, and to be nominated companies need to reach a minimum 70 percent of the criteria shown in Table 3.1.

The companies that have achieved minimum 70 percent in each of those criteria have their scores audited by an independent consultancy company in order to be on the short list for the award as shown in Table 3.2.

The years 2007 through 2009 represented a period of intense mergers and acquisitions. Table 3.3 lists the companies that have been awarded the seal.

The Essentials

In the age of knowledge, people—their hands, minds, and souls—are the most important assets in a company. The return on investment that an organization gets from its employees depends entirely on human actions, including its managerial capabilities. In the surveys conducted by Sextante Brasil, it becomes obvious that behind the excellent financial and market results of these best companies is a set of values and principles that guides management practices. The qualitative survey identified how these managerial practices are organized and implemented.

Company Mission, Vision, and Values

Each of these companies is clear about its mission, vision, values, and principles. The identified values include:

* Teamwork
* Respect for the internal and external client
* Innovation
* Respect for the employees
* Individual and group responsibility
* Common good
* Commitment
* Ethics
* Respect for the environment

Table 3.1. Specific HR themes for Best in Brazil Seal.

Profitability	> = 50%
HCVA per capita	> = 50
Investments on labor injury prevention	> = 75
Labor injury followed by medical license	< = 25
Severity of labor injury	< = 25
Occupational disease	< = 25
Overtime	< = 25
Labor suit	< = 25
Solidarity on labor suit	< = 25
Liability suits	< = 25
Voluntary dismissal	< = 25
Seniority	> = 50
Income equity (CTP) (remuneration)	< = 50
Internal income distribution (PLRE) results and profit sharing	< = 50
T&D investments	> = 50
T&D hours	> = 50
HR specializations	Specialist professional > = Management and administrative

Table 3.2. Candidates for short list.

Issue	Industrial Group	Number of Companies	Employees	Gross Revenue
2007	12	105	797.000	R$ 629 billion[1]
2008	09	77	873.000	R$ 669 billion[2]
2009	09	79	815.000	R$ 790 billion[3]

Exchange: [1] U$ 1,00 = R$ 2,18; [2] U$ 1,00 = R$ 1,95; [3] U$ 1,00 = R$ 1,83.

Table 3.3. Winners of the Best in Brazil Seal, 2007–2009.

Year	Company	Industry	Number of Employees	Localization
2007	CELG	Utilities	10.001–25.000	Belo Horizonte/MG
	Tractebel Energy	Utilities	501–1.000	Florianópolis/SC
2008	Ahlstrom Louveira	Pulp and Paper	1–500	Louveira/SP
	Carioca Catalys Manufacture	Chemical and Petrochemical	1–500	Rio de Janeiro/RJ
	Tractebel Energy	Utilities	501–1.000	Florianópolis/SC
2009	Carbocloro	Chemical and Petrochemical	1–500	Cubatão/SP
	Tractebel Energy	Utilities	501–1.000	Florianópolis/SC

In each case, it is considered critical that (1) all employees understand and, furthermore, commit themselves to the company's mission and vision; and (2) that they put these values into daily practice.

For these companies, HR is responsible for communicating these principles to every new employee, ensuring full understanding and maintenance. Management has the responsibility to disseminate and guarantee these practices in all levels of the organization. In practice, there is costant focus on adding value to all that is done. The realization of growth, shareholder return on investment, reputation enhancement, and sustainability of market share are reflected in the day-to-day actions and in the satisfaction of internal and external customers.

Furthermore, people management is the main pillar of the HR business. There is a connection across the HR department to all staff areas and business units. All units share the company's values. HR takes part in the company's strategic planning and, based on that planning, defines and rolls out its own supporting action plan.

Human Resources Strategies and Best Practices

The role of HR is to attract, maintain, develop, and retain people; strengthen attitudes and behaviors aligned to the company's strategy and culture; and give meaning to work, generating pride in the team's accomplishments, facilitating organizational changes, and fostering learning and human growth via new scenarios aligned to values and company culture.

HR's purpose, then, is to add value to the business and to its internal customers, employees, and managers. It is expected by the top executives, managers, and employees in general. HR pursues the following points of excellence:

* Alignment focused on the company's strategic planning
* Speed in problem solving
* High quality in techniques, methodologies, systems, and people support
* Information system to properly support strategic decisions

People are considered and managed as essential to support the business, which is fundamental to the success of both employees and the company. The transparency in all actions is also common in HR departments, though they adopt different processes, programs, and systems to attract and retain excellent people who are committed and engaged with the company through the following:

* Integration and company culture acquisition
* Performance development and evaluation
* Internal acquisition, career, and succession
* Leadership development
* Climate management and quality of life
* Communication: listen, listen, listen
* Learning organization

A Partnership Between HR and Executives

The human resources function acts as a strategic partner for the line managers, without paternalism or philanthropy, and is perceived and valued for its contribution to the organization. In all of its actions, HR works with simplicity and objectivity. There are no superpower programs; everything is simple, professional, and tailored to the company's needs.

In all of these best companies, leaders are responsible for people management and they share the final decisions with HR, which provides instruments, methodology, and systems to support the whole process.

Communications with the Employees

The best companies assume that communication is an integral part of achieving planned results. Key actions in this area are keeping the employees informed about all relevant matters, with speed and transparency, and evaluating the effectiveness of the ongoing process. There is freedom of expression in all levels, on all topics. Communications happen naturally and are multidirectional.

These best companies also understand that communication is not only an HR responsibility but also a function that the entire management team should be accountable for. Effective communications promotes engagement, respect, and commitment among employees.

Organizational Climate Management and Customer Service

All the best companies manage their organizational climate and show results above 80 percent for responses to the survey question, "Are you proud to belong to . . . ?"

HR, with the managers' participation, reports the results of employee surveys to the internal community, implements action plans as a response, and monitors the project results. For all companies, it is important that there be a healthy relationship between the executives and employees, in all levels and directions. Solid leadership is fundamental in this process, as good internal relationships.

Sustainability Actions

All companies follow sustainability guidelines that are part of a complete chain linking the internal community, customers/consumers/suppliers, and the external community/society/environment Guidelines for action start with employee participation: The social responsibility is shared, which enhances the employees' feelings of "belonging."

Going Beyond the "What" to the "How"

It is confirmed that management practices based on values and principles of sustainability lead to excellence in financial and social results. It is also evident that good companies wish to compare their results with their competitors. However, the best management practice is not always the same for those that operate in the same economic sector or in the same region. Best practices rely exclusively on an enlightened way of being, thinking, feeling, and wanting. This way is unique to each company.

It's important to go further than what has been done, however. It's imperative to understand *how* these results have been achieved. The "how" of good HR management naturally respects the individual company's particular way of doing business, so knowing the culture of an organization is essential to ensuring people's commitment to sustainable development. In these best companies, there has been a search for coherence between theory and practice. For them, success has been the result of healthy internal relations; engagement; and commitment to the common goal, a sharing of values and principles, and overall caring for the company.

More than systems and processes, it has been relationships that have made the Brazilian DNA workforce different. A good working environment and healthy relationships guided by respect and genuine interest promote the integration and strengthening of a group that feels proud to belong. Indeed, a group led by competent managers conjointly with a professional HR function can make a big difference, helping these companies achieve exceptional results. For this reason, they deserve the Best in Brazil Seal in People and Business Management.

CHAPTER FOUR

The New Face of Workforce Planning

"Strategic planning is worthless—unless there is first a strategic vision."

—JOHN NAISBITT

Until the late 1980s, workforce planning was a common activity. But with the layoffs starting in 1989 it disappeared for a dozen years. Just as we came out of the recession of the early 1990s, the dotcom mania struck. There was no way to plan in that feeding frenzy. Workforce planning was viewed as passé in the short period during which vast sums of venture capital were thrown at unsubstantiated proposals. It wasn't until around 2005 that workforce planning resurfaced, as management realized how essential it was especially with the talent shortages exacerbated by an unpredictable, rapidly changing global market.

The challenge now is how to make workforce planning effective today. Because of the high level of market volatility and the risk of bad decisions, we need as much insight into the future as we can assemble. Think back to the technological capabilities that existed in 1990. For instance, there was no Internet for collecting and sharing data. The PC software was not nearly as robust as it is today. The cost of computer memory was perhaps 100 times more than it is now. In short, we had rather basic tools at that time, even if we didn't recognize that.

The risk level that businesses faced was much lower twenty years ago, too. Globalization was just a word, and Chinese, Indian and the Middle Eastern economies were a fraction of the size they are today. Japan was a dominant economy about to fall into a ten-year recession. Labor in the

United States was readily available. In fact, we had more managers than we knew what to do with, so over the next five years we laid off a couple million of them. We thought we were busy then, but it was more a matter of managing a recession than trying to compete on the global stage.

Human Resources Versus Human Capital Planning

Strategic workforce planning is more than annual stargazing and budget building. By definition, it is a complex process that addresses both short- and long-term issues. Most important, and a characteristic that is sometimes ignored, strategic workforce planning is only as good as the operating model on which it rests. Absent a consistent, comprehensive, integrated model, workforce planning is bound to be suboptimized. We can't construct a complex modern building without architectural drawings, and we can't build a solid business today without a management model.

Models are common in organizations. Production has a model for managing material and processes. Finance has a model for managing cash flow. Marketing has a model for managing customer relations. Information technology has a model for delivering data and intelligence. However, human resources' traditional "operating model" can be compared to the man who jumped on his horse and rode off in all directions. We have thrown one solution after another in an uncoordinated, inefficient attempt to respond to the latest crisis; we have always been *behind* the curve—and consequently, we have seldom been creating competitive advantage with our HR efforts. HR people wonder why they are not respected, but let the record show that their track record has been far from stellar. Human resources—and by extension, C-level executives— need a model and a plan that shows the total scope of the problems as well as the opportunities. They need the tools for putting out today's fire and, as important, preventing tomorrow's conflagration. Now, they have it.

HCM:21, or the new HR model, is shown in Figure 4.1. This management model for human capital development is an integrated, comprehensive approach that aligns each HR function with the business vision, values, and plan, as well as with each other HR function.

A Small Case in Point

When I founded Saratoga Institute in 1980, I had a clear vision and a particular model in mind. The vision was to provide objective data about

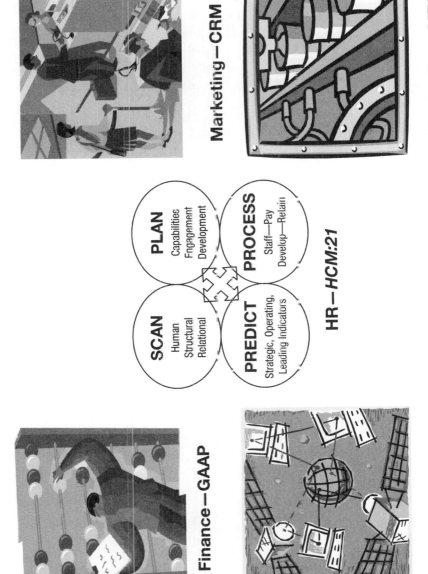

Figure 4.1 HCM:21® management model.

human resources services so that management could make better business and personnel decisions. The model was to focus exclusively on data collection and management, and pass up opportunities to become involved in recruitment, compensation, or training. This single-minded view of the model stemmed from a story I had read years before.

Two men were having lunch at a Wall Street restaurant when one asked the other, "Who is that man sitting along that wall?"

The other responded, "Why do you ask?"

The first man said, "Because almost everyone who has come in has gone over to talk to him."

The other said, "That is Mister Brown. People talk to him because he knows more about municipal bonds than anyone else."

The lesson for me was this: If I could focus my resources on becoming known for my deep knowledge of an important topic, people would want to talk to me. It is like the old saying, "Build a better mousetrap and the world will beat a path to your door." Adhering to my vision and sticking to my model led me to develop a worldwide reputation for measuring human capital management (HCM) that endures to this day. I recount this not to boast but to make the point that if you see an opportunity, and you build a vision and model around it, you will generate a competitive advantage that will be difficult for others to upset.

The Why of HCM: Capability Planning

Is it possible that HCM can be integrated with all aspects of today's constantly changing business initiatives? The answer is not that it can be, but that it *must be*. Yet, HCM can be integrated only if we think beyond HR processes. We must initiate a broad study of the marketplace, using advanced analytic tools to operationalize a new strategic model. So often we get lost in a problem, unable to see outside of it. This leads to patchwork, short-term tactical reactions rather than insightful, long-term solutions. Even when we put out the fire, the embers will reignite with the next day's crisis.

Typically, workforce planning focuses on matching the staffing requirements in business plans with the available labor pool and the expected growth and changes in staff owing to transfers, promotions, and departures of various types. From there, a staffing plan is developed for filling the holes. Unfortunately, quite often there is little coordination or planning between staffing and development. Siloed thinking minimizes the value of anticipating future outputs. This is industrial-era thinking that is essentially nothing more than truncated gap analysis. HCM:21

overrides this, once and for all time by providing the means for capability planning.

With the results of the environmental scan, described earlier in Chapter Three, you can begin to design a capability plan. Note that I have changed the term from *workforce* to *capability*. Workforce planning, as I mentioned briefly, is but a gap-analysis exercise. Although it deals with identifiable skills, the thinking is often restricted to filling jobs. But when you move to capability planning, your mindset expands. It goes beyond positions to be filled to building a strategic human capital capability. This might seem like a semantics game, but I assure you it most certainly is not. The lights go on and the energy rises as human resources people grasp the magnitude of difference here.

HCM:21's capability planning process is a new mental and physical technology. It is mental in that it fosters a different mindset, with the focus on knowledge and skill, not on job descriptions that will soon be obsolete. It is physical in that the operating system includes formulas and materials for carrying out the model in practice. A workbook is available with instructions and spreadsheets for implementing this model. You will find it in the appendix.

With capability planning, the focus is on the success of the organization. Your conclusions and recommendations are driven by the data you collected in the scan and your risk assessment. Remember, capability planning is a live, ongoing program. It doesn't happen once a year and then shut down, the way workforce planning does. Your organization must function at a high level, no matter what the future may bring.

The Segmentation of Skills

Capability planning starts with skills segmentation. While all people are important, all skills are not of equal importance. Treating the workforce like a monolith is absurd and costly. Instead, subdivide the workforce into four categories, in terms of valued capabilities:

1. *Mission Critical*. A few capabilities are absolutely key to ongoing success. If you think about it you know what these are. They can relate to technology, leadership, finance, sales, production, or anything else that represents a make-or-break situation. The question is, do you currently have sufficient mission-critical capabilities in place? Do you have backups being developed? This is where you start capability planning.

2. *Differentiating*. Given your current or desired future market position, which capabilities separate your organization from the competition? These can be unique technical, financial, service, or other skills and

knowledge that only your organization has or needs to acquire. These often augment the mission-critical capabilities, but are not identical.

3. *Operational.* Certain skills are necessary to keep the operation going. These are often characterized as administrative and maintenance, but also include technical skills. At times they are taken for granted or ignored. They need to be reviewed as insurance, as their absence would reduce efficiency, impair timely response to customer needs, and increase operating costs.

4. *Movable.* As markets, customers, and products change, some skills become less important or even obsolete. Companies sometimes forget this and allow these to remain, causing operational expenses to build. This situation became such a massive problem in the 1980s that American businesses had to lay off 3 million people to regain competitive cost structures. People in these positions need to be retrained, reassigned, or let go, and the processes outsourced, if needed at all.

So, the question is: What new capabilities do you need to acquire or build to meet changing market trends? Changes in technology, customers, market niches, competition, or other forces signal this need to develop new capabilities. At this initial point, you are better able to build the scenarios for planning, acquiring, deploying, developing, and retaining those new capabilities. Scenarios are stories or scripts that spell out potential future events. They can be best-case, worst-case, or probable-case scenarios offering a range of alternatives. In short, if you have several different views of how the future may unfold, you can better prepare for the eventualities.

The Scenarios and the Playbook

In the first essay in this chapter (see page 94), James P. Ware shows how to develop the scenarios and build a playbook for the future needs of your organization. The playbook concept is derived from sports, and the analogy to businesses is straightforward. Don't wait until the game starts to decide what to do. Depending on the conditions that develop and what your competitors try, you have to have an adaptable plan to carry out before you head out onto the field.

Succession Planning

Executive succession is a great concern for boards of directors, especially since the dotcom crash. Many companies have a senior management cadre that is ill prepared for its responsibilities. Is that the situation at your organization?

According to recent research, companies fall into three basic categories. First are the approximately 15 percent that have the cultural predisposition and systems needed to do succession planning effectively. These companies have a sense of career mobility and internal development. They also vigorously recruit and develop talent in every key area.

Next are the 50 percent that have some sense of a need for succession planning. They have taken a thoughtful approach to filling vacancies when they arise, and typically they engage in some management-development efforts. Last are the 35 percent of organizations where succession occurs largely by default. The companies may be growing too fast, may be financially troubled, or otherwise may lack the common sense or resources that effective succession planning and management development demand.

If these estimates are accurate, then approximately 85 percent of companies fall short in their efforts to deploy full, proactive, succession-planning programs—a problem only likely to grow increasingly evident as management and labor pools contract. It is also seen in numerous surveys of employee commitment. Without employee faith in organizational leadership, high turnover rates naturally follow.

Too often succession plans, when they exist, are not up to date and not relevant. The people responsible for succession planning do not always have an eye toward the future. And management development cannot be based on past experiences alone. By the time managers have a chance to put into play what they have learned, the procedures may be two to four years old. Also, managers often fail to recognize that the future seldom follows the forecast.

In 2007 and 2008, we surveyed over 1,200 companies regarding their planning programs.[1] A highlight of their responses is shown in Figure 4.2.

Our results showed that 54 percent of companies have ready backfills for fewer than 30 percent of their positions while 7 percent have ready backfills for 80 percent of their positions. Also, 54 percent have an active replacement plan for fewer than 30 percent of their positions while 9 percent have an active replacement plan for 80 percent of their positions. Lastly, 58 percent have fewer than 30 percent of positions trained for direct replacement while 6 percent have direct replacements trained for 80 percent of their positions.

The answers to these questions were compared with management practices and correlated with financial results.[2] This revealed that the companies that had at least 75 percent of their high-potential (Hi-Po) candidate-development programs fully operational, and where there

Figure 4.2. Planning practices of surveyed companies—selected questions.

1. For what percentage of your company's managerial positions do you have a replacement currently ready to backfill the position?	23%
2. Have you identified "A" players?	19
3. Is an annual succession-planning review included in your company's management staff planning program?	15
4. What percentage of your company's managerial positions are filled internally?	15
5. Do you maintain coaching or mentoring programs?	14
6. What percentage of your professional's personal objectives are expressed quantitatively and linked directly to corporate goals?	13

were replacements ready to step into mission-critical positions, the organizations saw a rise in revenue growth per full-time equivalent (FTE). The explanation for this is that Hi-Pos in mission-critical positions are the leverage that drives overall performance. Figure 4.3 shows that point at which succession planning practices begin to have an effect on revenue growth.

Given these findings, we have developed an advanced succession planning system built around four imperatives:

1. *Responsibility.* Assign a senior executive the primary responsibility for managing the system. This person must have the organizational power to keep the system on track and people being developed according to the needs of the organization and the prescribed plan.

2. *Identification.* Identify high-potential managerial and technical personnel as far down the organization as possible. As organizations become more complex, every manager and professional will be delegated greater discretionary power and faced with higher-risk decisions.

3. *Design.* Develop personal growth programs, and review and update the Hi-Pos' progress at least annually. Strategic capability implies that these people be exposed to a broad range of on-the-job experiences, as well as formal learning opportunities. Because the market is moving so rapidly, continual review and revision are necessary.

4. *Effectiveness.* Monitor advancements and their effect on top-line growth and accelerate development where necessary. All development

Figure 4.3. When succession planning affects revenue growth.

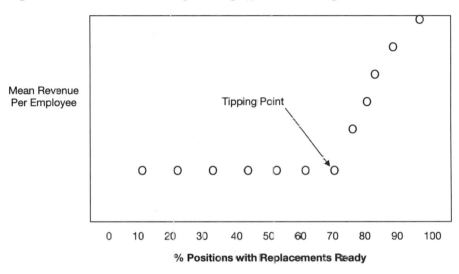

Mean Revenue
Per Employee

Tipping Point

% Positions with Replacements Ready

Source: Workforce Intelligence Report, 2007.

plans link up with the organization's strategic goals. Development is not about training; it is about sustained capability in the form of people who are intently knowledgeable and focused on purpose.

Although a senior executive is responsible for management of the succession planning system, ultimately accountability must reside with the CEO. It has become increasingly clear in recent years that management succession is a critical driver of sustainability. Despite—or perhaps because of—the inadequate planning that has characterized the past, boards of directors are starting to hold CEOs accountable for ensuring a continual flow of capable executives, managers, and high-skill professionals. Research has shown repeatedly a positive correlation between organizational performance and the CEO's commitment to management development. In the final analysis, the only corporate resource that matters is people; all other resources are depreciating assets.

Jumping Ahead of the Competition

It is possible to win—or at least be competitive—by getting the jump on the competition in the war for talent. To be proactive in your human capital management, you must:

* Have individuals readily available who possess the specific knowledge, skills, and personal qualities needed to assume key positions

* Ensure minimal downtime caused by positions remaining vacant or being covered by someone without the skills or with competing priorities

* Accelerate the time it takes for new persons to adjust to the new positions and/or corporate culture

* Significantly reduce the risk of costly hiring errors

* Achieve a higher talent retention rate

These proactive responses demand a well-thought-out, comprehensive view of the market and its forces. Your capability plans must be current and flexible, designed to move with both planned and unexpected change. The HCM:21 model does this, with its emphasis on scanning the external forces and internal factors that may impact the organization, followed by capability planning that considers the marketplace not only next year but five years out.

Notes

1. Workforce Intelligence Institute (Human Capital Source), Workforce Intelligence Report 2007, 30.
2. Ibid.

HOW TO PUT CAPABILITY PLANNING INTO PRACTICE

The essays that follow deal with scenario building, employee engagement, and paying for performance.

SCENARIO PLANNING: PREPARING FOR UNCERTAINTY

James P. Ware

As the new year begins, most of us are "on edge," knowing intuitively we're facing a future that feels more uncertain than anything we've ever experienced before. It's all too easy to become overwhelmed or want to crawl into a hole somewhere and just hibernate until the future arrives—for better or for worse.

Will the economy get better? Or worse? When? How will it affect you personally? How will your job change in the future (if it even exists)? Will your company thrive or struggle? What's going to happen to health insurance, Medicare, Social Security, climate change? How will terrorism, violent weather, or pandemics affect you personally, and your business? Will corporate profits ever return? Will average wages continue to drop in real terms?

We'd all love to know the answers to those questions and more, but, of course, if you did you would be rich and famous. More fundamentally, how can anyone predict or plan for a future so filled with uncertainty? The truth, of course, is that no one really can—in spite of what pundits claim, the track record of the so-called experts is dismal, especially over the past twelve to eighteen months.

It has been said that "the best way to predict the future is to create it."[1] However, as much as we'd all like to create our own future, that isn't a realistic option.

Historically, strategic planning was all about focusing your organization's attention on a particular marketplace and ensuring that you have the operational capabilities to compete effectively in that market segment. Most strategic plans make explicit assumptions about future trends, estimate probabilities, and include educated guesses about what's going to happen.

However, in today's highly volatile and unpredictable economy, assuming any kind of predictability in the marketplace can be fatal. Traditional strategic planning is worse than useless when dealing with the uncertainties of today's economy. Indeed, traditional thinking about the future, as if it were actually knowable, is downright dangerous. Most strategic planning approaches embody several fundamental assumptions that are patently false in the current business environment:

* Industry conditions are relatively stable and predictable.
* We can extrapolate current trends into the future with reasonable accuracy.
* Customers and competitors are well known and will remain so.
* Competitors play by the same basic rules that have governed the industry and its distribution channels in the recent past.
* There is one "right" picture of the future, and it can be predicted by the careful analysis of trends and their underlying drivers.

* Strategic planning can be done periodically (typically once a year) as a way to step back from daily operations and be reflective about the future.

The state of business today shows how totally irrelevant and even misleading those assumptions are. What we need instead is an approach to planning that moves at the speed of the Internet, embraces uncertainty, and prepares the organization to move in several different possible directions, sometimes simultaneously.

As a strategic planner, your task is to sort out which small number of possible futures is most likely to occur and how those alternative futures will affect your organization. More important, you need to develop a range of options (what we like to call a "playbook," to be described in some detail later in this essay), and determine the skills and resources required to cope with (or to create) any particular future scenario. This essay provides a brief overview of the only way to plan for uncertainty that I have any confidence in: scenario planning.[2]

Reinventing Strategic Planning

Scenarios are stories about the future that, when taken together, describe a range of plausible future states of an industry, its markets, and a particular business. Scenarios are a tool for dealing with rapid change, uncertainty, and inherent unpredictability. Scenarios are not *predictions* of the future; rather, they are images of *possible* futures, taken from the perspective of the present.

Because scenarios are developed explicitly to describe a range of possibilities, they enable managers to open their minds to the inherent uncertainties in the future, and to consider a number of "what if" possibilities without needing to choose and commit exclusively to one most likely outcome. Scenario analysis enables managers, business planners, and executive teams to develop multiple options for action that can be compared and assessed in advance of the need to implement them.

An effective scenario suggests critical implications for a business and contains personal meaning for the people who build it. Scenarios are useful tools primarily because they facilitate—indeed, *require*—a strategic dialogue about the unpredictable outcome of today's rapidly changing business environment.

Here's the way a special report on the future role of the chief human resources officer prepared for the Society for Human Resource Management (SHRM) described the authors' goal:

In contrast to the SHRM Workplace Forecast, the goal of this work is not to identify or trace out the trends that will likely unfold. These trends inform the scenarios presented here, but the focus in this report is much more on the uncertainties of the future. What is it that we don't know that could fundamentally change the environment in which we work? How could these uncertainties lead us to very different worlds that will require different capabilities for success?[3]

In fact, the scenario-building process enables you to uncover and consider near-term developments in your markets that are indicators of the larger trends that will eventually have a dramatic impact on the shape of your industry and your business. Scenarios also help managers envision future states that might seem highly implausible to a naïve viewer. And even if the scenario is implausible on the surface, it can serve to highlight possibilities for action that may someday become absolutely essential to the future of your business, or may stimulate innovation if the future they were created for never comes to pass.

Depending on a well-defined map of what amounts to an unexplored territory can be highly misleading. As a real-life example, here's a brief history lesson. When European mapmakers in the seventeenth century listened to the ship captains who returned from exploring the western coast of North America, they depicted California as a large island, separated from the western United States by a large unnamed body of water.

Although wrong, their logic was understandable. Sailing past Baja California, the ship captains had reported seeing nothing but water to the north. Then they traveled north in the Pacific Ocean to Seattle, where they entered Puget Sound, and once again they saw nothing but water. Based on their limited experience, it was easy to conclude that California was indeed a large island. The incorrect maps they produced led to incorrect—and sometimes disastrous—decisions by the early settlers of the American West.[4]

Scenario planning, in contrast, encourages a creative tolerance for ambiguity; and it enables an organization to consider what skills and resources it would need to compete effectively in each of the imagined alternative futures, as well as how it would have to change current practices to survive in that world. Finally, scenario planning provides executives with a sense of what events or patterns to look for as early warning signs that one or more of the projected scenarios might actually be starting to occur. This early sense of how the future is beginning to unfold amounts to a form of "anticipatory insurance."

Building Scenarios

While there are many different approaches to developing scenarios, my personal preference is to follow a three-stage process. The first step is to identify the most critical and potentially impactful unknowns—the things you know you don't know now but if you did know would tell you how to make effective decisions today about tomorrow.

The second step is to select two of the most critical of those unknowns—two uncertainties that are essentially independent variables. Each of these two dimensions of the future should have two equally likely but unpredictable outcomes (as far as you can tell at this point; if the opposite outcomes are not equally likely, the variable isn't really an uncertainty).

Then, once you've identified those two critical uncertainties, the third step is to set up a 2 × 2 matrix and look at the four possible combinations. You name them, and flesh them out to create four compelling stories that capture four alternative visions of the future.

For example, consider this scenario matrix for a project-based engineering company that is highly dependent on government contracts (Figure 4.4).

While this company's executives can't accurately predict or adequately control either government spending or the salaries they'll have to pay to attract and retain critical talent, they *can* prepare for each of these four possible futures by carefully considering their talent attraction/retention strategies, their business-development activities, and the range of possible macroeconomic trends that will influence both of these variables.

Figure 4.5 on page 100 identifies four scenarios describing very different future roles for the chief human resources officer (CHRO). These scenarios were developed in 2005 by a group of academic experts for the Society for Human Resource Management; the full report presents the four possible roles in greater detail.

In this exercise, the scenario planners selected two aspects of the future economy that they believed were indeterminable:

1. The prevailing kind of organizational strategy, either self-organizing or a more traditional, hierarchical approach

2. The global supply of talent, either scarce or in abundance

The scenario planners then developed four richly described and very different roles that senior HR executives might play in each of the four "worlds" that those two variables suggested. Here, for example, is a brief

Figure 4.4. AJAX Engineering future scenarios.

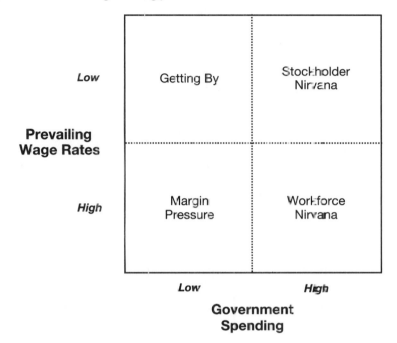

summary of the "caregiver" future as it was envisioned by the SHRM authors:

> Terrorist attacks and a desire for protection lead to the return of centralized, hierarchical organizations as companies create the structures needed to attract and retain workers. As the organization serves the role of a "parent," HR in this scenario is the keeper of the corporate hearth and provider of the many benefits the organization offers.[5]

Each of the four hypothetical roles for the CHRO is spelled out this way to enable senior executives and HR professionals to imagine the world in which that role would be appropriate. A story like this is far more interesting, and compelling, than a set of dry statistics or a sterile narrative about the projected future conditions, no matter how sincerely the planners believe that those conditions will prevail.

Once a set of scenarios like these has been developed, a strategic dialogue can begin in earnest. Which future scenario is closest to where you

Figure 4.5. Four possible worlds for the CHRO.

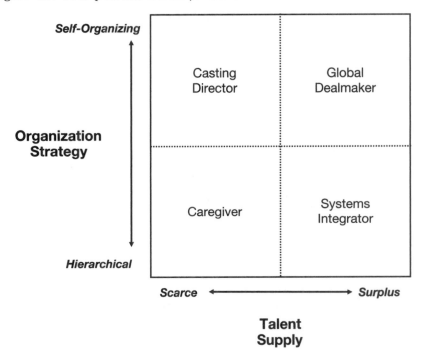

are today? Which one will you be in if the key scenario drivers—business trends, regulatory policies, technological innovation—continue their present course? Which "world" would you prefer to be in? Is there anything your organization could do to nudge the future in one direction or another? What new kinds of competitors could emerge in each scenario?

Most important, in which direction are the prevailing winds blowing? The real value in using scenarios is in identifying potentially useful strategies for moving your business into a more desirable future. Scenario building enables a type of war gaming well in advance of actual market competition.

From Scenarios to Playbooks

Once you have developed several plausible scenarios, what can you do with them? Scenarios are not an end in themselves, and if misused they can actually increase organizational risk. If you have developed several different but equally credible views of how the future might unfold, you might end up even more overwhelmed than if you had simply been sty-mied about where things might go. To avoid that, we recommend build-ing a "playbook" containing alternative scripts or action plans for the different futures you have described in your scenarios. We know of sev-eral organizations now using playbooks to develop multiple possible stra-tegic moves and to enable rapid implementation of the most potent ones. The playbook approach expands scenario planning into a complete, action-oriented management technique.

The Playbook Concept

Professional teams in most major team sports—especially those in time-based sports like football, basketball, and soccer—have used play-books for years. A playbook contains a series of different offensive and defensive plays that have been developed for a variety of different condi-tions. An effective playbook takes into account the unique strengths (and weaknesses) of the team; there is one set of plays for the first-string quar-terback (who may be a left-handed rollout passer) and a second set for the backup quarterback (who may be right-handed and more of a drop-back passer). Similarly, when the star halfback is in the game, the team will execute one set of running plays, and when he is on the sidelines, there may be a completely different running game in place.

The analogy to businesses developing future-focused strategies is straightforward. Like a football team, you can't afford to wait until the opening kickoff to figure out what to do; nor do you want to wait until you have only thirty seconds left in the game to figure out how to move the ball sixty yards downfield. Instead, you want to anticipate, develop, and practice (i.e., pilot) a series of possible strategic moves. Then, depending on the conditions that develop and what your competitors do, you can carry out one set of plans or another.

Or, if the competition does something unexpectedly, you can even "call an audible" at the last minute and execute it effectively because you have rehearsed it in advance. In addition, of course, when you know what strategic moves you want to be able to make, you know what skills and resources you will require to make the moves successfully.

Management teams that think of themselves as coaches planning for a championship game are more likely to succeed than those who "wing it" by acting predictably, randomly, or only in response to the actions of others. Working through in advance what "plays" or strategic moves you want to make under different conditions is by far the best way to prepare for the new, highly unpredictable "game" of business strategy. We have even seen some companies that engage in "scrimmages" whereby they explore several generations of strategic moves by imagining what their competitors will do in response to their initial moves, and then determining what to do next.

The Contents of a Business Playbook

A business playbook must be developed quickly, and it should be fully integrated into your organization's strategic planning and execution process. Ideally, building the playbook will involve the entire senior management team in thinking through the possibilities of market futures, strategic moves, and potential business outcomes.

From my perspective, a complete strategic playbook includes six basic "chapters."

1. *Analyzing the "Game."* The opening chapter includes a basic analysis of the company's business environment, focusing on the fundamental drivers of change, including those strategic uncertainties whose combinations lead to a set of plausible alternative futures.

2. *Assessing Our Competitive Position.* This chapter includes a thorough examination of the company's capabilities and limitations, with a particular focus on its position and power in its current channels. What is your present value proposition? Why do your customers buy from you and not your competitors? What are your capabilities and resources?

3. *Scenarios—Envisioning the Future.* This chapter contains documentation of the alternative futures that come out of the critical uncertainties defined by the scenarios you have created. These scenarios are most effective when they take the form of rich, detailed narratives that make the alternative futures come alive. In addition, more detailed economic analyses, customer profiles, and channel structures may also be described and discussed. This is also the chapter of the playbook where opportunities for changing the rules of the game can be identified.

4. *Plays—Setting Our Options.* These are the specific strategic moves that can be made within each scenario. In addition, indicators are identified—environmental factors that can act as signals that one or more of the alternative worlds may actually be occurring, or are becoming more likely. Here is where a potential sequence of plays can be outlined, helping to identify strategic priorities and interdependencies.

5. *Executing the Plays.* This chapter lays out the action steps required to execute each plausible or desirable strategic move. Here, the resources needed to execute each play are delineated, as are the managerial accountabilities for ensuring resource availability and actually executing

the plays. In addition, it is often useful to identify the consequences of both success and delay in executing each play.

6. *Tracking, Anticipating, and Acting.* This chapter includes the ongoing documentation of the plays as they are executed, and it contains updated environmental assessments as well as any new plays or counterplays as they are developed. It represents the regular, if not continuous, revision of the playbook. This notion of the playbook as a "living" document is critical—given the pace of change we live with today, any set of static plays will become outdated very rapidly.

It should be clear from these descriptions that creating and maintaining a comprehensive strategic playbook is no small undertaking. Yet, today's business environment does not allow any organization the luxury of taking a year, or even six months, to develop its playbook. The successful companies we have observed typically complete a first-draft playbook in twelve weeks or less. It takes a focused, high-energy effort to do so. A time-box approach—which necessarily limits the amount of detail in the initial version of each chapter and each play to what can be prepared in a short period—is the only way to get the job done in time to make a difference.

The Process for Creating a Playbook

We recommend developing a playbook in three phases:

* Phase One—Background research and scenario development
* Phase Two—Development of strategic options
* Phase Three—Acquisition of necessary resources and building of the capability to execute

Phase One—Background Research and Scenario Development

Phase One corresponds to chapters 1 and 2 of the playbook structure described previously, plus the groundwork for chapter 3. It involves conducting intensive background research into your industry, your current customers and channel partners, and your own business capabilities.

This phase typically begins with formation of an effective cross-functional playbook team that not only represents all the skills and perspectives needed to build the playbook but also has the credibility with senior management to ensure that its findings and recommendations are listened to and acted on.

Phase One includes asking questions like these:

* What is changing today about our customers, our competitors, our marketplace?

* What is our current position within our supply chain? What is keeping us where we are in the chain? What forces are changing our channel power relative to our suppliers, our customers, and—if applicable—the ultimate end consumers?

* What core business processes drive our industry and channel today?

* What kind of channel player do we want to be going forward? What are our ambitions?

Phase One generally concludes with a workshop with senior management in which these questions are addressed. Critical uncertainties are identified, and the senior management team itself explores scenarios of possible future operating states.

Phase Two—Development of Strategic Options

Phase Two, corresponding to chapters 3 and 4 of the playbook structure, should be completed within four weeks, if at all possible. The playbook team develops the scenarios in much greater detail, and for each scenario the team asks, "If this world actually happens, what do we need or want to do? What capabilities and resources are required to be successful?"

Other important questions to ask during Phase Two include:

* What impact would each scenario have on our existing resources, market position, and channel partners?

* How might our competitors react to each scenario? What opportunities and threats would their reactions create for us?

* How could our resources evolve or be transformed to take advantage of the conditions in each scenario?

* What competencies are required to be successful in each scenario? What will it take for us to develop or acquire those competencies? Can we afford them?

* What kinds of products or services would our customers value in each scenario? Can we create these offerings ourselves, or do we need new (or existing) partners to create them?

It's very important at this point to engage senior management across the company in playbook development. When done well, this participation produces rich scenario narratives, and the detailed playbook becomes the basis for extended discussion and even excitement within the operating units that will ultimately implement the plays. During this phase, the company sometimes discovers that some of the critical indicators it has identified as signals of the future are already occurring. Such discoveries can serve as powerful wake-up calls that action is needed, and quickly. Of course, they also help in narrowing the field of likely and feasible options for action.

Phase Three—Acquisition of Necessary Resources and Building of the Capability to Execute

Phase Three, corresponding to chapter 5 of the playbook structure, is also best completed within another four to six weeks. It consists primarily of working through the resource requirements and execution capabilities surrounding each of the strategic options that have come out of the scenario-building process in Phase Two.

Here the organization is doing something that looks and feels like traditional resource planning; it is sorting through the implications and consequences of each possible scenario. What makes this process different, however, is that no final or formal commitments have been made to any particular strategic move. Identifying the possible or most likely scenarios is not equivalent to predicting that they will actually occur, and describing a set of *possible* plays is not committing to execute them. Indeed, defining the resource requirements and costs of each strategic play is another consideration that will help to determine what actions management actually wants to take. The practicality and economic feasibility of developing or acquiring the resources is an important part of deciding which of the moves to prepare to take.

The first iteration of playbook development concludes with another senior management workshop, this time to consider the playbook as a whole, internalize the scenarios, evaluate the plays, select any plays you want to execute immediately, and plan investments in capabilities and resources that will enable strategic plays in the future.

The Strengths and Limitations of Scenario Planning

As a planning tool, scenarios have both strengths and limitations. Their primary advantages are as follows:

* *Plausibility.* No one is trying to *predict* the future. The focus is on the logic of the scenario, not on what someone believes will or should happen, but what *can* happen and why.

* *Creativity.* The brainstorming approach actively encourages out-of-box thinking.

* *Tolerance for Ambiguity.* By their very nature, scenarios teach managers that it is all right not to know "the" answer about the future. Perhaps the most important value of scenarios is that they shift the debate from "what will be" to "what if."

* *Seeing the Big Picture.* In laying out a range of possible futures, we become more adept at considering multiple variables, asking fundamental questions, and thinking open-mindedly about plausible alternative conditions. On the other hand, scenario planning introduces new kinds of risk into the way people think about the future.

There are several important limitations that you can ignore only at your peril:

* *Oversimplification.* You can't cover all the key uncertainties in complete detail.

* *Team Composition Interacting with Content.* The team members and their interaction during scenario building inevitably affect the visions the team produces. While individual involvement and group cohesion can create an enthusiasm and understanding that is then difficult to replicate across the organization, groups that fall into either interpersonal, special-interest bickering or "group-think" may actually interfere with productive planning.

* *Insight Versus Action.* The scenario technique works best in generating new ideas and leaps in understanding. But this doesn't necessarily lead directly to action and concrete change. It is too easy to become enamored of the scenarios themselves, and to gain false security from their documentation. But their only value lies in the way the company *acts* on the information and ideas the scenarios generate.

Summary

This is the value of scenarios: They have the ability to help you plan effectively for improbable and uncertain futures. Rather than selecting a most probable vision of the future and devoting all of your resources to a single, hard-to-change strategy, you can instead spend a small but significant amount of effort keeping your knowledge current in each of several different areas of concern—a range of possible futures.

The scenario planning process takes managers out of their daily routines, forces them to consider the underlying drivers that are causing change and uncertainty, and enables them to work constructively together to consider what might happen in the business environment. With this deeper understanding and broader anticipation of the future, they are then equipped to play out a range of potential strategies and sort out the implications of each strategy for the current business and its customers.

With a portfolio of strategic options in hand, a management team can determine the costs and risks inherent in adopting any one of them, or in trying several of them simultaneously. More important, the organization now has a much clearer sense of what factors in the marketplace matter, and can focus attention on the few uncertainties that will have the greatest impact on the future. With this knowledge of what to look for, the company is well positioned to move quickly to adopt a specific strategy, or make an aggressive move, as soon as it determines that the strategic indicators have moved in a given direction.

Building a playbook is not a simple task, but it is an extremely effective approach to anticipating how your business will be affected by the complex dynamics of a volatile marketplace. No one can predict with any confidence what the future in general will be like, and certainly no one but you can plan for how it might evolve in your industry and within your particular market segments.

As Louis Pasteur said, "Chance favors only the mind that is prepared." In the fast-changing world of today, the future may be almost completely unpredictable, but it is not completely random. Scenario analysis, strategic indicators, and playbooks are tools for increasing your odds of success (and survival). When you know your strengths and limitations, your sources of competitive advantage, and your strategic options, then playing the game well becomes much easier.

Notes

1. It is difficult to identify the original source of this idea, which has been repeated many times by many pundits. As nearly as I can tell, it has been attributed with roughly equal frequency to both Peter Drucker and Alan Kay.
2. Arie de Geus, Peter Schwartz, and their colleagues at Shell Oil in the 1970s are generally credited with being the "inventors" of scenario planning. Schwartz was also the co-founder (and remains chairman) of Global Business Network, today's undisputed home of scenario planning. And if there is a bible of scenario planning—what it's about, why it's important, and how to do it—it's Peter Schwartz's 1996 book, *The Art*

of the Long View (Peter Schwartz, *The Art of the Long View: Planning for the Future in an Uncertain World* [New York: Currency Doubleday, 1996]).

3. Robert Gunther et al., "Scenarios for the Future of Human Resource Management" (Executive Summary), Society for Human Resource Management, 2005.

4. This example comes from Eric Clemons, a friend and former colleague who teaches IT and Business Strategy at The Wharton School at the University of Pennsylvania.

5. Gunther et al., p. 12.

QUALITY EMPLOYEE ENGAGEMENT MEASUREMENT: THE CEO'S ESSENTIAL HUCAMETRIC TO MANAGE THE FUTURE

Kenneth Scarlett

Peter Drucker, generally recognized as the inventor of the modern organization, commented that the best way to predict the future is to create it. Perhaps he was thinking about the day CEOs would use predictive human capital metrics, or hucametrics, to sculpt their own business future. Thanks to advances in technology and greater scientific understanding of the value potential of human capital, that day has arrived for CEOs who are ready to proactively manage their human resources and their businesses using future-facing metrics. Here, I describe how having predictive data to put the right people in the right place, at the right time, with the right skills, at the right engagement level, so they can do the right things, serve the right customers, just in time, is the best way to create business success in these unpredictable times.

Hucametrics Explained

So what is hucametrics and what in the world does quality employee-engagement measurement have to do with predicting outcomes? Hucametrics (*hew-ca-MET-rix*) is the new science of tracking and applying human capital data to predict employee and business performance and cause and effect. Hucametrics is to predicting winning business outcomes as sabermetrics is to predicting the best courses of action to win baseball games and Numerati is to predicting customer purchase preferences. The assumption is that most, if not all, organizations have a signature set of data on their human capital that can be formulated to foretell the future and illuminate the best possible courses of action with a high degree of accuracy. These hucametric data sets, powered by quality employee-engagement profiles, can enable forward-thinking top managers to create their own futures.

Are You Ready?

In forty-five-plus years of employee attitude and engagement research, some interesting, reliable, and repeatable statistical models have been produced that are predictive of future business and employee performance. These models vary in complexity from basic to expert. Further, they seem to operate, if managed from the top of the organization, in virtually any size company or organization, provided the measures are statistically sound and separated into management, nonmanagement, and customer-contact groups.

I refer here to the *basic* hucametric predictive model as the CEO success formula:

$$\text{Competence} \times \text{engagement} \times \text{organizational opportunity} = \text{return on human capital}$$

Or, more conversationally put, "ready, willing, and able." For those who want reliable, forward-facing metrics to maximize the return on dollars invested in human capital, while synchronizing the organization's activities to delight the customer, this is as simple as it gets. Human resources' economic contribution is at the heart of maximizing the productivity of capital (profit), and human capital is usually the most expensive form of capital. It stands to reason that some foresight regarding the return on human capital has the potential of adding incredible value. So, in its complete form, the success formula provides CEOs with meaningful indexes and data columns that list the elements of each of these hucametric indexes on their computer spreadsheets each month, with a baseline ROI on human capital numbers and a projected ROI on human capital numbers. Each leader is accountable for each index in the formula for his or her group and for correlating those statistical relationships to group performance and data on business outcome. It is at the group level that many predictive linkages emerge and become actionable. Many organizations have some form of these hucametrics squirreled away, sitting idle, and they simply need to be gathered and mathematically calibrated to work in combination. But the CEO needs to get his or her hands dirty and drive it. But let's look at the CEO success formula in greater detail.

Competence—"Ready"

Think of competence in the organization as a collective rather than an individual phenomenon, where unity of effort is more important than the sum of the parts. That's why we have organizations: because one person can't do all the work. But too much emphasis has been put on individual/anecdotal talent management these days, at the expense of group engagement and unity of effort, which is where the real value and potential for predictability slumber.

Competence, for hucametric purposes, is the group's or organization's collective state of being adequate, well qualified, or masterful in performing a specific set of jobs or functions, measured against set standards, and in consistently and successfully achieving specific outcomes. It's a reliable statistical measurement of group performance against established or desirable business outcomes. The competence element of the equation can be derived from individual performance-appraisal scores (provided those scores reliably describe the actual level of performance), aggregated by work group, expressed as an index, and broken out by value-factor element. Experience has shown that the aggregated scores of management, nonmanagement, and customer-contact groups should be broken out and rolled up separately to make it easier to spot direct cause-and-effect links.

Figure 4.6 is an example of what the nonmanagement competence profile may look like.

For these statistics to be useful for predictive and intervention purposes, individual performance results should be aggregated by leader work group. We have found that most companies underutilize combined individual performance-appraisal scores and fail to adequately manage group performance totals. Often the valuable data get stuck in the human resources department rather than being sent to operating managers for data mining and correlation.

Figure 4.7 is what the top management group profile may look like.

Competency profiles, once calibrated properly, should statistically describe the competency of each work group, as well as the organization as a whole. Group competency scores can be classified into categories of less than adequate, adequate, well qualified, and masterful for purposes of skills training and transfer management. Over time, signature acceptable ranges can be established based on their correlations to desirable future outcomes.

Employee Engagement—"Willing"

How many times have we seen gifted athletes or persons of great talent become disengaged or even hostile toward the organizations that

Figure 4.6. Nonmanagement work group competence profile.

Competence Value Factors	0–100 Scale
1. Understanding individual and group work goals	79
2. Performance in accomplishing goals:	81
(a) Speed	61
(b) Quality	95
(c) Percent achieved	87
3. Opportunity to contribute	91
(a) Attendance	79
(b) Tardiness	99
(c) Percentage of daily uptime directly contributing to work goals, the welfare of the organization, and/or customers	96
4. Skill/achievement level	88
5. Scope of knowledge of products, services, customers, and potential new markets	66
6. Innovation events—implemented ideas resulting in saving time or money, better customer service, or finding new markets	21
7. Dedication to serve	45
COMPETENCE INDEX	67.29

employ them? They may be masterfully competent, or *ready,* to provide great talent, but they are emotionally *unwilling* to focus their talents and efforts for the economic benefit of the enterprise. It's like a champion race-car driver spending big money on a high-horsepower sports car and refusing to start the engine. The driver is ready but unwilling.

True measurement of engagement statistically describes this state of willingness and predicts the quality, speed, energy, and enthusiasm of human effort in the organization, independent of competence or oppor-

Figure 4.7. Top management competence profile.

Competence Value Factors	0–100 Scale &/or % Achieved
1. Organizational goals achieved	90
(a) Percent	85
(b) Quality	95
2. Human Capital Return on Investment	66
$$HCROI = \frac{\text{Revenue} - \text{Expenses} - \text{Pay} + \text{Benefits}}{\text{Pay} + \text{Benefits (all labor classifications)}}$$	
(Economic Contribution of Human Resources)	
3. Human Capital Market Value	71
$$HCMV = \frac{\text{Market Value} - \text{Book Value}}{\text{FTEs} + \text{Contract} + \text{Contingent}}$$	
4. Brand enhancement/customer loyalty increase	31
5. Profitability and return on human capital invested	45
6. Innovation events	91
7. Cumulative, company-wide engagement index	81
8. Cumulative, company-wide competence index	83
COMPETENCE INDEX	69.75

tunity to contribute. "Ready" without "willing" results in poor return on human capital because the capital sits idle. The expert race-car driver is going nowhere.

This is why the engagement element of the CEO equation given earlier must come from quality employee-engagement psychometrics—a rarity in today's euphemistic marketing-muscle world. Poor-quality attempts at measuring engagement are a massive problem affecting an estimated eight out of ten organizations in the United States alone. Faulty measurement disables management's ability to engage employees, which often is the root cause of companies going out of business. Based on our sampling, seven out of every ten CEOs are less than satisfied with the integrity of their measurements or the return value of their current employee-survey programs. That is, they don't believe that their surveys accurately measure engagement. Conversely, we have found that eight out of ten HR directors are satisfied with their surveys. That is, satisfaction is passive, engagement is active, and the emotional commitment of energy is toward reaching the goals of the enterprise. Thus, quality measurement of engagement is critical to employee survey values, workforce productivity, the future success of the business, and the successful application of hucametrics—so we need to examine this in some detail.

Cases of Mistaken Identity

Engagement is often mistaken for satisfaction in opinion, best-in-class, or business outcome surveys. As a result, management errantly embarks on fixing the wrong things in an attempt to positively engage more employees, often with deleterious consequences. Extrapolating from a reputable independent study,[1] over 7 million more employees in the United States became disengaged between 2005 and 2006. Clearly, this epidemic of disengagement is being fueled by mistaken measurement. Most surveys labeled "engagement" are, in fact, not.

Similarly, two fundamental precepts necessary to positively engage people are often ignored in the survey measurement: (1) employee sense of fair treatment underpins engagement (if people feel they are treated unfairly, there is less than a 15 percent chance they will be positively engaged), and (2) the things that engage people are different from the things that disengage them (the opposite of disengagement is not engagement, but no disengagement). Disengaged talent produces negative financial value. Figure 4.8 summarizes our findings, which describe how engagement factors and disengagement factors operate separately but interdependently.

There are a couple of things to note about these findings, based on Frederick Herzberg's Two-Factor studies and confirmed by our survey work: (1) positive employee engagement cannot be sustained if the preponderance of disengagement factors is not neutralized, and (2) to positively engage employees there is more than "one thing you need to know"—most disengagement factors must be neutralized before improvements in engagement factors can have a significant positive influence.

Figure 4.8. Effect of motivation and hygiene factors on engagement and contribution.

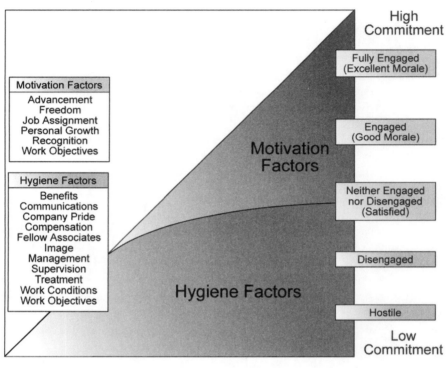

Source: Scarlett Surveys International, 2008.

Definition and Measurement of Quality Engagement

After many years of empirical instrument testing and measurement across many industries and cultures, we developed the following definition of *engagement* that is measurable, manageable, and predictive: *Engagement is an individual's degree of positive or negative emotional attachment to his or her organization, job, and colleagues.*

Notice that the above definition describes engagement as an individual phenomenon that varies in intensity from extremely positive to extremely negative. In the middle of the engagement spectrum is a neutral position that is often mistaken for satisfaction (and acceptably productive). The reality is that engagement—or, more precisely put, emotional attachment—is heavily influenced by employee experiences with employers; leadership interactions; policies and procedures; company image; and aspects surrounding the job, work, rewards, social camaraderie, and work environment.

Figure 4.9 illustrates engagement when expressed as an acceleration lever. At the front-forward position, there is a predisposed behavioral tendency that favors economic contribution for the organization. At the back-end position, there is a behavioral tendency that is detrimental to economic contribution. Individuals at the back end are disengaged. At the extreme back end, employees are actually hostile about constructively contributing to the economic benefit of the organization.

From this understanding and definition of engagement, Scarlett Surveys has developed fifteen global factors, or drivers, of engagement that are universal in their measurement application. Employee attitudes toward these drivers heavily influence their behavioral predisposition to economically contribute, add value, or not contribute. Thus, employee engagement can be measured by surveying employee attitudes about these drivers, using a battery of validated questions. Scored responses to these question batteries assess the emotional attachment level, judge the intensity of effort propensity, and predict future behavior.

The Identification of Engagement Drivers

So, how can CEOs apply this information to increase the ROI of human capital?

Employee engagement from the organization's point of view is the art of getting people to do whatever is necessary to ensure continuous

Figure 4.9. Accelerator for employee engagement.

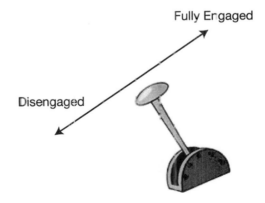

Fully Engaged

Disengaged

Source: Scarlett Surveys International.

high performance and the success of the business—and have them love doing it! The measurable definition of engagement—an individual's degree of positive or negative attachment to the organization, job, and colleagues—makes it possible to provide managers with trustworthy statistics as a means of improving their art. The group engagement index shown in Figure 4.10 is a summary score of how masterful they are becoming in the art of better engaging their people. The goal, of course, is to fully engage 100 percent of the people who are 100 percent competent 100 percent of the time.

The most common failure of management to engage employees is poor integrity of the survey measurement. Occasionally, in a workshop or presentation, I will ask participants to select from a list of immeasurable but pleasant-sounding employee engagement "definitions" collected from published Society for Human Resource Management information. I ask them to bear in mind that their selections will determine their company's leadership actions in managing people in the organization for years to come, in spending thousands of hours in discussions at meetings, and in determining the spending on human capital priorities. A couple of interesting things occur. Rarely do people from the same company choose the same definitions, and the most nicely worded but most immeasurable definitions are chosen more than 60 percent of the time. The point is this: Confusion in the marketplace is crippling management's attempts to successfully measure engagement and to use that data predictably to increase their percentage of engaged employees. Employee engagement is too often reduced to rhetoric ("I know it when I see it") rather than a reliable statistical measurement upon which to base performance standards, make leaders accountable, and continually increase return on human capital.

Similarly, most employee surveys do not contain the complete set of fifteen engagement drivers (even though they may get at some elements or derivatives of engagement). The harm is caused when follow-up managers prioritize an incomplete or incorrect list of drivers that, when engaged, actually disengage employees. This predicament is commonplace with satisfaction surveys that measure factors that, in reality, are entitlements and hygienic oriented. Prioritizing and activating those survey results do not have a positive correlation to improving the number of positively engaged employees.

In a recent podcast interview I was asked why there are fifteen engagement drivers. My response was, "I wish there weren't, because there are more questions to ask, more psychometrics to get right, and more factors to manage; but we can empirically prove there are fifteen, just as Frederick Herzberg proved there are fifteen." The interviewer's

Figure 4.10. Nonmanagement engagement sample.

Sample Company

FACTORS: OVERALL vs. GROUP

January 2008
Non-Management

	Critical Range	Overall Results	Group 01	Group 02	Group 03	Group 04	Group 05	Group 06
AER* Index	67–79	73	65	88	65	81	78	66
Percent with poor attitudes	40–20	28	25	0	(50)	13	22	(60)
Number of participants		193	12	7	10	8	18	5
COMPANY PRIDE	82–93	80	57	100	68	100	86	70
VICE PRESIDENTS AND ABOVE	53–65	69	67	88	63	77	58	73
DIRECTORS	50–86	67	43	93	50	60	80	57
COMPANY IMAGE	58–73	61	47	79	42	77	66	47
INFORMATION	64–77	73	60	100	63	87	81	67
TREATMENT	53–66	65	61	80	48	69	74	40
ADVANCEMENT OPPORTUNITIES	48–62	56	63	76	45	79	65	63
COMPENSATION	45–63	52	64	45	35	50	52	90
BENEFITS	72–86	87	97	95	73	90	92	100
WORKING CONDITIONS	70 81	84	90	79	83	91	83	78
FELLOW ASSOCIATES	78–86	87	79	93	83	89	94	93
JOB ASSIGNMENT	78–89	73	47	95	67	94	69	60
WORK OBJECTIVES	62–76	73	69	90	55	75	88	27
MANAGER	69–80	82	78	98	78	76	93	58
PERFORMANCE FREEDOM	76–85	83	76	95	83	85	89	70
PERSONAL GROWTH	68–79	65	32	93	78	91	63	70

*AER = Associate Engagement Research.

Source: Scarlett Surveys International, 2008.

response provided a good summary of reality: "I guess that's because people are a lot more complicated than we want to believe." What we are dealing with is an accepted widespread lack of integrity in engagement measurements, which originates from faulty definitions—that is, does the instrument correctly measure employee attitudes toward proven engagement factors and calculate a reliable numerical index predictive of future behavior?

Now that we're experts in employee engagement measurement and its predictability value, let's move on to the next hucametric.

Organizational Opportunity—"Able"

Dr. Frederick Herzberg once commented, "If you want someone to do a good job give them a good job to do." This statement lies at the heart of what organizational opportunity is all about: putting the right people in the right place at the right time doing the job or working for the cause they love.

Organizational opportunity metrics are a bit trickier to gather than those for competence and engagement, since they aren't wholly available off the shelf. In his recent book *Outliers*, Malcolm Gladwell describes how opportunity in addition to competence and engagement (he calls it "luck") help people and groups succeed. GE did some good practical work on organizational opportunity some years ago. It took data from performance appraisals, placement tests, and employee surveys relating to job fit, productivity, personal growth, and personal goals to formulate group indexes and manageable individual work plans that were matched to customer engagement, future customer demand, and potential new markets. GE was one of the first organizations to realize that organizational opportunity—giving people a chance to contribute to the max and have unlimited success—could predictably maximize their return on human capital and grow their business exponentially. GE forced its managers to figure out innovative skill-building career paths for each individual in their groups so that their "double O" group index would be higher and their bonuses bigger. As a result, a good brand was made great, and innovations and new start-ups became commonplace, all while running low operating costs and achieving high return on human capital. But the CEO drove the process.

Our research over the years has revealed that, by and large, people go to work for economic stability, to find out who they are (personal growth), and to achieve and be recognized for those achievements. Company owners, on the other hand, want people to come to work to add more economic value than they are paid. The two motivations can be bridged through organizational opportunity.

Figure 4.11. Nonmanagement work group organizational opportunity profile.

OO Factors	0–100 Scale
1. Job Fit	89
2. Achievement	61
3. Recognition	40
4. Responsibility	75
5. Advancement Opportunities	60
6. Personal Growth	70
7. Freedom to Perform	40
8. Maximized Contributions	40
OO INDEX	59.38

Take, for example, our race-car driver. He is "ready" (he is a certified, competent master race-car driver with a great car), he is "willing" (he is fully engaged racing cars), but he is required to work concessions at the track instead of getting the opportunity to race. His organizational opportunity score would be low and his return on human capital score would be low.

The method we have used successfully to measure double O is to extract data from engagement survey results in the following areas: job fit, achievement, recognition, responsibility, advancement, growth, freedom to perform, and a self-classification question involving contribution. Figure 4.11 above is an example of a nonmanagement work group organizational opportunity profile.

The Return on Human Capital Predictor

Based on the example in Figure 4.11, using the index scores of the nonmanagement group, let's take a look at how things multiply out:

(Competence) 67.29 × (engagement) 73 × (organizational opportunity) 59.38 =
(potential HCROI) 291,685

This translates to a PHCROI index average of 66.56. Both number results are useful. The 291,685 can be compared to current revenue per employee, human capital ROI, human capital value added, and human capital market value (see *The ROI of Human Capital* by Jac Fitz-enz, pp. 35–38) every time the CEO success hucametrics are gathered until some type of predictive relationship is established, overall and at the work-group level. After the first round of measures, there should be sufficient data from the group profiles to establish some predictive trends.

The index average can be used to measure leadership performance, company-wide, in maximizing return on human capital. You can use it as a summary score for leadership effectiveness and as an essential quali-fication for promotion.

Hucametrics—Where Do I Start?

The value proposition is this: If the CEO does not embark on huca-metric modeling, his or her organization's chances of continuously thriv-ing in this age of short product and service life cycles, extreme market shifts, and economic uncertainty are substantially diminished. Driving a car looking out of the windshield gives someone a much better chance of arriving at the intended destination on time and alive than using the rear-view mirror. As the car increases in speed, the rearview person's chances of avoiding obstacles, staying on the road, and arriving safely diminish substantially. This is the case with today's flat-world market speed. His-torical and even current financial accounting and operating statistics have us looking out the back and side windows as the speed of markets increases and the likelihood of going in the wrong direction or hitting something we didn't see is certain. Foresight eats hindsight for breakfast. The business disasters at GM, Ford, and Chrysler are harbingers of what's in store for companies that disregard hucametrics.

This basic CEO success equation should be just the beginning in the modern organization's quest to harness and apply human capital data to reduce uncertainty and shape its own business future. But hucametrics can't get stuck in numerically challenged HR departments. Think of it as a science that requires someone's full attention to get the signature cause-and-effect models right. It's more than just about making money; it's about promoting human excellence and eupsychian leadership. It's about creating wealth with people, rather than by using them.

For hucametrics to really work in an organization, CEOs need to own the data and appoint a numerate human capital (HuCap) manager who reports directly to them. The HuCap manager should supply the data matrices, explain them, and make them predictive and reliable. Like a business GPS system showing the road ahead and the alternative routes, the HuCap manager is responsible for developing signature predictive cause-and-effect profiles, eventually correlating hucametric data with Numerati data to predict the most efficient deployment of human resources to best engage the customers. Similar to the "quality czars" of the 1980s who made quality predictive and American businesses competitive again, the HuCap manager of tomorrow will make return on human capital predictive, will make investors more knowledgeable, and will make businesses more successful.

Note
1. The Conference Board, TNS survey of over 5,000 U.S. households.

TRULY PAYING FOR PERFORMANCE
Erik Berggren

Performance management is one of a manager's most perplexing tasks. The reason that managers and supervisors have a difficult time conducting performance appraisals is twofold: psychological and systemic. In the first case, many cultures, particularly for America's individual-based all-are-created-equal value system, there is an underlying belief that criticizing another person's performance is unacceptable. When organizations force this task on supervisors, those employees' anxiety levels elevate. In the second case, the system and the tools we give supervisors to do the job are problematic. In my years of running HR departments, every compensation manager I hired wanted to change the performance-appraisal forms. My response was, "Go ahead if you must, but it is not going to make any difference." The problem is not with the form; that is simply a scorecard. The problem is with how we manage performance.

—Jac Fitz-enz

Paying for Performance

The standard system of performance management is flawed. Theoretically, we pay for performance; actually, we pay for many things, and performance is one item that is often far down on that list. To begin, we all know the reasons that people receive salary increases of one level or another:

*   Fear of confronting employees whose view of their performance is much higher than that of the rater
*   Fear of losing employees who would be dissatisfied with the rating and subsequent salary increase
*   Lack of sufficient room in the salary system to truly differentiate between levels of performance

The list goes on. In contrast, the most effective systems I have seen in the past forty years—and there have been few—all have one common trait: They connect individual and group performance with the organization's key performance initiatives. There is no break in the linkage. Most organizations claim that they align the top goals with employee performance, but close scrutiny reveals gaps and misdirections as the goal imperatives cascade down from the top to the middle and bottom.

If you ask top executives if they have fully aligned organizations and if they pay for performance, they throw back their shoulders and proudly say, "Of course, that is my job." But when you empty the room and turn off the cameras, the shoulders come down and the truth comes out: "We try, but we don't always succeed." In too many cases that is a gross understatement. If workers had any other option, they would rebel. Unfortunately, the next company they go to has the same flawed system.

Why is it that intelligent, talented, experienced executives cannot build and manage aligned systems that truly reward people for their performance? Like most solutions, the answer is in the question and the key word is *alignment*. If the line from the corporate goals to the individual performance is skewed or broken, the system breaks down. And why, so often, is that line skewed or broken? It is a lack of discipline backed by naïveté.

I once had a somewhat heated argument with a CEO who believed— so he said—that all you needed were good people backed by resources and they would work it out. He could not see that everything that works well runs on a system of consistent and coherent processes. No, that attitude is an abdication of executive responsibility. I suspect he didn't want to confront something in which he was not proficient—that is, managing systems. He was a financial wheeler-dealer, not a leader and manager. Eventually, his company fell apart, and he moved on to ruin another company.

Research has consistently shown that companies that set and maintain an alignment from top to bottom, and that pay for performance based on employees' meeting objectively stated goals, outperform the market.

Performance Management: How to Really Pay for Performance

Performance reviews are a fundamental aspect of managing individual and company performance. As organizations grow larger, the link between individual performance and organizational performance becomes more obscured by size, systems, and processes. In a company of one, a person working for him- or herself, it is clear that company performance is largely determined by the performance of that person. In a company with thousands of workers, the contribution of each individual is not always so clear, yet motivating and maximizing the performance of individuals is critical to company performance.

Every Person Counts

Too often, the focus on individual performance is lost because people are aggregated into numbers. These numbers are important for perspective—in fact, people costs make up as much as 70 percent of operating costs. There is no doubt that people are supremely important to both output and cost; however, managing people in aggregate as an expense is a surefire recipe for poor company performance. Everyone in a modern organization is connected.

Companies are under increasing pressure to make big decisions regarding their people. Uncertain economic times and changes in the environment are forcing companies to adjust their staffing, reduce headcount, and realign their resources for the future. Furthermore, companies are under pressure to make these decisions quickly enough to respond effectively to the changing environment. Those companies with great human capital management will be able to make these decisions intelligently, with real data on individuals. Companies without great systems for managing people and performance-related data will default to managing people in aggregate. True workforce optimization is not possible without meaningful, accessible, and relevant data on individuals.

SuccessFactors Research and Dr. Jac Fitz-enz conducted a study called "How Smart HCM Drives Financial Performance," which clearly showed that companies that maintain a focus on the individual perform better than those that do not. This study looked at high- and low-performing companies to see how the talent-management processes of high performers differed from those of low performers. The results speak for themselves:[1]

1. 67 percent of companies with stronger financial performance cover all managers and some levels below with the performance management system. Only 28 percent of the weaker performers do.

2. 44 percent of the stronger performers have 100 percent aligned goals at the managerial level. None of the weaker performers do.

3. 63 percent of the high-growth group review employee performance more than annually. Only 22 percent of the low-growth companies do.

Companies with performance management, goal management, and succession management outperform those that do not—it is that simple. Performance management provides individual benchmarks relevant to the worker. Goal management provides a context within which to act and get everyone on the team on the same page. Succession management provides a framework for moving individuals to where they might have the greatest impact in the organization. Of course, the data are the real power behind these talent-management applications.

    *   *Performance Management Systems.* From a people perspective, isn't it fair to say that an individual should get clear expectations on what he or she should accomplish? Think about playing a sport without understanding the rules of the game. How are success and defeat to be measured? In most situations, business is a team sport. Team sports have the added dimension of different roles, with some players on offense, some on defense.

These individuals need to know how they are doing and how to improve. This is why success in different positions is measured differently. In ice hockey, a goalie is measured by different metrics than is a forward offensive player. A strong performance management system measures individuals with relevant metrics, and these metrics are transparent and effectively communicated to the individuals in order to set clear expectations.

    *   *Goal Management Systems.* Of course, team sports are won by teams (individuals acting together toward a common goal), not by individuals. Where performance management provides individual benchmarks for success, goal management links individual performance with the goals of the team or organization. Players on the field need a context for making decisions. If athletes were rewarded only on success in their roles, and not on the success of the team, then teamwork would break down. Goal management puts action into perspective for individuals, and

also ensures that everyone is contributing to the team goals, or the objectives of the organization.

✻   *Competency Management Systems.* How do you build a successful team? Sports are fairly straightforward. In American football, if you need a great receiver, you look for someone with the speed and agility required for the role; the competencies required to be a great receiver are obvious. With some thought and planning, smart companies also can identify the competencies required to succeed in various roles, and place and develop talent in those roles accordingly. Competencies are one of the few reliable leading indicators of performance. People with the right competencies for a role are more likely to succeed in that role.

A Real Performance Review

A real performance review is much more than a form, or even process. Many companies look at a performance review as an appraisal, but it is really much more than that, as shown in Figure 4.12. It is the single most powerful tool for driving the performance of an individual in an organization, and it will likely have substantial repercussions on pay, future promotion, and (therefore) the engagement of the individual.

The automation of a form is the start of a performance management process, not the end. A well-rounded and complete performance review has these three components:

1. *The Dialog.* The line of communication between a manager and his or her direct reports is the start of all performance reviews. The dialog is an ongoing conversation between manager and employees, with the purpose of establishing clear expectations and goals, and trust through transparency.

2. *The Data.* All too often a performance review is distilled down to a single appraisal that is either too generic or too narrow in scope to truly perform a meaningful assessment. The performance review is a time to pull together and rate the employee on all of the dimensions mentioned earlier. Review the progress the individual has or has not made on the goal plan, assess his or her competencies, and measure the individual contributions. Only with comprehensive data can meaningful decisions be made.

3. *The Direction.* If a performance review does not provide direction for both the manager and the employee, then the process itself has little value. The employee should be left with a clear impression of where he or she has excelled and where improvement is needed. Furthermore, the

Figure 4.12. Performance review functions.

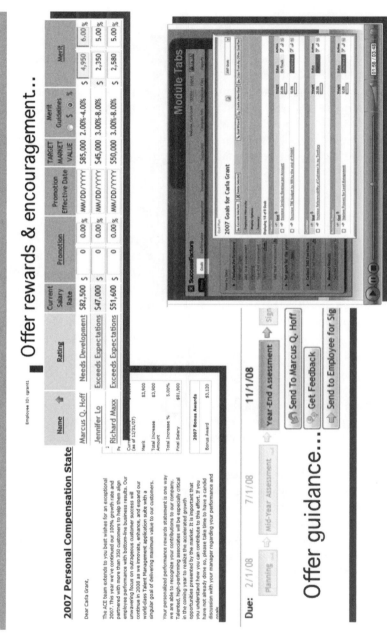

Goals & competencies drives the performance review hence a pay decision

Offer rewards & encouragement...

Offer guidance...

Source: SuccessFactors, 2008.

individual should not only have an idea of how he or she is doing in the current role but also where he or she might go elsewhere in the organization. Managers should get a clear idea of not only how their people are performing but also where each individual can make the best contribution for the company.

Why is there so much focus on transparency and direction? In addition to being smart tactically—employees will find it harder to complain if they know what is expected and where they are going—it is also smart from a performance perspective. Both clear links between individual goals and company performance and having a clear career path are strong drivers of employee engagement. Then, organizations are pushing performance directly through the review process, as well as through potential increased employee engagement.

Make It Count: Strategic Applications

The performance review, done correctly, is the foundation for making strategic people decisions. In isolation, it provides the tactical benefits of managing the performance of an individual. But what if the data could also be used to save the company millions of dollars in compensation cost by providing a global view on pay versus performance across the entire organization? This is just one potential strategic application of performance review data. Use performance management data (which, remember, should include goals, competencies, and workforce planning data) to drive real value creation in your organization.

There are several rules you can use to ensure that you get the most from your performance management data.

Never, Ever Do Compensation Planning in a Vacuum

Compensation is the clearest and most direct reward that companies control, and it is one of the most effective levers for motivating individual performance. Compensation is also supposed to represent in some way the value that an individual adds to the company—people are supposed to be paid what they are worth. Compensation largely determines the cost of people (including benefits, time off, and other perks). Few things are as critical to a company as getting its compensation right, and you must not get it wrong.

The only way to really understand if you are compensating an individual appropriately is with access to detailed performance review data on that person. Of course, the labor market will set a wide range that is appropriate for a given role, but these broad categories do not provide real insight into the contributions of individuals, regardless of their roles. If someone is contributing much more than a typical person in his or her role, that person should be rewarded, even if it pushes the individual over that role's pay ceilings. (Ceilings are ridiculous things anyway; if someone is performing and contributing extraordinarily, artificial boundaries should not dictate the compensation.)

Real performance review data allow managers to set pay accordingly, to truly pay what the employees are worth. The value of an integrated system extends even further; with analytics and comparative functions, managers can see how the pay is spread, how it compares to that of others in the organization, and what a global view of compensation in the company looks like. Having a global stack ranking of performers can help in determining appropriate compensation levels, and it has the added benefit of highlighting high performers throughout the company. The value of this data review is illustrated in Figure 4.13.

Never Do Layoffs Without Performance Data

Earlier I mentioned the folly of managing people by aggregate; there are few scenarios where this is more likely to happen than in the case of

Figure 4.13. Effects of merit increase on net income.

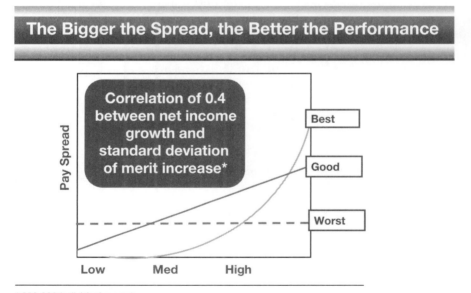

* 239.000 individual records
  41 public companies

Source: SF Research Analysis, 2008.

layoffs. Presumably, layoffs happen because the company is spending too much money or because revenues have dropped, usually owing to changes in the external environment. Financial pressure drives managers to make cost-cutting decisions quickly. Where people are managed as costs, bad decisions result. People create the value in modern organizations; they make the products and intellectual property, sell to and support customers, and ultimately build the top line.

Take, for example, a typical layoff scenario. All departments are ordered to lay off 10 percent of their staff. But what if one department was extremely high performing? Why lay off any of the high performers? Global performance review data can help companies avoid these scenarios by allowing them to do real performance-based layoffs. Don't lay off aggregate groups; lay off the low and middle performers who aren't contributing. In uncertain times you want to keep your strongest people to keep your company performing and ready to emerge in a position of strength when the economy recovers.

Fill Here, Fill Now

Use your performance review data to drive the internal fill rates in your company. Hiring from outside of the company is costly. External hires are unknown quantities, typically have longer ramp-up to productivity times, and are generally much more expensive than filling an open position with an internal promotion or lateral move. Of course, companies need and should want some external hires for fresh ideas and to expand the workforce, but finding the right balance between internal and external fills builds impressive cost savings and has the potential added benefit of increasing engagement. As I have mentioned, career pathing is an important driver of employee engagement. Furthermore, flexibility to move people around the organization allows managers to put talent where it can make the most impact.

The power of real performance review data is in the objectivity and transparency that the data bring to the process of filling positions, making promotions, and arranging lateral moves. Slackers cannot hide when performance is being accessed continually and comprehensively. Politics and favoritism can be curtailed. Objectivity and transparency are the building blocks of a high-performance organization. Progressive organizations don't "manage turnover"; they "optimize their workforce"—a much deeper and more impactful action that sets the company up for long-term success.

Quantitatively Driven Performance Management

As Dr. Jac Fitz-enz taught over twenty years ago, it's not about the form—it's about the usage of data. What is important is consistency, or having a systematic approach to managing performance and having a sound process that drives the right behavior. Quantitative, objectively driven performance management simply provides you with the most strategic data to manage the business. Those data are key to motivating your managers and employees to use the system, and to make the strategic data easy and rewarding to act upon. You cannot hand businesspeople a solution with poor processes and complicated forms and expect them to use it. Simplicity is the key to getting the most strategic benefit from the process and to beating your competition while making work a better place for individuals in the process.

Pay is an extremely sensitive issue for employees, and it serves several purposes. It is a scorecard that allegedly reflects one's contribution to the organization. It is supposedly a fair assessment of reward that matches the market. It is a measure of comparative equity across the workforce. Mostly, it is a highly personal matter. Get the pay wrong and very little else matters. The connection of pay to performance is probably the most important issue that management must master.

Note

1. Erik Berggren and Jac Fitz-enz, "How Smart Human Capital Management Drives Financial Performance," SuccessFactors, 2006.

THE SLIPPERY STAIRCASE: RECOGNIZING THE TELLTALE SIGNS OF EMPLOYEE DISENGAGEMENT AND TURNOVER

F. Leigh Branham

There are two ways to look at what is often called turnover, or attrition. One is the negative perspective of turnover whereby we track turnover rates. The other is the positive viewpoint of *retention*. If we focus on keeping people whom we need, we will have better results than if we view the problem from the turnover side. In order to be preventive and predictive, however, we have to reverse-engineer the concept of turnover. Questions such as who is leaving, when in the individual's career is he or she jumping ship, and what is the reason for quitting paint a picture of turnover. This gives clues as to what you can do to retain such people. It is almost always better to view a problem from the positive rather than the negative side.

Engagement can also be viewed from two angles—an employee's feeling engaged with the company in general and the results of engagement that lead to exceptional performance. The first view is passive, akin to job satisfaction. The second is active and drives value. For both retention and engagement, the challenge for supervisors at every level is to pay attention before the fact rather than after, when it is often too late.

Disorder and Disengagement

The phrase "attention-deficit disorder" can be used to describe a much broader range of phenomena than its usual psychological meaning. In today's business climate, it certainly applies to a reduced focus on employee retention. One CEO described how he saw the situation: "Most of my CEO friends at other companies are 'high-fiving' each other in celebration of the fact that their employees are once again 'tree-hugging their jobs.'" In other words, many leaders and managers are finding good news where they can in the down economy.

But there is a downside to the relief of not having to work so hard to retain talent: Many managers are paying ever less attention to their front-line workers. And the timing for that response couldn't be worse. Economic contraction demands that managers work harder than ever to coach, manage, and engage all who report to them. And yet, the human response, regardless of one's level, is to turn inward and worry about one's own job and survival prospects.

With employee disengagement already hovering somewhere between 40 and 75 percent in most companies (depending on which survey is used), we don't need any new reasons not to pay attention to people management. We already know that while more than 80 percent of employees leave their jobs for reasons unrelated to pay, a large majority of managers still believe that pay is the main reason employees leave.[1]

This disconnect between manager belief and employee reality strongly suggests that many managers are failing to see the daily opportunities to reengage employees through recognition, performance feedback, career discussions, increased responsiveness to work-life issues, job redesign, and the full range of "soft" solutions. The good news is that these solutions are relatively inexpensive, and are well within managers' spheres of influence and control.

The Unfolding Model of Employee Disengagement and Turnover

Most new hires are highly engaged on day one, so why do so many become less engaged during the ensuing weeks and months? And how do we get leaders and managers to pay more attention to the signs of employee disengagement before it's too late to do anything about it?

Knowing the causes of employee disengagement doesn't guarantee that managers will recognize the signs of it. Nor does recognizing the signs guarantee that managers will care enough to do anything about it. But what is helpful is to better understand the dynamics of how employees disengage and leave their jobs.

No one has done more to help us understand these dynamics than Dr. Thomas Lee, business professor at the University of Washington in Seattle, who has spent much of his academic career studying how and why employees make the decision to leave their jobs. Dr. Lee's major finding is not a surprising one, but it is sobering nevertheless: that an employee's departure, from first thought to final action, is typically not a sudden decision; it is a gradual process that may take weeks, months, or even years.[2]

The down staircase in Figure 4.14 shows the intervening steps, from initial engagement through final departure. An employee typically starts a new job with great optimism and enthusiasm. Some are able to sustain

Figure 4.14. Steps in the disengagement-to-departure process.

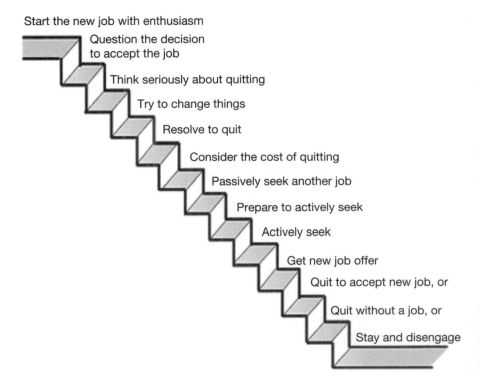

Start the new job with enthusiasm
Question the decision to accept the job
Think seriously about quitting
Try to change things
Resolve to quit
Consider the cost of quitting
Passively seek another job
Prepare to actively seek
Actively seek
Get new job offer
Quit to accept new job, or
Quit without a job, or
Stay and disengage

their enthusiasm. Others become disillusioned by the job or other workplace realities, which they may tolerate for long periods, during which time they typically withhold effort and show less enthusiasm. Eventually, the employee may, or may not, begin an active search for another job, receive an offer, and leave. And as we know, as the saying goes, some employees quit and leave while others quit and stay ("warm chair attrition").

The Two Distinct Phases of Employee Departure

Dr. Lee points out that there are two distinct phases that occur between the moment an employee starts thinking about leaving and the employee's last day. Phase 1 is the time that passes between an employee's first thoughts of quitting and the actual decision to quit ("I'm outta here!"), which Dr. Lee calls the "deliberation phase." Phase 2 is the time between the employee's decision to leave and the actual leaving—the "action phase." In this phase, the employee begins updating the resume; telling friends he or she is looking; and checking online job listings (often on company time), contacting recruiters, applying for other jobs, and interviewing.

The following brief comment from a post–exit survey respondent gives us a glimpse into how the cognitive, but emotionally charged, deliberation process begins and evolves: "After the merger I gave it a year to see what the company would be like, and I tried to keep my attitude positive, but things were no different, so I started looking." Another departed employee said that he actually first started thinking of leaving after he was promoted and no letter went out announcing the promotion, which he took as a personal slight. Things went downhill from there:

> I first started thinking seriously about leaving later, when I asked for more responsibility and was turned down. What made it even tougher to take was the fact that I had left my wife and family behind for a year to work abroad for the company. I felt they owed me a new opportunity. But, instead of getting the job I wanted, I was transferred to another department. That's when I made the decision to leave.

In reviewing the comments of exited employees, it is easy to see a "last straw" phenomenon in many cases, as they reveal what pushed them over the edge from deliberation to action:

* "I wasn't being challenged. And then I came across payroll information while doing some project costing and discovered that I

was paid less than 15 percent less than everyone else in my group. That was the turning point."

* "I was happy there two years ago, but my manager left and my new manager was not a good mentor or coach. She was just coasting to retirement, but she was moody and unprofessional. And then one day she yelled at me. I went to her manager about it, but she just excused her behavior, saying 'That's just the way she is.' That was the last straw for me."

* "My head of our department changed and I felt the new one didn't seek my input or recognize my contributions. Then, the work started becoming more administrative than technical. I felt like I was just shuffling papers and not designing anything. That's when I started looking elsewhere, and a co-worker referred me to the company I now work for."

Dr. Lee's studies have shown that 63 percent of all employee decisions to leave are precipitated by a "triggering event," or turning point of some kind, such as:

Realizing they are underpaid compared to others doing the same job
Realizing they are not in line for promotion
Being pressured to make unreasonable family or personal sacrifices
Being asked to perform a menial duty (e.g., clean bathroom, go
    shopping for the boss)
Petty and unreasonable enforcement of authority
Being denied request for family leave
A close colleague quitting or being terminated
A disagreement with the boss
A conflict with a co-worker
An unexpectedly low performance rating
A low pay increase or no pay increase
Being passed over for promotion
Realizing the job was not as promised
Learning that he or she may be transferred
Replacement of the hiring boss with new boss the individual doesn't
    like
Being asked to do something unethical
An incident of racial discrimination or sexual harassment
Learning a leader is doing something unethical

Some additional interesting findings reported by Dr. Lee are that relatively few triggering events are pay-related. About 20 percent of departing employees leave without having another job in hand. Temporary, part-time, and marginal workers are more likely to quit suddenly or impulsively after experiencing a triggering or shocking event. Lastly, many employees keep an eye out for other jobs while working, and they decide to interview for outside opportunities just for practice, to create a "plan B," or to test their marketability.[3]

In my own research into why and how people leave their jobs,[4] I have some findings of my own to report:

* The triggers that caused respondents to start thinking of leaving were mostly push factors that the organization could have taken steps to address before it was too late. About 53 percent said their decision to leave was motivated primarily by their job dissatisfaction, while only 10 percent reported that their decision was motivated mainly by an outside offer. The remaining 37 percent said their decision to leave was based on a combination of push and pull factors.

* Pay was the deciding push factor for only about 12 percent of survey respondents. While most of us believe we should be paid more, some people really are underpaid compared to similar positions in their industries or within their companies. "Pay not based on performance" and "unfair pay practices" were also frequently mentioned as push factors.

* Disappointment with senior leaders was the number-one push factor cited as the major motivation for leaving. In the post-Enron, post–Wall Street collapse era, it is not surprising that employees might be more jaundiced and inclined to lose faith in senior leadership. And as we know, senior leaders' decisions and mindsets either determine or influence most other push factors, such as insufficient pay, lack of work-life balance, unhealthy or undesirable culture, excessive workload, uncertainty about the future of the company, lack of open communication, and pay not based on performance.

* Most survey participants experienced a turning point or "last straw" in their final decision to leave. Almost 60 percent said they experienced such a triggering event.

Some of their verbatim comments include:

"Being told that my best skills were the ones I needed to work on"
"Seeing an unethical manager be promoted"
"Company owner swore at a customer in an open Internet forum"
"Promotion denied; found out that boss did not even show up to promotion meeting"

"The arbitrary termination of half of the employees within one week"

"Obvious favoritism to co-worker"

"Berated by SVP who made me feel incompetent for making a small mistake"

"Incidents in which good people were fired and destructive people were promoted"

"Was directed to break federal law and commit crimes"

Some other findings include that 65 percent who voluntarily left did so within one year of starting to seriously consider leaving. And 71 percent of employees surveyed said they were giving less effort on the job during the period they were thinking of leaving. Likewise, 77 percent reported that they were looking for another job while still employed, and 66 percent had already accepted another position when they resigned. About two-thirds felt that their employers could have taken some action to make them change their minds and stay.

To Reverse Disengagement and Turnover, Watch for the Signs

As you might expect, the chances of a manager's re-recruiting and successfully gaining renewed commitment from an employee during the action (job-seeking) phase are greatly reduced. This is why it is important for managers to be alert to the signs that an employee is just starting to disengage—when there is still time to do something about it.

So, what can managers do about it? First, and most important, they can observe the signs—some subtle and some not so subtle—that employees are in the downward spiral of disengagement and possible departure. There are three kinds of signs to watch for: behavior-based, event-based, and data-based.

Behavior-Based Signs of Departure

Employees' nonverbal behavior is the most basic and easiest of the three kinds of signs to observe. All that's required is for managers to get up, get out, and walk around, and open their eyes and pay some attention to their direct reports. Here are some common signs that an employee may have experienced a triggering event and is thinking of leaving, or at least starting to disengage:

Avoids eye contact

Stops smiling or greeting

Gives less energy and effort

Arrives later

Leaves earlier
Has bursts of anger or frustration
Participates less in meetings
Exhibits passive noncompliance
Exhibits active resistance
Is absent more often
Misses deadlines
Applies for other jobs internally
Increases community involvement and networking

Event-Based Signs of Departure

Some event-based signs may not indicate that the employee is disengaged, but they may nevertheless precipitate thoughts of leaving. The following types of triggering events are not preventable and exert more of a pull on the employee:

Marriage
Pregnancy
Inheritance
Personal or family health crisis
Spouse or partner having job opportunity in another city
Reaching eligibility for retirement benefits
Last child leaving home
Paying off the mortgage
Acquiring a company

If an employee is already somewhat disengaged or dissatisfied with some aspect of the job or environment (push factor), a pull factor such as one of those listed above may be just the nudge he or she needs to move on. Yet, when asked in exit interviews why they are leaving, these employees, not wanting to burn a bridge, are more likely to offer the pull factor as the main reason rather than divulge the contributing push factor. As a result, many root causes of turnover remain hidden and unresolved.

Other triggering events are clearly more of the push variety and are definitely preventable:

Conflict with manager
Being ignored or discounted by manager
Manager leaving, getting new manager
Valued co-worker leaving
Conflict with co-worker
Being passed over for promotion

Career advancement being stalled or blocked
Loss of confidence in senior leaders

These kinds of events may be the most difficult for managers to see or acknowledge, as the managers may, in fact, be the root of the problem.

Data-Based Signs of Departure

The third kind of sign that may help in anticipating employee disengagement and turnover is available to us by reviewing data typically kept in human resources records. Like all signs and indicators, any one or two of the following data points may be meaningless, but when combined with others from the first two categories, they may add up to a flashing red light:

Absenteeism record
Tardiness record
Vacation days not taken
High turnover in the employee's demographic group, type of position, or location
Declining performance ratings
Survey data showing low levels of engagement in employee's unit
Employee being paid less than others at same level
Employee having longer than average tenure in same position
Being at or approaching historically high-turnover tenure "window" (e.g., second or third year)
Having had short tenure at previous employers or in previous jobs
Employee having record of frequent internal job postings
Employee not having received performance review
Employee having record of filing employee relations grievances

This list is not comprehensive, but it is representative of the kinds of data that may be available from one company to the next, depending on company size, and the availability and relative sophistication of HR information systems. An important advantage of HR data is that they can also help pinpoint trends indicating that groups of employees in various job categories, geographic locations, or under the supervision of certain managers may be at risk.

Can We Really Predict Turnover?

As Yogi Berra supposedly remarked, "Predicting is hard . . . especially about the future." We need all the help we can get in predicting whom to hire, much less who will stay. But this is still not a science. Theoretically, a manager could assign points to all the warning signs for a given employee, then add them up to see which ones fall into yellow, orange, and red alert groups. The logical next step would be for the manager to sit down with employees in the red-alert category first—assuming, of course, that the manager wants to keep them and cares enough to keep them engaged. If so, Figure 4.15 may be a helpful tool for diagnosing which employees may be most at risk of leaving.

It should be noted that B performers are valued, steady, and not dispensable—and are well worth your efforts to keep and engage them. So are many C performers, who have simply been placed in the wrong jobs, mismanaged, or undercoached. To use the chart, simply list the names of your direct reports in the appropriate boxes, based on your evaluation of their performance and how at risk of disengaging or leaving they may be, based on your awareness of the signs presented here.

As an example, suppose you have noticed that Joe, one of your A performers, has stopped sending you e-mails in the last two weeks and has stopped speaking up in meetings. You began seeing these changes the day one of Joe's closest peers left the company. Joe has been working sixty to seventy hours a week to meet a critical project deadline and has not taken a vacation in two years. So, is Joe a high or a medium risk? It probably doesn't matter. What matters is that you care enough to notice and have a talk with Joe.

All managers of people need to keep their antennae up for signals

Figure 4.15. Disengagement diagnostic matrix.

	High Risk	Medium Risk	Low Risk
"A" Performers			
"B" Performers			
"C" Performers			

that a valued employee may have experienced a disappointing shock or a gradual accretion of last straws. Because it is often hard to read the feelings of employees from the looks on their faces, and managers are sometimes too busy to read every available sign, they should simply have regular check-in meetings with their direct reports.

Many employee disengagement-and-departure cycles can be reversed if managers will only care enough to sit down with the employees at some point in the hidden-from-view deliberation process and say the following: "I value you as an employee and want to keep you. How are you feeling about things in general?" That simple question may well open a discussion that can lead to a resolution of the precipitating issue.

When you consider the gradual, unfolding nature of employee disengagement, there can be but one conclusion—there is urgent need to initiate discussions and actions to engage and reengage employees, and the daily opportunity to do so is ever present. The good news is that most valued employees can be reengaged and retained with the right kind of attention, concern, and willingness to take action. But first you have to see the signs.

Notes

1. Leigh Branham, *The 7 Hidden Reasons Employees Leave: How to Recognize the Subtle Signs and Act Before It's Too Late* (New York: AMACOM, 2005).
2. Thomas W. Lee et al., "An Unfolding Model of Employee Turnover," *Academy of Management Journal* 39 (1996), 5–36.
3. Ibid.
4. Data based on my ongoing analysis of almost 300 post-exit surveys, conducted on my Web site, http://www.keepingthepeople.com/survey Start.cfm.

CHAPTER FIVE

Collapsing the Silos

"For every failure, there's an alternative course of action.
You just have to find it."

—**MARY KAY ASH**

Everything that happens in an organization, from an individual's decision to act to the outcome of a major initiative, is the result of a single or, more likely, multiple processes. All processes share a fundamental three-part model consisting of inputs, throughputs, and outputs. Human capital management, especially the HCM:21, provides a new view of these processes, and in the bargain collapses the silos that characterize yesterday's organizational structure. The result is a means for process analysis and process optimization that makes the HR function part of corporate strategy.

Any Process: Input, Output, Throughput

At the individual level, inputs are made up of a person's background, such as past experience, education, knowledge, and current behavior of his or her family, friends, and the constantly changing phenomena that make up this world. Often ignored in the layman's analysis of a person's behavior and decision making is the individual's value system, personal health, career interests, ambitions, and goals. Other inputs include what a person takes in from his or her environment, which includes both the behavior of others and any observances of the surroundings. Behavioral data include the actions of co-workers, as well as inputs from outsiders such as suppliers, vendors, consultants, competitors, or people whom the individual meets in the course of the day outside of work. Direct data include observations of internal events, the reading of reports, and information from the external world. Externally, the state of the economy, political trends, and even the win-loss record of a favorite team can influence a person's state of mind, and hence his or her reaction to incoming stimuli. For example, you know that when you are tired, sick, or depressed, you feel stress much more readily than when you are fresh, well, and happy.

Throughputs include the actions and methods in a process. This category covers variables such as policies, procedures, systems, tools, and information applied to the process deliberations, decisions, and actions. Also included is feedback from previous experience concerning related issues. For example, if you input to an ongoing process, what is the result? Usually, someone takes whatever you do and incorporates it into his process. Your output is that person's input.

This transfer of energy can make or break relationships, and on a grander scale, it can make or ruin a company. It is what makes organizations efficient, effective, and sustainable or not. Things don't just happen—people make them happen through processes, as Figure 5.1 shows. Is your contribution to the process well received and appreciated? Or is it ignored or denigrated? Your answer will influence the way you act the next time you deliver your product or service. It also influences your perception of your value, and here is the core of the antipathy toward the traditional human resources department.

The programs and services of HR are inputs to the workload of line managers and employees. Too often, however, we intrude on these managers (in their view), asking them to fill out new forms or take on new

Figure 5.1. Staffing process model.

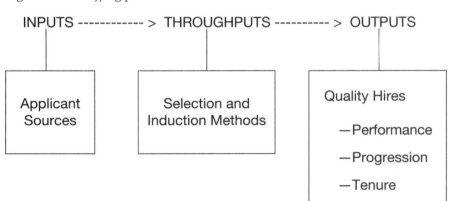

processes for which they see little or no value. Their job is to get their work done, to meet their commitments, and to be accountable for certain results. Human resources is a nuisance to them, rather than the business partner HR claims it to be.

Turn the tables and consider this instead. You are a manager in the midst of a stressful, complex situation, in which you need to produce something quickly and accurately. Along comes someone with a question, a request, or a demand that you stop doing your job to satisfy his needs instead. It doesn't matter that the individual is offering or requesting something that is important to you or to the organization. He's still a pest and doesn't show concern or respect for your needs. To make matters worse, when you have a problem sometimes they quote policy rather than help you solve it. Now, do you understand why people claim to hate HR? If this is the situation at your organization, then you need to consider process analysis.

Process Analysis for Human Resources

Periodic process analysis can greatly increase both efficiency and effectiveness. Process analysis received a great deal of attention in the 1980s, with the quality movement. Then, it was all about how to lower the cost and improve the timeliness and quality of manufacturing processes. It spawned the Six Sigma phenomenon that eventually reached staff functions such as accounting, information technology, and human resources. Shortly after that came reengineering. Again, this movement started in manufacturing and eventually moved to functions such as call centers, where high volume, high cost, and high value were obvious conditions. In the case of human resources management, reengineering could be applied to planning, hiring, paying, developing, and retaining talent.

Human resources does not have the volume of transactions that manufacturing has except perhaps the human resources function in an employee call center, yet the impact of HR processes on internal operations can be significant. Consider the effect that substandard staffing or inadequate training programs can have on an organization's operations. A more obvious example is payroll processing. Although typically housed elsewhere, this aspect of HR includes processing changes in wages or salaries and forwarding them to an outsourcer or the accounting department. Regardless of its location, payroll processing can be optimized. For example, we have had occasion to run process analytics for payroll and have found vast differences in procedures across companies, with the cost to cut a paycheck ranging from about one dollar per check to ten times that amount.

Chapter Four looked at the process of workforce planning. The inputs were data from external and internal sources; the throughputs were the identification and analysis of human, structural, and relational capital and their interactions. This analysis showed that outputs could be changed from simply filling gaps in the fabric of the workforce to building a capability system. The values added were twofold. One was the change of focus from structure-bound gap analysis to a human capital management that could generate sustainable strategic capability. The second was a change from an annual plan to an ongoing analysis of the cost and productivity of the workforce. These are no small differences. They are an order of magnitude higher and of greater value than the traditional workforce planning model. Such is the importance and value of process analysis.

A New Staffing Process

In large companies, the staffing function is often divided into sourcing and selection. Some staff members spend all their time finding and exploring sources of new applicants. Then, selection teams take those applicants through rejection or offer of employment. In smaller organizations, a staffing person is responsible for the entire process. In either case, though, process analysis is important, for one very good reason.

Over time, or under high-stress conditions, the repetition of an act can become so ingrained that a person stops using his or her best thinking and relies on past experience. The individual claims not to have the time to analyze, plan, or change; yet, he or she always seems to find time to do it over when the established process fails. In line repeatable assembly jobs, the process is fixed by engineers and the workers simply follow the procedure they are taught. In professional service functions, such as staffing, one expects the provider to use skill, experience, and imagination to carry out the process in the most effective manner. This is necessary because in the latter function, there is often significant choice and variance in methods or procedures. These variations can be internally generated by the demands of the hiring manager or externally influenced by the availability of skills in the job market and/or the uniqueness of applicants.

For the most part, career recruiters use not only past experience and developed skills but also an awareness of the demand:supply ratio to do their job well. Nevertheless, anyone who does the same task day after day is susceptible to falling into a routine that is not necessarily the most effective. Process analysis can be helpful in increasing the yield, reducing the cost, or improving the end result (the output).

Applying process analysis to staffing, HR can determine that the inputs are job applicants who come through sources such as advertising, job boards, agencies, and employee referrals. The throughputs are the selection and orientation or induction methods, and can encompass individual and group interviews, testing, assessment, and onboarding. I include onboarding in the throughput because I don't believe that the new hire is truly on board until he or she has gone through an inductive process. I have seen cases where new hires leave on the first break or at lunch during an onboarding program. So, you really don't have a new hire until that person reports to the supervisor involved.

Extending the Staffing Process from Hiring to Management

There is a small problem, analytically speaking, when you evaluate someone's work history and then report the individual as a good or bad hire. Once the new hire joins the organization, the staffing function's job is completed. Thereafter, the person's performance and tenure are influenced by his or her interactions with others in the organization. This is no longer a hiring issue; it is a management issue. Having said that, HR can still apply the HCM:21 process optimization model and obtain valuable insights, not only into the process but also into the management of the ensuing output.

There are firms that offer to run a source analysis for a client, and these have value because they show the client which sources tend to produce the better-quality applicants. They also purport to show which sources produce the better employees. However, here is where I disagree. The output of a staffing process depends on the input and the throughput methodologies, as well as on subsequent internal circumstances. It can be a rash judgment to evaluate new hires strictly on the basis of the source from which they came.

For example, one source might produce a highly qualified candidate, but the selection process may frustrate the candidate before he or she can reach the job offer so, in evaluating the hiring process, you have to add on-site enhancers or barriers. I had such an experience early in my career, when a family friend arranged an interview for me with a successful international company. I could have handled the job in question, but by the time I had met three managers, I was so put off that I passed on the opportunity.

Figure 5.2 is a list of people hypothetically hired two years ago for a given mission-critical job group. We started with mission-critical jobs because they have the greatest effect on the organization. After you study

Figure 5.2. Staffing process analysis.

JOB GROUP	SOURCES						METHODS					RESULTS			
NAME	**N**	**M**	**S**	**E**	**J**	**W**	**I**	**G**	**T**	**A**	**O**	**B**	**C**	**P**	**T**
Al		M					I		T			2	2	1	1
Bea					J		I	G	T	A	O	2	2	2	2
Cee				E			I	G		A	O	3	2	3	2
Didi	N						I	G	T	A	O	2	2	2	2
Earl					J		I			A	O	1	1	1	2
Frank					J		I		T			2	1	1	1
Gina						W	I	G		A	O	3	2	1	2
Hal		M							T	A	O	2	3	3	2
Isaac			S				I	G		A	O	3	3	2	2
Jon				E			I	G	T	A	O	2	3	2	2
Ken	N						I		T			1	2	2	1
Leo	N						I		T			1	1	1	1

N = Newspaper, M = Prof Magazine, S = Search, E = Referral, J = Job Board, W = Walk-In

I = Personal Interview, G = Group Interview, T = Test, A = Assessment, O = Onboard/Induct

B = Performance, C = Pay Increases, P = Potential Rating   Score: 1 = low, 3 = high

T = Tenure: 1 = left, 2 = stayed

the figure for a minute, can you see which source produced the best results in terms of performance, progress, potential, or tenure?

For the sake of brevity, let's confine the evaluation of this process to tenure. At first glance, you might say that newspapers are not a good source, since two (Ken and Leo) out of three (Didi) left the organization. Indeed, this is what a source analysis might conclude. However, if you look at the selection methods, you might focus on the correlations between individual and group interviewing, or on who was tested or assessed and the subsequent performance or potential. You could also look at onboarding. Here, you see that Didi went through onboarding and is still here (two versus one). Ken and Leo did not, and they have left, voluntarily or involuntarily. If you push a bit further, you see that everyone who went through onboarding is still with the organization, and everyone who did not get onboarded is gone.

This is a valuable insight, isn't it? You can continue to look at other sources and methods for additional information. If your sample has a

large number of hires, you need to conduct some type of statistical procedure, such as a regression or clustering, to draw out the critical variables.
In the end, you will discover which combination of sources and methods
were the most effective in terms of each result. Clearly, this knowledge is
invaluable when it comes to developing a strategic staffing program. Also,
it guides HR in cost management. In the end, you have both cost and
performance improvement.

A Broader Future View

To take this further yet, you can build a model that brings into play additional future variables. To do this, you look at factors outside of the past
hiring experience. For instance, by studying the environmental scan
described in Chapter Three, you can at least hypothesize about the future
effects of external market forces beyond the available labor supply. Obviously, if you have determined that the economy is trending strongly
upward, this suggests that the demand:supply ratio will change in the
near term.

Other forces, such as competitor actions, entering new markets, new
laws, or technology changes, will also affect your efforts to fill mission-
critical positions. For a long-term view, you could study trends in college
graduates and their fields of interest. Are young people majoring in disciplines you need, or not? Through experience you can put the ranges of
these effects on the external forces and construct algorithms. Now, HR
can truly become predictable.

By way of explanation, an algorithm is simply a formula or an equation that contains a set of variables. These variables are arranged in such
a way as to predict certain outcomes for a given interaction of variables.
For example, take a look at a possible equation:

$$O = S \times M -/- E \times I$$

The variables are:

O = the predictable outcome
S = source of applicants
M = selection methods
E = various external forces (economy, competition, education
trends, technology) that are given weights based on their
estimated strengths
I = various internal factors (state of finances, development
investment, turnover rate, etc.)

The multiplier and positive versus negative factors suggest the judgment of the person conducting the analysis. In time these will prove accurate or they can be modified until a valid, reliable algorithm is obtained.

When faced with the task of process analysis, some people invariably say they don't have time to do this. It is clear that they will lag behind those who take the time to learn how to do the job, and this gives the latter a competitive advantage. Remember that America experienced massive losses in market share during the 1960s and 1970s, which spawned the need for quality improvement. It seems that we have to hit bottom sometimes before we can recognize that analysis is essential for continued growth.

Within the human resources function, this decline is already under way. In 2000, the first major HR outsourcing contract was signed. Today, many companies have pushed record keeping and payroll processing outside their buildings. Other HR functions, such as staffing and training, are also being restructured and in some cases outsourced. Remember, there is a truism in economics: The work will always go to the source with the lowest cost and best quality. If HR does not adopt process analysis, it will continue to learn the hard way as its role diminishes.

Other HR Applications for Process Analysis

Process analysis and optimization can be applied to HR functions that go beyond staffing. Training and development and retention programs are also being analyzed by various organizations.

Trainers have maintained for decades that the value of their programs cannot be measured. This idea, however, has been refuted many times in the work of people like Jack Phillips at ROI Institute, as well as in my publications going back as far as 1994.[1] In the latter case, I collaborated with a group of trainers from a dozen companies to develop an evaluation model for training. This model was tested in a wide variety of training programs, and in every case the model was able to determine the dollar value of the training event.

In another application of process analysis, Figure 5.3 displays a brief example comparing the impact of training events from different sources on different job skills, looked at before and after performance. It also shows tenure as a possible variable for correlation.

In this example, you can see that all the persons using self-directed materials have stayed with the organization. A secondary analysis of those persons might reveal something unique about them that could be applied to other issues. For example, they may be highly motivated and ambitious. You'd want to look at their backgrounds for tips on possibly

Figure 5.3. Learning process analysis

	LEARNING SOURCES		RESULTS
	Internal	External	Impact
Key Skill 1: Database Admin	I F M X C	O E S T U	B A T
C. Able	I X	E T	1 2 1
G. Baker	I X	E T	2 2 1
H. Fox	I M	E S T	1 2 2
J. India	I M X	E U	2 3 2
Key Skill 2: Operations Controller	Internal	External	Impact
M. November	I M X	E	2 3 2
O. Sierra	I M	E	1 2 2
P. Tango	I X	T	1 2 1
R. Lina	I M X C	U	1 2 2
Key Skill 3: Process Supervisor	Internal	External	Impact
M. Belta	I C	S	2 1 2
W. East	I F M C	T	2 3 2
Z. Braver	I F M C	E	1 2 2
Y. Dong	X	T	2 2 1

Internal Sources: I = Informal OJT, F = Formal OJT, M = Self-directed materials,
                    X = Computer based, C = Corporate college
External Sources: O = On-site, E = Off-site, S = Seminars/conferences,
                    T = Trade school, U = University classes
Results: Performance (B: below, A: after: 1 = Low, 3 = High
                    T = Tenure: 1 = Left, 2 = Stayed

fast-tracking them. Those persons using other sources have a mixed record of performance and tenure. Do you see any other tendencies?

After thirty years of doing this type of analysis, I still don't understand how HR managers can claim to manage a function when they have no data on process or results. Exactly what is it they think they are managing? If the sales manager couldn't tell us how much his people sold and at what margins, would we believe he or she is managing sales? The same goes for production data and results. Yet, HR people shrug their shoulders and still expect to be invited into the conversation.

Turnover Analysis

In 1981, Motorola bought the computer company where I headed the HR function. Bob Galvin, the CEO of Motorola, told me that he considered preventing the loss of a valued employee as a management defect. Twenty years later, Mr. Galvin had retired and Motorola went through the hiring and layoff cycle that cost the company over $1 billion. This event was a symptom of a larger management issue that seemingly has never been resolved. The company has gone through a series of short-tenured CEOs and has continually lost market share. To me, it is a dramatic case of what happens when there is no clear HCM strategy backed by effective execution of the process; the company heads down a slippery slope at ever-increasing speed.

The loss of highly trained and skilled people is truly a management error. Unwanted turnover spawns a loss of the time and money that had been invested in training and mentoring. No matter the state of the organization, turnover should be limited to the uncontrollable and involuntary. I am assuming that you have some type of engagement and retention program under way. The question is: How effective are these initiatives? You can start your analysis by segregating the turnover into controllable and uncontrollable. Sample categorization of each is shown as follows:

Controllable	Uncontrollable
J = better job offer	F = family status change
S = better salary offer	R = relocation
C = change of career direction	S = return to school
T = lack of training opportunities	L = leave of absence
D = dissatisfied with supervisor	IP = involuntary: performance
W = dissatisfied with co-workers	IB = involuntary: behavior

There can be many other reasons for turnover, but these are the most common. You can also trace related issues such as tenure, or years of service at time of departure. The state of readiness should be noted, however. In which cases was there a person prepared to step into the vacated spot? Remember, gaps in performance cause customer losses. In the case of each departure, you could follow up with the relevant department in sixty days or so to determine what the immediate impact was of that loss of personnel.

With the data, you can go back to your engagement and retention processes and reassess their effectiveness. For instance, what are the data telling you about your hiring and induction methods, development opportunities, compensation, interpersonal relations, or supervisory leadership? Outcomes can often be the result of interactions between these and other variables. How do you stop the bleeding? What are or were the inputs and throughputs for those activities? If the sample size is large enough, you might be able to run some statistical analysis to show how you can optimize those processes.

The Integration of HR Services

The greatest leverage opportunity for HR managers can be found in how their services are delivered. Almost all HR departments—read over 95 percent—deliver in a fragmented manner. That is, each function, from planning and staffing through compensation and benefits to development and relations, operates in its own silo. Although there is a general HR plan, each function develops and delivers on its own time schedule, with little or no regard for what its sibling functions are doing. If you doubt my claim, ask yourself how often staffing, compensation, and development synchronize their offerings. Development usually knows little of the quality of new hires or the introduction of new pay plans. Likewise, compensation looks only at pay and benefits, neglecting to include development and employee relations investments in a total-rewards system.

Service integration is absolutely essential to high performance. It improves efficiency through synchronized activity of various groups within a functional unit. Proof of the value of an integrated approach comes from Dick Kovacevich, retired CEO of Wells Fargo Bank. In a March 2007 interview by *USA Today*, Kovacevich was asked how it was that Wells Fargo sold more products and services per customer than any other major bank. His answer was succinct and to the point: "The first thing we've got to do is not to have silos. We had to design our culture and systems to focus on the customer, not on the product line. We reward the behavior we want, which is getting all of our customers' business."[2]

Rather than have the bank's various departments—that is, commercial loans, branch offices, credit cards, treasury, mortgages, etc.—attacking the customer one after another, Wells Fargo set up a system wherein all departments work together for each customer. The same idea would be much easier for an HR department, where all functions are closely related to each other. Figure 5.4 is an example of an integrated, synchronized delivery system.

Underlying an integrated system is the operating dictum of synchronization. Not only do the various HR units recognize their interdependency, they also realize that their delivery should be timed with each other. This builds a natural harmony that is often missing. The classic example is the orchestra, wherein each section knows when it is to enter and leave the musical line. If the timing is off, so is the rhythm and phrasing. Of course, the conductor is there to cue the entrances and exits so that this doesn't happen.

Figure 5.4. Integrated delivery system for HR function.

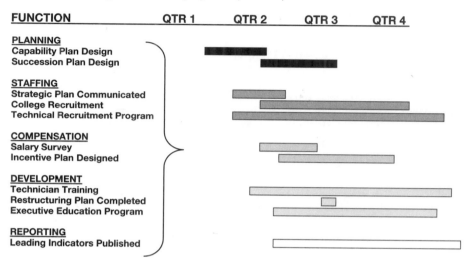

In Figure 5.4, you see that different activities are timed to start at different times. This synchronization of delivery requires an integrated HCM strategy. It ensures that employees are signaled by a service at the right time. Clearly, planning precedes staffing and staffing leads to training and development. What the figure can't show are the many specifics that need to be synchronized. For example, when the staffing function is taking on a major hiring project, it should talk with whoever handles onboarding, as well as alert L&D to the impending arrival of new people who will need various developmental experiences. Likewise, compensation needs to review its structure, processes, and pay systems to support the mass hiring effort. By integrating around a common goal and synchronizing service delivery, the organization presents a united front that produces the optimum result.

The secret to integrated, synchronized delivery is leadership on the part of the CHRO. Functional heads are not asked to give up their autonomy. There should be no loss of discretion or power with little personal value in return. The CHRO, with CEO support, must lead by showing how integrated and synchronized delivery is best for the managers, employees, and customers. As Peter Drucker has said, the purpose of a company is to create a customer. And by doing what is best for customers, employees at all levels ensure that they are most likely to keep their jobs.

Notes

1. Jac Fitz-enz, "Yes You Can Weigh Training's Value," *Training*, July 1994.
2. Greg Farrell, "CEO Profile: Richard Kovacevich," *USA Today*, March 28, 2007.

HOW THEY ARE APPLYING IT

The essays in this chapter are case studies of the application of human capital research to manufacturing, supply-chain management, and time and labor data analysis. These stories show how process analysis can be applied, using the principles of human capital management.

ROBERTA VERSUS THE INVENTORY CONTROL SYSTEM: A CASE STUDY IN HUMAN CAPITAL RETURN ON INVESTMENT

Kirk Hallowell

Although many human resources professionals continually call for a standard set of metrics to track HR services and demonstrate return on investment, no one has stepped up to the challenge. During the 1980s, at Saratoga Institute, we introduced a set of metrics that we continued to publish for nearly twenty years. Still, the Society for Human Resource Management (SHRM), the national professional society, chose not to endorse those or any other system, leaving the profession without a standard method. That is the equivalent of there being no Generally Accepted Accounting Principles (GAAP) for accounting. This essay, therefore, offers some alternative ways of conceptualizing and measuring the return on human capital from a perspective parallel to tangible capital investments.

By way of making the point here, I use as an example the experience of the Sundance Distribution Center, which decided to build a new facility in central Michigan. If investments in human capital cannot be linked to financial returns with valid and reliable methods, the current accounting methods for depreciating or appreciating tangible assets cannot be applied. The metrics and/or the rules of accounting must be modified if a new way of thinking about investing in people is to be applied and sustained.

Different Expenditures, Different Measurements of ROI

Human capital expenses, including payroll, benefits, and training, constitute as much as 70 percent of corporate budgets. The absence of consistent metrics and the fact that spending in human capital is expensed rather than depreciated create a mindset that impedes corporate leadership from managing, measuring, and maximizing the return on investment in human capital as they would any other investment in tangible assets. Four human capital performance metrics are suggested here as superior alternatives in measuring and managing return on investment in human capital, with direct relationship to standard ROI analysis.

Sundance Distribution Center is a $2 billion consumer products company with distribution centers in four states. Based on a five-year strategic business plan, Sundance decided to build a distribution center in central Michigan. The business case for the distribution center was clear: A center in this geographic area would decrease transportation cost and time to delivery while increasing product throughput to an emerging market base. The initial proposal to build the center included detailed business plans with a strong business case, detailed market and competitive analyses, and financials including capital investments, risk analysis, and projected return on investment.

The business plan for the distribution center included $20 million to acquire the land, build the facility, and equip the physical plant. The business plan also addressed staffing the center for the first year. In this case, the plan anticipated a staff of 125 employees. With an average cost to hire or transfer at $1,500, initial training at $1,500, and an average salary and benefits package of $38,000 per employee, the initial human capital investment for the first year of the plant was $5,125,000.

While investments in tangible and people assets were directed at the same business outcome, the accounting process for each investment was remarkably different. The costs of hiring, compensation, and training people were expensed and they impacted Sundance's balance sheet immediately. The investment in the physical plant of the distribution center was listed as an asset, and was to be depreciated over thirty years. Various categories of equipment will be depreciated over respective depreciation schedules. As a result of these accounting procedures, the expense of the physical plant captured on the balance sheet would be significantly less than the initial investment in human capital, even though the total investment was far greater. This fact, however, would pass relatively unnoticed in Sundance's report to stockholders.

The Perennial Accounting Problem

Investments in buildings and equipment are assets, while investments in people are expenses. This is consistent with over a century and a half's worth of accounting principles. But what happens to the financial value of these two investments over time?

From the moment construction is completed, the physical asset of the distribution center will incur maintenance and utility costs to minimize deterioration. As the building, equipment, computers, office furniture, and other tangible assets age, they decrease in value. Within a period of time, most of these physical assets will completely lose value and eventually will need to be replaced. In the case of our $20 million distribution center (excluding the value of the land on which it is located), its value is likely to drop by 30 percent in the next ten years and may incur $20 million in maintenance and utility expenses during that same period of time.

The strategic value of the distribution center is to increase distribution efficiency, speed, or throughput that will result in an ROI in capital investments. Without a commensurate investment in human capital, however, the distribution center offers nothing more than enclosed space, motionless equipment, and inventory. The people operating the center will also incur expenses as time passes. Each employee requires pay, benefits, training, and human resources administration to keep the center operational. Unlike physical assets, however, the value of human capital will increase over time. As each employee gains experience in managing and operating the center, his or her talent and expertise grow. If training and management efforts are successful, people-driven processes will become more efficient and quality will improve. In the end, individuals will increase their ability to add value to the organization while the predetermined investment in salary, benefits, administration, and training will remain relatively constant. If the return on investment in the distribution center is driven by people, why is this investment listed as a nondepreciated expense in the quarterly report?

The solution to this problem is clear: Modify the metrics and/or rules of accounting to reflect a new way of thinking about investing in people. In this case study, we compare the return on investment in two entities within the Sundance Distribution Center: a new inventory control system and Roberta, a new freight team associate. Four human capital metrics are suggested as viable analytic devices to track return on investment in both of these entities over time.

The Inventory Control System

As an integral part of the plan to increase efficiency and throughput in the distribution center, the site plan includes a state-of-the-art inventory control system. It features handheld scanners and a central software package that ties directly into Sundance's enterprise resource planning system. Based on anticipated needs, the system design specifications and performance standards are set. Requests for proposals go out to a variety of vendors and a competitive bidding process ensues. Eventually, a vendor and system are selected, and the final bid amount is included in the budget.

In planning the anticipated return on investment in the scanning system, the financial analysts considered the cost of purchase, the cost of physical implementation, and the cost of training associated with getting the system up and running. As the system is implemented, it will take time before the return on investment is realized. It is not until the system is fully functional and accurately tracking inventory and orders that the full financial return on the system will be realized.

The *relative* return on investment in the scanning system can be tracked as illustrated in Figure 5.5. In the initial installation of the system, there is a net financial deficit created based on the investment to procure the system shown at Point A. As the distribution center begins operations, time and resources are invested in implementing the system,

Figure 5.5. ROI in the inventory control system.

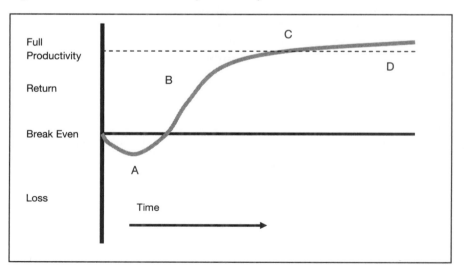

articulating outputs with order entry and inventory control processes. As the various bugs are worked out of the system, and the system begins functioning as it was intended, the efficiencies are realized and the target level of production is gradually achieved (Point B). Eventually the system is operating at design parameters defined in the operations plan; we may refer to this as "full productivity" (Point C). Additional steps to optimize the system may gradually increase the return on investment over time.

Roberta

Parallel to the investment in the inventory control system, an employee named Roberta enters the workforce at the distribution center as a freight team associate. Roberta begins her work by moving through a period of onboarding, which includes job orientation and initial training. This process is captured from a return on investment perspective in Figure 5.6 as "Roberta's Learning-Value Curve." Moving through orientation and initial training classes, Roberta incurs a cost in payroll and benefits rather than generates revenue (Point A in Figure 5.6). As Roberta gains her bearings and begins to understand her job requirements, she is able to fill orders and track inventory by understanding the order fulfillment and shipping process while mastering the inventory control technology used in the center. Again, parallel to the implementation of the inventory control system, Roberta's economic contribution to Sundance

Figure 5.6. Roberta's learning-value curve.

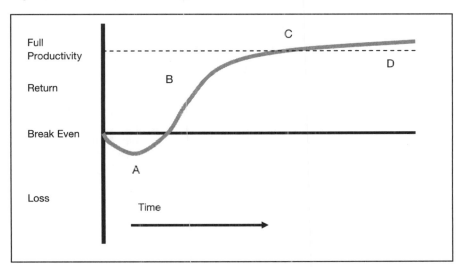

is realized only as her actions conform to the expectations of her job description, and this will take time to accomplish.

As Roberta gains competence in her position, she adds value to the organization at a rate higher than her salary and benefits, and she creates positive economic return (Point B). At this point in Roberta's tenure, training adds substantially to her capacity to return value to the company. While formal training is critical, the main source of her ability to create value is on-the-job learning. She will increase her skills and proficiency as she encounters errors and learns how to prioritize her tasks. She will master complex social networks of peers and supervisors to get problems resolved and tasks accomplished more efficiently. Other than training costs, Roberta's increasing value to the organization does not require an immediate increase in rate of investment.

From an investment perspective, the period of time that it takes Roberta to reach a break-even point and then move to a point of meeting or exceeding productivity expectations is critical. This part of the appreciation process reflects Roberta's learning-value curve. The curve will likely be steep at first and level out over time (Point C). Once Roberta meets a criterion-based level of performance defined as "full productivity," her learning curve will directly reflect the value she creates for the company.

Four Human Capital Performance Metrics

The learning-value curve provides a way of thinking about how human capital appreciates over time. Representing the curve graphically allows us to visualize the effect of various conditions that could impact return on investment. The learning-value curve also introduces the possibility of measuring ROI in human capital with a new set of performance-based metrics. Each of these metrics considers individual and environmental factors that impact the creation of value in human capital over time. Each metric is designed with these three principles in mind:

1. Each of these metrics is *event driven*. Effective assessment of ROI is determined by *how* and *when* measurement takes place. In the case of other capital investments, it is not useful to wait until a quarterly profit-and-loss statement is issued to respond to a serious financial issue. Human capital metrics must also provide timely, goal-directed information that is not constrained by the schedule of an annual or semiannual performance review process.

2. These measures are constructed to be *clear and practical*. Any measurement system that cannot be quickly understood by every individual in the organization from C-suite to associate is not likely to have impact.

Measurement systems that require excessive data collection and report routines that are not seen as relevant to work will quickly collapse under their own weight.

3. These metrics focus on *points of highest leverage* for gain or loss of ROI in a human capital system. A successful measurement system will include fewer strategic measures.

These three principles also lend significant support to the idea of linking development of human capital directly to dollar figures. Because the measures outlined are event driven, measures and financial transitions can be more carefully defined. By integrating competencies with performance, assessment of productivity can be both forecasted and validated. Because measures are clear and practical, the measurement and reporting process should be accessible to all levels of the organization. Finally, given the fact that over 500 human capital and HR metrics have been identified, the four metrics listed here represent a "short list" based on leverage to support evaluation and continuous improvement of human capital systems.

Performance Metric 1: Time to Full Productivity

Roberta's learning-value curve will continue to increase over time and reach some level of sustained value. A particular point in this value-appreciation path will be objectively defined in terms of productivity, skills, and knowledge achieved. This point is labeled "time to full productivity" (TFP; Point C in Figure 5.6). TFP is a critical metric of human capital appreciation, as it has the potential to focus and direct investment strategies.

Roberta's assent to full productivity parallels the implementation of the inventory control system. As the system is implemented, a series of prescribed steps, parameters, and procedures are determined to ensure that the system is operating effectively. Integration with existing software and overcoming user errors take time and intention. In the same way, Roberta's orientation to her position will depend on the training, support, and her own motivation to reach her goals.

A challenge is to define TFP in a clear and objectively measurable way. Quality and productivity measures are lagging indicators of ROI. Technical and leadership competencies, as well as quality of relationships with her boss and peers, predict Roberta's future performance and her contribution to the overall performance of the center. Established research has indicated that the *potential* to reach superior performance may be determined by reliable assessment of validated competencies for a particular job or job class.

Of course, no set of competencies, however rigorously assessed they might be, ensures performance. Performance is a transactional concept. Roberta may come to her position with well-established competencies and experience that support performance-differentiating behaviors on the job. If she is undermined by a political agenda, demotivated by a dysfunctional manager, thwarted by lack of training and support, or does not fit with the values and culture of the organization, Roberta may fail in her position regardless of her competency.

Roberta's ability to reach full performance is determined largely by her own motivation and her ability to find the resources she needs to be successful. The end goal of full productivity needs to be carefully defined and quantified by line management and human capital professionals. The path to that destination should be determined by Roberta in collaboration with her supervisor. A clear process and shared expectations enable the supervisor to move from a directive to a facilitative role.

If we apply the impact of Roberta's example to many hires, we can quickly see the potential value of any human capital investment that will shorten employees' TFP. Strategies for decreasing TFP include:

* Integrated talent development systems

* Selection for competencies and adaptive learning skills

* Competency-based training

* An aggressive onboarding process

* Early identification of development needs

* Candid and frequent performance feedback

* Incentive-based pay

Also, looking at environmental issues such as work process flow, equipment, and resources necessary to support work performance will contribute to productivity.

If effectively implemented, the value of TFP as a measure is that it drives ownership of the measurement process down into the organization. Many performance management systems do this by asking employees to create personal SMART (S = specific, M = measurable, A = attainable, R = realistic, T = timely) goals aligned with company strategy. In some cases this can be an overly ambiguous task. A competency-based definition of "full performance" defined for specific jobs would provide greater clarity and consistency of these goals. A SMART plan aligned and integrated into an onboarding process with specific performance goals linked directly to competency development would create an objectively assessable target for TFP.

Performance Metric 2: Quality of Hire

Just as a variety of inventory control systems would take various amounts of time to implement based on their complexity, level of customization, and eventual depth of implementation performance, individual employees will reach full productivity at different rates. Each individual hire will have a different starting point, shape, and trajectory of the value-learning curve in TFP. While there are many different factors that determine the starting point and shape of the learning-value curve, quality of hire is the strongest. Quality of hire includes the degree of employee *fit* with the organizational culture and the *readiness* to assume job accountabilities. Quality of hire is typically determined by several variables:

1. Key experiences related to the job responsibilities
2. Evidence of past performance
3. Competency assessment of both baseline and differentiating competencies
4. Adaptive learning skills
5. Personality variables measured by validated assessments

Quality of hire may vary greatly based on the sourcing of candidates. If successful, measures of quality of hire will help predict both the starting point and shape of the learning-value curve. Employees with key differentiating competencies as assessed in solid recruiting and selection methods will reach TFP more quickly and efficiently.

Consider the learning-value curves of Roberta and two other employees, shown in Figure 5.7. Maria enters the freight team associate position with three years of experience in distribution, strong interpersonal skills, and technical competencies related to inventory control and related software applications. Clearly, her learning-value curve starts higher and she reaches full performance sooner. In contrast, Zack is a recent technical college graduate with little work experience and competency deficits in planning and organization. Zack will require more training and closer supervision, thereby extending TFP. A proactive assessment of quality of hire will yield information to guide development strategies aimed at increasing value of human capital.

Quality of hire also creates a compelling financial case for differentiation of compensation based on capability relative to TFP. If a new hire's

Figure 5.7. Comparative learning-value curves.

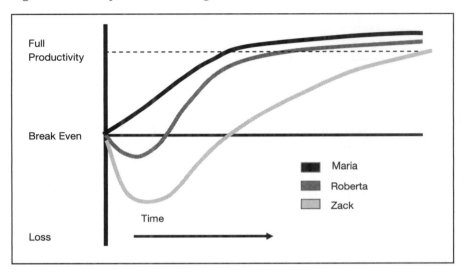

TFP is three months faster than a colleague's, then significant differences in pay at job entry may be justified. Reaching full performance criteria indicates that the initial investment in compensation has paid off and a raise is justified.

Performance Metric 3: Quality of Promotion

As the throughput in the distribution center increases, the demands on the original inventory control systems increase substantially. The number of hand scanners needs to be augmented, updates on pricing structures need to be more streamlined, and articulation with existing ERP infrastructure needs to be updated. It is decided, based on financial analysis, that an investment in a system upgrade is warranted. New system parameters are created and upgrades are installed. The result is increased capacity, accuracy, and efficiency of the inventory control process.

When we think of Roberta's return on investment for Sundance, a system upgrade is analogous to a promotion for Roberta. As a human system, Roberta increases her capacity to produce value to a point where it makes financial sense for her to manage the action and priorities of others. A promotion is a sort of system upgrade that enables Roberta to influence and direct a broader bandwidth of actions within the distribution center. By providing feedback and support, delegating tasks, and improving processes in ways that impact many others, Roberta has the opportunity to have an exponentially greater impact on ROI.

It is well established that one of the most challenging events in career progression is to move from an individual-contributor role to a supervisor role. In addition to increased accountability, an employee moving into a role as supervisor must shift from a reliance on technical, administrative, and functional competencies to command and managerial competencies. In many cases, new managers may be supervising employees who were formerly peers, significantly challenging their motivation and courage. It is not surprising that many employees struggle or fail in this transition. The process of developing management competencies can be enhanced by training, coaching, and consistent feedback.

Quality of promotion depends on new investments in human capital. Before exponential ROI can be realized, a promotion typically results in a dip in the learning-value curve. Cost of salary and benefits also increases with promotion. This new level of investment will create a dip in Roberta's learning-value curve, as shown in Figure 5.8.

At the beginning of her promotion process, Roberta's immediate performance may be impacted by transition issues, need for new supervisor training, or a need for advanced technical training. It will be a matter of learning and integration with time before Roberta's new potential as a supervisor provides a return on investment. If the promotion is success-

Figure 5.8. Roberta's learning-value curve through promotion.

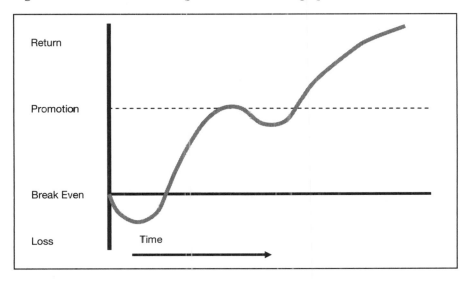

ful, not only will Roberta's learning-value curve increase but also her newly developed competencies will impact the productivity of her direct reports, as well as the other systems and processes she influences in the distribution center.

With increased potential for ROI of a promotion, there is also increased risk for loss. All of the characteristics of increased influence on people and processes also increase the opportunity for compounded losses. Poor decision quality, inability to manage conflict, lack of organizational savvy, or ineffective communication skills can have a devastating effect on performance, leading to loss of human capital ROI. Any behavior that leads to employees' being less engaged and committed to their work can have a far-reaching impact on productivity. Any leadership behavior related to a productive employee's leaving the company results in a substantial loss of human capital investment. These possibilities suggest that leadership potential might be evaluated through assessment tools prior to the promotion. A manager's estimate is not always the most valid or reliable assessment tool.

Performance Metric 4: Quality of Separation

If Sundance's inventory control system was to fail for any reason, the economic impact would be sudden and potentially catastrophic. Orders would not be filled quickly and accurately, customers would not receive shipments on time, and the credibility of Sundance in the competitive market would be shaken. If a failure or a disruption in the inventory control process was to take place, there would be a careful analysis of the failure and immediate action would be taken to restore the system to full operating capacity.

If Roberta was to leave her job for any reason, there would also be an immediate economic impact for Sundance. Key information about customer accounts and projects would not be available and immediate activity on her day-to-day accountabilities would cease. Eventually other members of the freight team would compensate for her absence. There would be workarounds, and redundancies in training and experience in the freight team would pay off. Because the economic impact of Roberta's departure would be less immediate and systemic than the loss of the inventory control system, Sundance's response to the loss of this asset may be less focused and intentional.

This is a profound oversight, in that loss of human capital can have an immense impact on economic return. Because this return is not managed and measured actively, the extent of the economic impact is not known. Therefore, the fourth key metric of ROI in human capital is quality of separation. When an employee like Roberta leaves an organization, ROI in human capital is potentially decreased in at least five ways:

1. All potential for that employee to add economic value from his or her direct action ceases immediately.

2. All investment in training, on-the-job experience, and internal network creation is lost.

3. A new investment will be made in replacing the employee if the organization is to sustain productivity or grow.

4. There is risk to profitability through breaks in customer relations and loss of potential revenue streams.

5. The employee may go to a competitor, taking valuable intellectual capital and client relations with him or her.

Intangible costs of separation include the impact on other employees' morale and productivity.

All organizations have some degree of turnover. Excessively low turnover is not necessarily good from a performance standpoint. Not all separations result in net loss of human capital. The quality and reason for separation are critically important. If a person is fired from his position owing to poor performance or unacceptable behavior, this may be a short-term loss in the cost of replacement. In the longer run, it is a benefit. Poor-performing employees fail to return value and they absorb capital that could have been invested in employees with stronger potential.

If Roberta leaves for issues beyond the company's control, such as needing to relocate, family issues, or retirement, there is little the organization can do. For example, Roberta might need to leave her position in the distribution center because she has to take care of an ailing parent in another state or she wants to return to school. An involuntary separation of this type is a loss of human capital, but it is the natural cost of doing business.

Analysis of separation from a quality perspective is critically important. Voluntary separation is the highest leverage point for loss of ROI on human capital. Individual separation cases may have a large impact even when overall retention rates are high. Failure to systematically track the frequency, quality, and drivers for separation can lead to significant mismanagement of human capital.

Of course, to this point, our metrics have looked at productivity from the perspective of the organization. We have not carefully considered Roberta's motivation and drive to reach full productivity. We will consider this in detail next.

The Role of Line Leadership in Human Capital ROI

One of the limitations of a human capital investment strategy is that it is often determined by the HR function. While a focus of expertise and experience is necessary to create sound development practices, the accountability for human capital ROI has been shifted away from the people who can have the biggest day-to-day impact on performance—line managers. If people development is seen as someone else's task, it is unlikely that managers are going to prioritize people-development processes. Moving human capital performance metrics into the realm and accountability of line managers will result in a realignment of this priority.

For instance, if Maria's manager is held accountable only for production and quality of output, contributions to human capital in the form of training, feedback, and development will not receive the same priority as immediate productivity. In contrast, if Maria and her supervisor are challenged to create a development plan for her to get to full performance quickly and effectively, investment in human capital makes sense from both of their perspectives.

Implementing human capital performance metrics also reinforces a systemic view of human capital strategy. The data used to measure time to full productivity, value of full productivity, quality of hire, quality of promotion, and quality of separation require information from across the organization. Each of these measures reflects the collective work of recruiters, hiring managers, learning and development, and organizational development professionals, as well as line managers. Data resulting from these measures have the potential to drive the kind of deep, cross-functional conversations about talent development that can result in effective and sustained process improvement.

Linking ROI in Human Capital to Dollar Amounts

It is a natural tendency in measuring return on investment in human capital to derive a specific percentage of return based on dollar amounts. For example, the training evaluation approach developed by Phillips[1] is focused on isolating the impact of learning on financial performance and reporting ROI figures in dollar amounts. The four performance metrics defined in this essay have the same potential with specific limitations.

Isolating the impact of any particular variable on financial performance in a highly complex business environment is difficult. For example, TFP, or the attainment of a specific competency profile by freight team associates, could be correlated to quality and productivity measures for the entire distribution center. If a supply line shuts down for some unrelated reason and halts distribution of a large volume of product, human capital variables could be largely irrelevant to the center's overall drop in performance.

Time to full productivity, value of full productivity, quality of hire, quality of promotion, and quality of separation offer some opportunities to place dollar amounts on the cost of or return on events within human capital investment. For example, the replacement cost of a high-quality employee can be figured in approximate dollar amounts by adding the direct and indirect costs associated with hiring, training, and onboarding a new employee. Estimates of 75 to 125 percent of annual salary may be conservative if costs to rehire and lost opportunity costs are included.

A Call to Action

Facing a downturn in the current economy, Sundance's leadership has been forced to make challenging decisions about managing costs. Share price is tanking, and there are immediate pressures from Sundance's board of directors to cut operating budget. Knowing that the capital investment in the inventory control system is a sunk cost, and that cost is being depreciated, it makes little or no sense to eliminate any investment in the inventory control system. Because the salary, benefit, and training costs associated with Maria are expensed and Sundance's total spend for human capital is approximately 60 percent of operating budget, it is far easier to justify terminating Roberta as an opportunity to reduce expenses. This decision-making process is currently being repeated across the globe.

There is little doubt that downsizing is an inevitable part of an economic downturn. It may be impossible for a business to stay intact if it cannot meet cash demands for payroll. At the same time, executive leaders who make decisions about headcount reduction based on an expense perspective of human capital rather than an asset perspective are perilously endangering the future growth potential of their organization. Recognizing that human capital as an asset requires time to build capacity and value, making decisions to reduce headcount without accounting for the commensurate investment in restoring human capital when economic conditions change indicates a lack of financial rigor that would not be accepted with investments in tangible assets.

In response to this challenge, three specific opportunities emerge:

Opportunity 1: *Define consistent human capital metrics.* Develop specific processes and procedures for defining full performance for jobs or job classes, and determine net contribution for an employee who is operating at full potential.

Opportunity 2: *Define human capital management strategies.* Define human capital management strategies that yield the greatest impact on reducing time to full productivity as key leverage points for increasing ROI on human capital.

Opportunity 3: *Analyze separation data as an asset loss.* Separation of productive employees represents a profound loss of human capital and severely impacts the potential of future returns. Risk analysis on head-count reduction should be conducted, with the same finical rigor as decisions on any other capital investment.

I am currently working on each of these opportunities. If you have interest in collaborative efforts to develop these, additional information is available at matchpointcoaching.com under the Human Capital Analytics tab.

Note

1. J. J. Phillips, *Return on Investment in Training and Performance Improvement Programs* (Houston, Tex.: Gulf Publishing, 1997).

THE TREASURE TROVE YOU ALREADY OWN

Robert Coon

Capital-intensive industries make extensive use of statistical analysis regarding structural issues. They recognize that their cost structure can be effectively managed through the utilization of predictive analytics. However, on the human side—which makes up 15 to 30 percent of their operating expense—analysis is virtually unknown. Here, I apply the value of predictive analytics to the transportation and logistics industry. In two examples, I point out how, just as the company analyzes its structural costs in an effort to be competitive, there are human capital variables that also affect competitiveness and profitability.

Predictive Analytics from Existing Data

Predictive measurements are mandatory in any resources-dependent industry today. Extensive "use statistics" are commonly collected in the transportation industry to determine future consumption needs. Operating resources must be anticipated and ordered far in advance: Fuel futures are purchased six months in advance; replacement tires are stockpiled per usage projections; lubricants and spare parts are preordered to anticipate maintenance schedules.

How, then, is it that the transportation industry, by and large, is not using similar processes to analyze and predict the acquisition, utilization, and replacement of its most important resource—its employees? Why hasn't this industry adopted similar predictive metric processes for human capital?

The first user resistance to metrics always begins with, "But our company hasn't collected any human capital data, so how can we even begin?" The more positive approach is to realize that the company is sitting on top of many more data than it will ever need to start the metrics process.

Compile the Data

Start with the many information fields usually contained in the current human resources information system, or HRIS. Standard within PeopleSoft/Oracle, SAP, or almost any other personnel system available today are collection fields on hiring and placement, promotion and assignment, termination and outprocessing. Used (and could be used) data fields are available to record a broad spectrum of employment process details.

For example, faced with the current shortage of tractor-trailer drivers nationwide, a large freight trucking firm recently began an intensive campaign to improve its recruiting success. It began by studying why applicants chose to accept its job offer and join the company. The purpose in finding the most effective "attractors" was to better the recruiting process. At the same time, experiencing constant turnover among its current drivers, it also needed to know what factors would better help retain its best qualified employees. Here, the purpose was to identify the most compelling "retainers," and the corollary was to learn if the "attractors" were related to the "retainers."

Delving into the personnel database for its current employees, this company found that it already had many data points to consider, including job information (position titles, levels, job groups) and assignment data (location, shifts, typical runs). Its HRIS contained personnel background data (education, prior experience, skill levels), as well as individual differentiation factors (age, sex, EEO class) as examples. The HRIS also recorded similar information on all terminated drivers, plus remarks on their expressed reasons for quitting—data that could be completed or expanded by supervisory records and notes.

Interestingly, the staffing department had similar information in its applicant tracking system (ATS) on drivers who had turned down employment offers, including their expressed reasons why. In addition, there were driver-satisfaction and commitment data collected by the employee relations department as part of its periodic employee surveys. All this information had been in the HRIS for years before anyone thought to use it.

An initial review of the data led to several interesting findings and predictions. For example, newspaper advertising for driver positions was found to be costly and ineffective. The data projected that job availability was better advertised by posters displayed at interstate truck stops, job signs placed in front of freight terminals, and increased word of mouth through employee referrals.

Interpret the Data

Now the challenge changes from what data you have to what information you need to fill in the gaps in knowledge. In this example, from statistical analysis of the already available information came a formulation of two additional sets of desired data. The first was specific hiring questions that could be answered by truck drivers who had recently accepted or rejected employment offers. The second was more detailed retention questions that could be answered by drivers who had been with the company for eighteen to thirty-six months. Incidentally, this time frame was found in the initial analysis to be a driver's most critical decision period about continued employment with the company.

The supplemental data led to other interesting findings and predictive factors. For example, availability of new trucks played a bigger role in job offer acceptance than previously believed. Likewise, future wage progression was more important to drivers than starting pay levels. Beyond that, company stability was even more important than compensation. Now, instead of management's gut feelings about what were employees' decisional factors, there were valid and relevant patterns, clearly identified and later applied to recruiting and compensation plans.

As more and more data points are added to your existing findings, you will find new statistical relationships and predictive correlations. After implementing the actions predicted by this company's analysis, the results flowed directly and positively to the bottom line. Specifically:

* Recruiting methods became more effectively targeted.
* Applicant flow increased by 25 percent.

* Hiring costs were reduced by one-third.

* Key employee retention increased over 12 percent.

* Turnover was reduced by 48 percent in the first year alone.

Perhaps even more important to the growth and stature of this human resources department, the same analysis was requested by the engineering and operations departments of the trucking company for their hiring and retention programs.

The Memphis Experience

Memphis, Tennessee, heralds itself as the "Distribution Capital of the USA." This thriving city is at the crossroads of several key interstate highways and cross-country rail lines. The Memphis Airport is the home hub of Federal Express. Now every national transportation, warehousing, and distribution company has a presence in this greater metropolitan area.

In the many square miles between the airport and the back of Elvis Presley's Graceland, an immense industrial warehousing complex grew up in the past decade. Street after street is now filled with brand-new, gigantic, single-story warehouses. Each is an attractive modern building, each is neatly landscaped, and each has a HELP WANTED sign planted in front. Each offered the same per hour starting rate for warehouse workers, and each found itself competing for the same applicants in a shrinking labor market. By the mid-1990s, Memphis was running out of distribution workers.

A while back, a billion-dollar global logistics firm located in several of these warehouses recognized the immediate need to take a more proactive stance. Its question was, "In the sourcing, hiring, and onboarding process, what were the common factors shared by our best performing employees?" To answer this question, the HR staff sought to discover actionable correlations among recruiting sources, hiring methods, selection processes, and employee performance.

In any standard process analysis, there is an input, a throughput, and an output component. In this case, the output of the best employees could be identified by the most recent performance appraisals recorded in the HRIS. Likewise, the input of recruiting sources was recorded on the ATS, while the throughputs of selection methods and onboarding were found in employee record jackets. Again, this process started with personnel data already on hand, just waiting to be utilized.

The Buried Treasure

There were several interesting and unexpected results of this analysis, which led to some dramatically effective process changes. For example, the input process review found that:

* Most of the best performers had been working at other companies in the immediate area when they applied for work there.

* Most warehouse applicants would not travel great distances to get to work.

* The applicants learned of job openings primarily through signs on the building or from employees, not from newspapers or magazines.

* Good employee benefit plans were key to the applicants' decisions to change companies.

The throughput process review found that:

* Good warehouse applicants preferred to be interviewed in person rather than filing online applications.
* The informal warehouse setting where the applicants would be working was a stronger recruiting location than formal off-site job fairs.
* The applicants usually filed their applications late in the afternoon—that is, just after or before their work shifts at other area employers.
* The most effective interviews were conducted by hourly lead employees rather than salaried supervisors.

The Actions Taken

In response to these findings, HR began a new recruiting program centered on the theme, "How would you like an exciting place to work, with great benefits, right in your own neighborhood?" This question appeared on a large billboard near the entrance to the industrial park and was repeated on flyers posted in all nearby restaurants, diners, and stores. Informal open houses, complete with warehouse tours, personal interviews, and even some snack food, were scheduled for Tuesdays and

Figure 5.9. Reasons employees stay or move on.

OPERATING LEVEL WORKERS		
ATTRACTORS	STAYERS	REJECTORS (Negative)
Facility location	Benefit plans	Promotional opportunity
Benefit plans	Vacation and PTO	Growth and development
Pay for this job	Approachable supervisor	Responsive management
Approachable supervisor	Supervisor competence	Work and OT scheduling
Company stability	Safety/work conditions	Tactful disciplining
Management loyalty	Communications	Management leadership
Normal work hours		

CLERICAL AND ADMINISTRATIVE STAFF		
Job security	Approachable supervisor	Performance-based rewards
Current pay	Flexible work hours	Promotional opportunity
Company stability, loyalty	Trustworthy supervisor	Earnings potential
Trustworthy supervisor	Personal concern for me	Co-worker attitudes
Vacation and PTO	Leadership skills	Development opportunity
Supervisor communications	Vacation and PTO	Chance to learn new skills

SALARIED PROFESSIONALS		
Trustworthy supervisor	Approachable supervisor	Performance-based rewards
Company stability, loyalty	Flexible work hours	Company loyalty to employees
Supervisor communications	Trustworthy supervisor	Promotional opportunity
Current pay	Responsive supervisor	Fair increases
Performance-based rewards	Management leadership skills	Upper-management trust
Upper-management leadership	Supervisor communications	Earnings potential

Thursdays from 3 PM to 7 PM to catch every day or afternoon shift change in the area. Lead employees were trained in interviewing and were provided question templates. A special employee benefits information packet was prepared for all attendees.

Within the first two months of these process changes, applicant flow increased over 20 percent, as had acceptances of job offers. Even more impressive, and as predicted, after the next review cycle, high-performing new employees had increased over 35 percent.

The message here is that data mining can be accomplished by your company, just starting with the treasure trove of data you already have in HRIS, payroll, and related systems. Using process analysis and distributive statistics such as discussed previously, you can begin to develop similar predictive metrics for the human capital in your company. In this constantly changing and ever-challenging business world, you cannot afford to pass up analysis of your treasured data.

Another Experiment

During this same period, HR conducted an extensive study of why people joined, stayed, and left. Figure 5.9 on page 173 summarizes the results.

As the figure shows, the general finding was that applicants are attracted by one set of factors, stay because of another, and leave for a third. From these results, one thing is clear: Although there are tendencies dependent on position level, there is no universal reason for joining, staying, or leaving an organization. However, it is also clear that, with a bit of data organization and analysis, you can make significant, trend-changing decisions regarding your own organization's hiring and retaining of talent.

WAKING THE SLEEPING GIANT IN WORKFORCE INTELLIGENCE

Lisa Disselkamp

There has never been a wider gap between what is possible and what is practiced in workforce management than there is today in the area of time and labor data. The tools exist, the data are within reach, and the audience is primed for improving the use of intelligence about workforce performance and cost. Yet there is a significant disconnect among these three components, leaving the potential for improved workforce intelligence sitting dormant. Can employers be rewired to use the power of data analytics to improve their management of human capital?

Employers have been collecting and reporting information about their workers for ages. The origins of payroll and accounting, bookkeeping, and paper and coin currencies can be traced to the beginning of civilization and have evolved slowly over time to what we have today. Although the practice probably dates back many thousands of years, the earliest disbursement records still intact are stone tablets from Athens dating to 418 BC.[1] Fast-forward to the end of the nineteenth century and we have the first mechanical devices for collecting workforce information—time clocks. These time clocks offered employers advancements in efficiency and accuracy, but the devices themselves were transactional, not intelligent. Time-clock technology remained relatively stagnant for nearly ninety years.

In the late 1970s, the first intelligent time-clock device was born when Mark Ain put a microchip into a time clock. During the last thirty years since then, there has been a rapid progression of new technologies to collect work-time data and develop the computer systems that support these technologies. Features in these devices now validate data, integrate the data with other business systems such as scheduling and accounting systems, and share the data across wireless networks from remote locations—all means that have dramatically enhanced the employer's ability to obtain accurate, meaningful, and timely information. Today, workforce management systems have evolved into sophisticated, intelligent, real-time business tools.

Workforce management systems have been transformed from processes for collecting and reporting information about workers and costs to tools for analyzing, reacting to, and improving how the workforce is managed. The latest additions offer management the ability to forecast and strategize how to effectively deploy and compensate people. But the key word here is *offer*. While software and hardware vendors have produced these powerful analytical tools, and with limited success have sold them to their customers, there remains a chasm between what is available and how it is used.

Opportunities Lost, Technologies Not Used

Outside the functional business units that own workforce management systems such as timekeeping, leave and attendance, labor scheduling, and payroll, people are becoming increasingly accustomed to the benefits of business intelligence and predictive analytics. In operations, managers follow lean methodologies that use production and quality data. Retailers and call centers employ sophisticated traffic modeling to guide them in decision making. An entire industry has developed around analytic tools for the financial markets so that anyone can access market data and trade investments from home. Every day, consumers are receiving their utility bills presented in graphic formats that show usage trends over time. And finally, advertisers and politicians alike use charts and statistics to support specific messaging being sent to their audiences. It is evident that people are familiar with the symbols of technical analysis, believe in the science of data collection, and often rely on data and signals to make important decisions.

However, within the realm of workforce management processes and decision making, predictive analytics is slow to be adopted. Companies resist at a variety of levels to transition toward methods of analysis, decision making, and control that are based on the collection and assimilation of meaningful information about their people. Perhaps one of the most glaring examples of this resistance is labor scheduling. The industry today boasts many sophisticated and interactive scheduling products that allow companies to apply the principles of supply and demand, cost containment, and employee satisfaction to their staffing process. Yet senior-level executives worry about its cost-effectiveness and front-line workers require talking points and cultural reprogramming to allay their fears and avoid "technology mutiny."

On average, companies spend 36 percent of their revenues on human capital expenses, but only 16 percent of them say they have anything more than a moderate understanding of the return on their human capital expenditures.[2] In other areas of time and attendance, despite strong suspicions or evidence that there is room for improvement, most employers neglect embracing the power of analytics. Yet, there are technological solutions to common workplace problems.

Punch Clock Abuses

A prime example of a common problem left unsolved is the neglect of methods to monitor and influence employee behaviors around reporting nonworked time (or paid time off), or punch-rounding abuse. The data can be easily analyzed and controls within the timekeeping system can be designed to influence and curb these behaviors.

We evaluated a sample of employee punches at one employer and found a significant spike in punches right at 00:23 minutes. For the minutes leading up to 23, punch activity showed a noticeable decrease. At 23 minutes, the employees' time was rounded up to the half-hour mark, and hence, they gained 7 minutes of paid time. When we looked at the individual employees and found many who consistently punched every day right at 23 minutes, that finding proved that employees were gaming the rounding rule to gain the 7 minutes every time they punched out.[3]

Figure 5.10 represents how employees at the organization were abusing the punch-rounding rule across the board. Hourly workers took advantage of the rounding rule that rolls the time forward to the next quarter hour. Employees punching at these "change points" (8, 23, and 53 minutes) gained 7 minutes per punch. The dark bars represent employees who punched at the change point and gained 7 minutes of nonwork paid time; the light bars represent employees who punched right before the rounding occurs. The difference in the two shows how

Figure 5.10. Abuse of rounding rule.

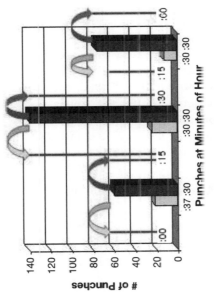

Punch rounds up to <u>next</u> 15-minute mark

Punch rounds down to <u>previous</u> 15-minute mark

Source: Client-based research by Athena Enterprises, 2009.

employees are waiting for the change point in order to gain the 7 minutes of paid time.[4]

Of course, it can be argued that this rounding mechanism works to the company's advantage as well. Employees' time can be rounded down in a way that shaves minutes off what they have worked. In theory this may be true, but only for the computer. People aren't computers, and they quickly learn how to "work the clock" to their advantage, and they do so with abandon. The cost of this unmanaged "leakage" quickly adds up. In fact, industry estimates place intentional and error-driven time theft in the range of 1.5 to 10 percent of gross payroll, costing U.S. businesses hundreds of billions of dollars each year.[5]

Many workforce management technology implementations suppress—intentionally and unintentionally—the deployment of the most powerful features in deference to the demand for "on time and on budget" project objectives. When business leaders seriously consider what they are potentially missing without analytics, they will demand that someone answer the questions: What are we missing? and, What areas of our business lack tools or strategies to drive improvements?

The answer to these questions is active time and labor intelligence, and full usage of the available time and labor management tools. For this employer suffering the punch-rounding abuse, the solution was to turn on the system to flag the abuses (reporting late arrivals and early departures, especially those near the change point), to restrict the most flagrant violators (configuring clocks to prevent frequent rounding abusers from punching in early or late), and to produce desired behaviors and outcomes (reducing the number of employees who gamed the rounding rules and decreasing the amount of money spent on rounded time not worked).

This example demonstrates the power to capture, predict, and influence employee behavior, ultimately saving the organization money and increasing productivity. In this case, analytics allowed the owners to hone in on the problem, measure the impact, and improve performance.

Overtime and Absenteeism Problems

Two other examples of underutilized analytics relative to time and labor management are found in the areas of overtime and attendance. Overtime is often dealt with as a stand-alone figure managed in reactionary mode—a set dollar amount or a percentage of total hours—or subjugated to the demands of production. Supervisors are simply told to "keep overtime in check." An intelligent, holistic approach to controlling overtime, while balancing the demands of operations, isn't possible without effective analytics.

Few organizations track on their balance sheets the cost of absenteeism arising from the direct and indirect costs of dealing with workers who don't show up for the day's work. The lack of measurement of this workplace malady demonstrates that, despite having systems that easily track work activity, mature policies around absence benefits and processes, databases with the requisite cost values and totalizers, and a subtle acknowledgment that there is a cause and effect, applying a scientific methodology to managing the impact of attendance and overtime is far from routine.

On average, employees take 1.25 extra days of leave time per year. This is equal to 0.48 percent of total payroll.[6] The good news is that both overtime and absenteeism can be successfully managed when labor analytics are part of the solution. Further, improving either will have a positive impact on the other, as there are correlations between absenteeism and overtime.

The most basic forms of intelligent workforce management deliver data that notify managers about employees who are approaching overtime, and they rank employees by their hourly rate or total hours worked when replacement workers must be called in. Further up the maturity curve, workforce analytics allow managers to zero in on trends in overtime and the root causes of excessive hours, so that action can be taken to resolve the problems. This is accomplished in a variety of visual formats—data tables, bar charts and graphs, detailed reports for drill down, and trend alerts (arrows, buttons, and automated e-mails). One product, for example, alerts the user when hour milestones are reached, and it allows them to quickly drill down into the specific group, time, and events that have led up to the overtime situation. The analysis can easily draw a line directly to a cause, such as high absenteeism or unexpected demand.

These systems are also integrated with other business systems and they relate workforce activity to key performance indicators, such as production volume and quality of equipment delays. For the first time, there is a convergence of the human capital side—what is known about people and labor cost (HR and payroll)—with the operations side, or what is known about output, workplace rules, and revenue. The result is a new, comprehensive understanding of the human capital factor in a business.

Over time, the findings are built into better planning and faster reactions to ensure that a business more successfully meets the demands of production at lower cost. This is the purpose of workforce intelligence: learning more about the real-world relationships among people, the work, and the result. It's not just providing more knowledge of what has happened or is happening, but additionally offers a greater ability to be prepared and to realize the outcomes that are desired—this is the mission objective of labor analytics.

Future Applications

What is so special about workforce intelligence? Today's labor analytics peel back the relativism that exists in labor management decision making and processing. Our time and labor management analytics deliver an assessment of critical, real-time business information that is objective, factual, and aligned with short- and long-term organizational objectives. Analytics also uses statistical analysis to make raw data meaningful and relative. While production and financial areas have long been using these techniques, the labor area has not been truly addressed. Now that the data are available, quantifiable, and relatable, the tools can be applied to human capital. The challenge is for people to be willing and able to adapt to these methods.

Workforce analytics technology has arrived; systems are available and ready to run. Its applicability is indisputable in the absence of any competing methods for capturing and leveraging workforce intelligence. However, its power remains in large part hidden under a blanket of institutional habit, skepticism, and neglect. Aside from Dr. Jac Fitz-enz, where are the academics conducting scholarly research into the potential uses of these tools? Too few business leaders are clamoring for more intelligence about their people. What must come next is an acknowledgment of this frontier and fervor for its exploration.

I predict that professors, researchers, and thought leaders will begin to develop a body of knowledge around the new data and their applications in the workplace. Practitioners can support these efforts by spreading the word about their successes to help other businesses understand what is involved in making the transition to this new way of managing their business. Each of us can draw on our use of similar sciences to improve our use of equipment, supplies, and finances to help us acclimate to this new environment relative to people.

Employers seem hesitant to embrace the new technology. Yet, when they do, they will find that the tools are a natural device for overcoming the negative effects of managing people with processes that have been mostly relationship based, home grown, and intuitive rather than scientific. Rewiring our people management methods will transform our organizations as we take analytics into action and position time and labor management technology as a proactive, forecast-based tool for managing the workforce with intelligence.

Notes

1. Lisa Disselkamp, *No Boundaries: How to Use Time and Labor Management to Win the Race for Profits and Productivity* (Hoboken, N.J.: John Wiley, 2009), 285–86.
2. Mercer Human Resources Consulting and CFO Research Services, 2003, #NB, p. 59.
3. Disselkamp, *No Boundaries*, 115.
4. Ibid., 116.
5. Acuity Market Intelligence, *Biometrics: High-Value Workforce Management—The Critical Role of Biometric Time and Attendance to Workforce Management Solutions,* white paper, February 2008, p. 116.
6. Nucleus Research, G45, July 2006.

CHAPTER SIX

Turning Data into Business Intelligence

"If you can't explain it simply, you don't understand it well enough."

—ALBERT EINSTEIN

People are either the largest or the second largest expense of an organization. This is increasingly true as technology has shifted work from muscle to brain. Individual understanding and discretionary decision making depend on accurate, timely, and predictive information. Human capital analysis and predictive measurement can provide this information and are, therefore, critical for business success in this global marketplace.

There are many reasons for human capital analysis and measurement to be so important today:

1. If you don't *measure* it, you don't know what is actually happening. Anecdotal reports and personal observations are full of errors and lead to misinterpretation.

2. If you don't *understand* it, you can't control it. How can you control a situation that has been viewed subjectively, vaguely, and inconsistently?

3. If you can't *control* it, you can't improve it. Management is about dealing with and promoting positive change. This demands standardized benchmarks.

Your business decisions should be based on empirical data. Analytics promotes accuracy, consistency, and a broader view of the effects of HR services. Analytics are bias free and credible. The numbers require little translation; they speak for themselves.

Just What Are Metrics?

The term *metrics* evolved from the work we started in the 1970s. It wasn't called metrics then—just "measurement." Over time, the term *metrics* started to be used, and by the late 1980s, many people claimed that they were doing metrics, albeit at the most basic level. By now, the term has been loosely applied to any application of numbers. So, just what are metrics?

Metrics are numbers that indicate how well a unit or an organization is performing in a specific function. The numbers provide a context around which performance can be analyzed more precisely than through anecdotal commentaries. Metrics can be expressed as percentages, ratios, complex formulas, or incremental differences. They can be individual or aggregated, and can be tracked over time to show trends.

Performance objectives should always have some quantitative aspect to them to promote a common basis for judgment. Qualitative data such as employee or customer satisfaction levels or quality judgments can be used to augment cost, time, and quantity numbers. Lastly, each metric or set of metrics should have an owner—that is, someone who is accountable for the quality, timeliness, and relevance of the data. Running numbers for the sake of having data in case anyone asks is a paranoiac waste of time. Metrics that are not used quickly become a burden on those who have to collect and publish them. In short, data for their own sake are an expense and efforts to collect them should be minimized. Data that can be turned into intelligence for decision making, however, can be valuable.

There is no shortage of data in corporate management systems. The numbers can be drawn from two sources: internal and external. Internal data sources are payroll, HR functions, employee surveys, ERP systems, production, financial statements, and marketing and sales data. External data sources are industry benchmarks, labor market trends, government databases and reports, competitor actions, survey research, and the Internet.

Avoiding Common Metrics Mistakes

Quantitative and qualitative data can generate value or create confusion and miscommunication. Simply collecting a mass of data not only has no value, it can lead to frustration and poor decisions. Some of the common mistakes made concerning metrics include:

1. *Confusing Data with Information* We can bury ourselves in data, with the erroneous assumption that we know something. Uninterrupted data collection is a worthless, make-work dust-gathering expense. The basic question is: What will you do with the data once you have it?

2. *Valuing Inside Versus Outside Data*. Basically, no one in the organization cares what is happening with the human resources function. All they want to know is what value HR is generating for the company. This is an extension of the activity versus impact mistake. Report on human capital, the employee activity, rather than on human resources, the department activity.

3. *Generating Irrelevant Data*. Presenting metrics on topics of no importance is useless. It simply clouds the issue, showing that you don't know what you are supposed to be contributing. Metrics must answer relevant business questions rather than just be a data dump. More data are not necessarily useful data. Focus on collecting and reporting only important business data.

4. *Measuring Activity Versus Impact*. A common tendency is to report costs, time cycles, and quantities without describing their effects. I call them intermediate metrics. My basic test question is: What difference does it make? What is the result? If the data do not show some positive or negative effect, why report them?

5. *Relying on Gross Numbers*. Averages mask effects. If you reduce a large number of outcomes to an average, you have no profile of the phenomenon. What are the mean, the median, the mode, and the percentiles? Are all data points bunched around the middle, or are they spread across a wide range? Average cost and average turnover are meaningless.

6. *Not Telling the Story*. We can gather a mass of data and display it in colorful charts, graphs, and tables, but in the end, does it tell the story of what happened, why, when, where, how, and to whom? Data are not intelligence. Data are expense. Intelligence is value. Don't report something if it does not tell a story.

7. *Analysis Stagnation*. What are you going to do with the data now that you have it? What are the implications of the data? How can you use it to spur action on the part of management or employee groups? Is the story compelling to someone who has a line responsibility? Does it guide the line person in solving problems or exploiting opportunities?

Second-Generation Metrics: Benchmarking

Benchmarking emerged from basic metrics in the mid-1980s, when we published the first national human resources financial report (HRFR) under the sponsorship of the Society for Human Resource Management. *Benchmarks* are comparisons between companies on various dimensions: industry, location, size, or growth rate. They help managers evaluate their work to some degree. The shortcoming of benchmarks is that the comparisons are sometimes invalid. During stable times, in small markets benchmarks can be useful. However, as markets have grown, fragmented, and globalized, benchmarks are often irrelevant. Even two small companies in the same area may be so different as to make most benchmarks misleading.

Benchmarks can yield views of broad trends across industries or regions, however. They can show that costs generally are moving up or down, time cycles are either growing or shrinking, labor availability is shifting in some way, or other basic factors of business are changing. Although they describe change, they do not reveal the reasons for the change unless you begin to apply analytic tools. In summary, benchmarks are better than focusing only on internal trends, but they must be used with caution. To obtain value from benchmarks, you need to know a lot about the companies used in the comparison. Just because they are in your industry that does not make their numbers comparable. Let's look at an example.

Assume you want to know how you compare on the amount of money invested in L&D. In order to draw intelligence from benchmark figures, you need to know many things, such as:

* What costs are included: centralized and/or decentralized expenses, self-directed and classroom, conferences, executive education, mentoring, and so on?
* What percentage of the total workforce is contract, seasonal, or temporary?
* How is the total expenditure allocated across sales, production, technology, management, and leadership programs?
* What are the organizations' hiring and turnover rates?

You can see how benchmarking is a complex matter, not to be entered into lightly. Misunderstanding or noncomparable data can cause more problems than they solve.

Third-Generation Metrics: Predictive Analytics That Yield Business Intelligence

To learn why some situation is changing, you need to move up from metrics and benchmarking to statistical analysis, which then ultimately leads to prediction and optimization. Figure 6.1 shows this progression from basic metric reporting through analytics to predictability and optimization.

Figure 6.1. Degrees of analysis and business intelligence.

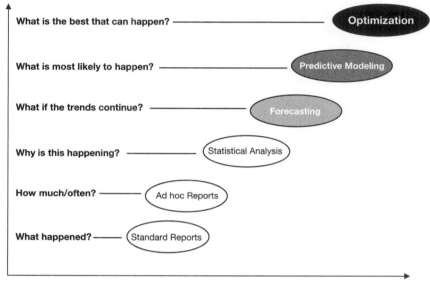

Degree of Analysis

Degree of Intelligence

Data or metrics alone do not help management make effective decisions. For that, you need to upgrade to analytics and eventually to business intelligence. This is where the value of HCM:21 comes through. Analytics requires building data warehouses by collecting information from ERPs and HR transactional systems, financial, sales, and production systems. Data integration emerges through querying and reporting, with its limitation being only that it tells what has happened in the past—it is a rearview mirror. But moving through analytics helps you understand outcomes and forecast opportunities. The more competitive and global business becomes, the more you need forecasting, predictability, and advanced modeling. Slowly, organizations are beginning to embrace the need for and see the value of these more sophisticated applications. But let's first see what is entailed with analytics.

Understanding Predictive Analytics

Data terms as used in the general marketplace are often incorrect or misleading. It is worth the time to review just what the terms truly mean. Here are two:[1]

    *   *Correlation*. When two events move in the same direction concurrently, they are viewed as correlated. This does not mean that they are necessarily related. It certainly does not mean that one causes the other. In a famous example by Bontis, age and obesity are shown to be correlated with heart attacks. He states that 'age is an antecedent to obesity which is the direct driver of heart attacks. The path from age and heart attack is not statistically significant even though it is correlated."

    *   *Causation*. In a more complex example, diet, fitness, and genetic predisposition are added to the mix. All of these also correlate to the propensity for heart attacks. Studies show that the influence of genetics is significant, but nothing can be done about that. So, Bontis moves to the next most significant variable, which is fitness. Each time a new variable is added the interrelationships of all variables becomes more evident.

    Now, apply that to a human resources service such as staffing, as was discussed in Chapter Four. There are multiple inputs to that process, including many applicant sources, various selection methods, the use of onboarding or not—all of which might be causally related to various outcomes. How do you know which variables have an effect on the outcomes? To make the problem more complex—which it is—the outcomes go beyond simply the immediate quality of the hire. They can also include ratings of potential, length of service with the organization, performance, flexibility, salary progression, and so forth. Causal modeling that we call *process optimization* reveals in any given situation which are the driving or causal factors. In addition, it shows which combinations of variables make for the most effective outcome. The small example of process optimization was seen in Chapter Five, Figure 5.2.

The Need for Integrative Measurement

Step back and think about human resources services and ask yourself how they affect your organization's operations and strategic key performance indicators. *How* does it matter if you can hire the best talent on the market, when you need them, pay them at market levels, build their skills to suit your needs, and then retain that talent? Can you see the difference this makes in any function in your organization? Would it be useful to truly know what is likely to happen when you make investment decisions? Everyone would say yes. So, why aren't you applying the best process logic and analytic technology to fulfill this critical requirement?

    Failure to have top talent in place impairs operational outcomes. Shortfalls in production, sales, accounting, and information technology naturally impede accomplishment of strategic KPIs. The logic is unassailable. The reason we have not come to this realization and built an integrated measurement system with a future focus is twofold:

1. *We are siloed.* How often do we hold meaningful conversations at the operating level among sales, finance, operations, IT, and human resources? My experience is that at the C-level, there is often a lot of finger-pointing when it comes to discussing failure to fulfill a KPI. At the operating level, the conversation rarely exists. Ask yourself: When was the last time I really talked across mid-level groups about how they were affecting each other's operations and how they could do it better? And then set up some metrics to monitor progress toward improved operations?

2. *We are obsessed with the past.* Almost all our data look backward. They report what happened yesterday. There are few, if any, data systems that have the capability to predict the future. Those that do, such as employee surveys, engagement scores, and readiness tables, are viewed as reports of past or current status. Their implications for future success are not recognized or vigorously pursued. And what is more important and useful—reporting on the past or predicting what is likely to happen in the future? HCM:21 leads us to understand not only today but also what we can do to optimize for tomorrow.

Figure 6.2 shows the links among strategic, operational, and leading indicators.

Connecting the Three Levels of Metrics

The following are some common metrics for each of the three levels. Do you see connections where one variable might affect another at the same or different level?

Strategic Level

> Revenue per FTE
> Total labor cost (payroll, contingent and contract worker pay, benefits excluding consultants) as percentage of revenue
> Total labor cost as a percentage of operating expense
> Benefits to revenue expense percentage (total benefits cost as a percentage of revenue)
> Benefits to operating expense percentage (total benefits cost as a percentage of operating cost)

Figure 6.2. Three-point integrated measurement system.

Mission-critical turnover rates: manager and professional (can be
broken out, voluntary and involuntary)

Diversity representation at executive, manager, exempt, and
nonexempt levels (percentage of executives, managers, exempt,
and nonexempt employees by diversity group)

Diversity turnover at executive, manager, exempt, and nonexempt
levels (turnover among diverse groups by executive, manager,
exempt, and nonexempt levels)

HR Operations

HR operating expense percentage (HR expense as a percentage of
operating expense)

Human resources expense per employee

HR employee ratio (HR headcount divided by total headcount)

Total training and development investment

Training and development cost as percentage of payroll

Time to fill nonexempt positions

Time to fill exempt positions

New hire quality (performance rating by supervisor ninety days after
hire)

Any other HR process metrics

Leading Indicators

Leadership survey score

Engagement survey score

Readiness rate (percentage of mission-critical positions with at least one Hi-Po person ready to step in) (executive, managerial, key professional)

Learning and development investment per employee

Learning and development investment as a percentage of payroll or revenue

Commitment level (percentage of employees reporting intent to stay at least three years via survey)

General turnover rate (exempt and nonexempt; can be broken out, voluntary and involuntary)

Great place to work (percentage of employees rating company as good or great place to work)

Do you see how changes in the leading indicators might affect the operational or strategic level? Figure 6.3 adds examples of variables in the three levels, with arrows indicating that analytics, and eventually algorithms, can point to the relationships among the variables.

Figure 6.3. Connections between variables.

Business Intelligence: The Ultimate Goal

When data are aggregated from various sources, they begin to take on meaning beyond just the raw numbers. And this is where business intelligence (BI) begins. BI allows organizations to collect, organize, integrate, and deliver reports that uncover hidden connections in the data. Predictive analytics reveal the return on HR services and investments in programs for human capital improvement. It not only predicts the likely outcome but also checks the validity of the results. It is where metrics, benchmarking, and analytics take us.

Human capital management today is fundamentally about risk. Evaluating risk requires a view over the horizon. Just as insurers and banks need to look at risk, so does the human capital manager. The effects of bad hires, incentives that don't produce, and late delivery and ineffective development programs can have a deleterious effect on a business. Predictive analytics leading to business intelligence can help avoid such shortcomings.

BI built upon predictive analytics provides visibility and insight into organizational and market activity that supports human capital management decision making and resource allocation. BI supports management through various tools, including comparative analyses, event management, data integration, and displays such as dashboards and scorecards.

At the End of the Day

The only way to do something is to do it well. That means to *finish the job*. My wife says that men operate on the 80 percent rule when asked to perform a household task. For us men, good enough usually is good enough. But in business, good enough leaves you in the pack. And as some wag once pointed out, if you are not the lead dog on the sled team, you spend your time looking at some other dog's rear end.

Although an organization is an open system, affected by external events as well as internal policies and practices, it is helpful to also focus on the interactions within. In this case, I mean the three arenas of strategic, operational, and leading. To omit any one of these is a serious mistake. In particular, to ignore that operational performance has an effect on future events (leading indicators) is obviously absurd, and no one would admit to it. Yet, it happens.

We make decisions today without regard to the future because of the pressures of the moment. Routinely we bastardize quarterly data to suit a financial report, praying that we will somehow make it up in the ensuing quarter. That is probably not going to stop as long as we must pander to the financial analysts who drive stock prices. Unquestionably, this system reeks, but it is our system and we have to live with it for the foreseeable future. So, where does all this leave you? It depends on whether you want to be the lead dog. If you don't care about your market position, then do whatever suits you. On the other hand, if you aspire to lead, then you have to pay the price. America was based on the principle that a person can be anything he or she wants to be if he or she is willing to work for it. In the war for talent, if you want to be the market leader, you have to do what is necessary. My business experience, now in its fifth decade, has taught me to address *all* issues: strategic goals, daily operations, and future signs. And look at them within one integrated model.

Note

1. Nick Bontis, "What's Measured Counts: Human Capital Management Using Causal Models," *Genera Insight*, 2008.

HOW TO INTERPRET THE DATA

Data analysis does not always require complex statistical procedures. If the sample population is small enough you can usually see the point. Simple averaging also records a lot. Means, medians, and modes can tell you how a population is distributed. But, if you want to be predictive, you will need statistics. The following three essays are examples of how to apply metrics and analytics to make a difference.

PREDICTIVE ANALYTICS FOR HUMAN CAPITAL MANAGEMENT
Nico Peruzzi

Prediction: It's the brass ring reached for by so many, yet grabbed by so few. What will happen next? How can I better plan for the future? These are questions often asked but rarely accurately answered. Data abound in the modern corporation, yet most of this potential information just sits on the shelf. That which is accessed is given only a cursory look, with people extracting very little of its potential value. In this essay, I discuss how the data can be better used—how it can be used for more of its worth. To achieve this goal, I describe using statistical methods for the purpose of predicting outcomes that will be helpful in the field of human capital management.

Understanding the Variables of Predictive Analytics

For the sake of those less familiar with statistics, let's start with the basics. A company has loads of data, so how can you break it into manageable pieces? One of those ways is by viewing it in terms of variables.

Variables can be thought of as "fields" of data, or individual pieces of data; typically, they are the columns on a spreadsheet. All of those columns—age; gender; years of service; education; performance score A, B, or C; and so on—are the variables. Why call them variables? Because they are not constants—the data for each of these variables vary for each case (think of a case as a person). Breaking the mass of data down into variables is a first step in getting a handle on the information that likely sits before you.

Categorical Versus Continuous Variables and Levels of Variables

Variables come in different types. The simplest way to break them down is to determine whether they are categorical or continuous. As the name implies, *categorical* variables are made up of types, classes, or categories. Think about the variable "gender." It has two categories—male and female. Continuous variables, on the other hand, are numbers or numerical. Anything you would report as a number is a continuous variable. Years of service could be one continuous variable; numeric age would be another.

Another word to keep in mind when talking about categorical variables is *level*. The concept of levels doesn't make much sense for the variable gender, but something like performance might be measured in categories of "high," "medium," and "low" or "past," "present," and "future." Each of these categories is considered a level of the variable called "performance" or "period."

How Variables Relate to Each Other

Well, that's the central question. If you can figure out how variables relate to each other, you can gain greater understanding of the way things in the system under examination work. There are two major ways to think about how variables relate to each other: interdependently and dependently.

Interdependence Techniques

These techniques are used to see how things relate to each other (or group together) when there is no direction to one's hypothesis or assumption. I say "things" here because this class of techniques allows one to look either at the relationship among variables or at the relationship among cases. The two most common interdependence techniques that you will come across are factor analysis and cluster analysis.

Factor analysis deals with variables and tries to answer this question: Are there groups of variables that hold together (i.e., are highly correlated with each other), such that they reveal an underlying theme? For example, say that there is a scale measuring the culture of a workplace. The scale is made up of twenty-five questions, and employees rate each question on a scale of 1 to 5 as to how much it applies to the workplace. Factor analysis allows you to see if certain types of questions hold together. For example, perhaps there are a few questions that highly correlate with each other, and all appear to have to do with company ethics. As opposed to declaring that there are subscales of the survey based solely on one's content expertise, factor analysis helps you determine if the world really does stack up that way in this specific company. Figure 6.4 shows this relationship.

Beyond the benefit of revealing underlying themes in a series of questions, factor analysis also serves the important role of data reduction. As the term implies, you can take a large number of variables and reduce them to a more manageable and coherent set of factors (think: composite variables that capture the essence of all the variables that make them up). Less is often more in regard to data; you want to simplify and look for parsimony. Factor analysis has various statistical flavors. Most commonly, continuous data are used; however, there are techniques that deal with categorical data.

Cluster analysis works with cases instead of variables. Recall that cases are people—the rows in your database. Cluster analysis looks for groups of people that have similar data across a range of variables. The people in a group (called a cluster) have characteristics similar to each other, and they are different from the people in other clusters. We're not just talking about cross-tabs here (such as "men look like this and women like that"). And we're beyond multilevel cross-tabs, such as slicing by gender and department to look for differences. Cluster analysis is a multivariate technique that takes into account lots of variables at the same time

Figure 6.4. How questions come together to make a factor.

to find those that best group like people and discriminate them from other groups.

An example of cluster analysis is as follows: You have distributed a comprehensive performance survey and you want to understand whether there are certain types of people who have similar characteristics, as measured by all the items (variables) in your survey. Cluster analysis might reveal a variety of employee types, thus helping you better understand your employees. We give descriptive names to clusters that help us sum up the essence of the group. In this example, you might end up with "new hires who are on an upward path," "marginal performers with long tenure," and "nonadvancing managers." Figure 6.5 shows the named clusters. Cluster analysis can work with either continuous or categorical variables. Again, the specific statistical technique will differ; however, either type is workable.

Dependence Techniques

Dependence techniques are used when you try to predict some outcome based on some number of predictors. To begin, consider the differences between predictors and outcomes. Remember that predictors and outcomes are just variables. When conceptualizing predictors and outcomes,

Figure 6.5. Example clusters.

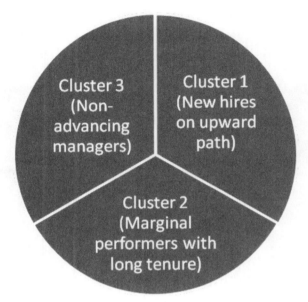

it's easiest to think directionally for a moment, as shown in the equation in Figure 6.6.

Predictors fall on the left side of the equation and outcomes on the right. One imagines that the combination of some number of predictors "leads to" the outcome. Perhaps, for example, years of service and job satisfaction relate to productivity. Note that, although you are imaging directionally, you need to remember that these techniques are based on correlations, and the old caveat still holds that "correlation does not equal causation." You might talk about years of service and job satisfaction as leading to productivity, but you are simply saying that they are related.

Figure 6.6. How predictors conceptually lead to outcomes.

The most common dependence techniques you'll run into are multiple regression and discriminate function analysis. Here is where the fun really starts.

The key aspect of *multiple regression* is that your outcome is a continuous variable (numeric). If, in the example, productivity was rated on a numeric scale from 1 to 10, you could use multiple regression to determine which predictors were most influential in increased productivity, as shown in Figure 6.7.

Discriminant function analysis, on the other hand, is used when the outcome variable is categorical. Imagine that productivity is simply rated high, medium, or low. You can still determine which predictors are most influential; however, your outcome scale is simply more crude than a numeric scale. See Figure 6.8.

DISCRIM, as it is known in stats circles, has a "cousin" technique called MANOVA (Multiple Analysis of Variance). MANOVA is sort of DISCRIM in reverse. Instead of thinking about which variables are the strongest predictors of a certain category, MANOVA asks: What are the differences between these groups? For example, you might want to know the main differences between people in two different departments. DISCRIM doesn't make sense, as you are predicting which department people are in; instead you are asking about the differences between people in the departments.

Figure 6.7. The concept of multiple regression.

Figure 6.8. The concept of discriminant function analysis.

Decision Trees

A family of techniques that use visual branching diagrams, *decision trees*, show how certain predictor variables lead to a specified outcome variable (often called a *target variable*). Both categorical and continuous variables can be used as both predictors and outcome. Examples of techniques include Chi-square Automatic Interaction Detector (CHAID) and Classification and Regression Trees (CART). These techniques are conceptually similar to the dependence techniques mentioned; however, the statistical algorithms driving the outcome are unique.

To put this into practice, you might use CHAID to see which variables best predict that people fall into the highest category of employee performance. Imagine that performance has been broken down into "high," "medium," and "low." CHAID could help you identify the categories from certain categorical variables and/or the number of certain continuous variables that are most predictive of someone's ending up in the "high" category. This relationship is shown in Figure 6.9.

Figure 6.9. An example of a decision tree analysis.

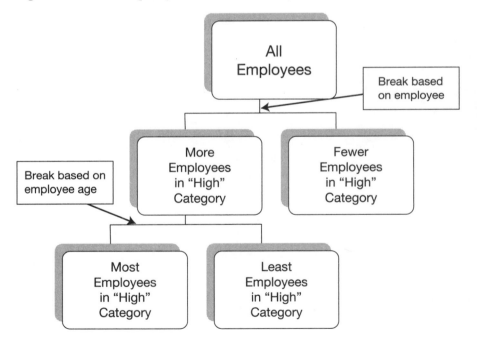

Going from Ideas to Variables

I have described different types of variables and ways to determine how they are related. This information is important so that you can take one of the most important steps in the predictive analytics process: connecting your questions (hypotheses) to the variables.

The process of moving from a research question to a concrete plan for measuring and analyzing data is called *operationalization* (to make measurable). In this phase, you ask yourself how you have or would measure your concept. For example, suppose you want to study productivity. Great—but what does productivity mean? Do you have some data in hand that measures it? If so, you have a starting point. What does the data look like? Can you conceptualize (organize) it as variables? Are the variables continuous or categorical?

If you don't have any data, you need to collect some. Perhaps you can run a survey. As you write your questions, keep in mind how the data will come in. For instance, take the survey yourself and put your data in a spreadsheet. What are your variables and are they categorical or continuous? If you know concretely what the variables look like, and you have a hypothesis as to how they might relate to each other, you are ready to collect that data and run some stats.

Caveats for Variables and Data

Here are some important precautions to keep in mind when you look at your variables and the data they contain. First, make sure your variables are *relevant* to your hypothesis. Don't collect extra data to fill out an unclear objective. Keep the project simple, relevant, and focused.

Also, missing data can be a pain and potentially weakens your end product. Try your best to collect *complete* data from each case (person). Don't have *too many*, rather than too few, *levels* in your categorical variables. If you are extremely specific, or granular, you might end up with very few people in a category. However, you can always "collapse" the category with another one later (e.g., take "junior manager" and "senior manager" and collapse them into "manager"). You cannot, however, "break apart" a previously identified variable (e.g., take "manager" and turn it into "junior manager" and "senior manager").

Continuous variables provide more opportunity to find differences than do categorical variables. Statistics are driven by "variance" (variability in cases). Continuous variables provide a more granular rating and, therefore, more opportunity to spot differences. That being said, it is often impractical to collect continuous (numeric) data; the desire for continuous data needs to be balanced with practicalities of measurement.

The more data, the merrier—usually. Two caveats here. First, if you have to collect fresh data, there will likely be practical constraints in the amount of data you can collect. Second, having more data makes finding statistically significant differences easier, which is a double-edged sword. It's nice to pick up fine differences; however, tiny differences that raise the statistically significant red flag may have no practical value.

Checklist for Using Predictive Analytics

* Start with your objective(s): What do you want to find out in a strategic sense? What is your hypothesis? Keep it as simple, specific, and actionable as possible. **Many studies have been ruined by lack of specificity and practicality.**

* Operationalize your hypothesis: How will you act on the information that you pull in? Translate the theoretical/strategic words into variables. Determine whether you have the data or need to get them. Are those variables you just operationalized available?

* Understand your variables: Which are continuous and which are categorical? What are the levels of the categorical (classes) variables and the scales of the continuous variables?

* Determine the technique that fits your hypothesis: Call in your local statistician for help. Explain your goal and let the statistician find the best way to obtain a valid and actionable result.

* Collect your data and run your stats: A discussion of data-collection methods and details of analyses are beyond the scope of this essay.

* Balance statistical with practical significance: Especially with large sample sizes, statistical significance may appear. Always ask yourself if the difference is large enough to matter.

* Tie the findings back to your original questions: Okay—what now? Given that each question was a practical one in the first place, now is the time to take some action based on the findings.

USING HUMAN CAPITAL DATA FOR PERFORMANCE MANAGEMENT DURING ECONOMIC UNCERTAINTY

Kent Barnett and Jeffrey Berk

It's no surprise that our world is enveloped in uncertainty. Economic uncertainty has reached levels not seen since the Great Depression. It is during these times that informed decision making is most urgently needed. Today's decisions create tomorrow's consequences. This essay focuses on how data are needed to make informed decisions about human capital and how the data should drive a process whereby human capital performance is managed by data, not by emotion or subjectivity. Here, we summarize the economy's current state, articulate the business case for measurement as a catalyst for performance management, present practical ways to gather and use data in decision making, and offer case examples of how organizations are driving decisions with data today.

An Economic Overview

As we write, the economic front is staggeringly different from how it was at the turn of the century. The economy has ground to a halt and evidence suggests that the current recession may be like a long, cold winter: bitter and unpleasant. The S&P 500 has dropped by over 40 percent, an unprecedented $700 billion bailout was passed by Congress, industries from financial services to the automakers are lining up for government aid, and unemployment is rising at a fast rate.

However, if we are observant, we may find that investments in human capital are not being banished, by any means. Smart organizational leaders are urging others to use this time to recruit and develop the right people needed for future success. For example, in a November 10, 2008, advertisement in the *London Times*, a full-page ad written as an open letter to UK employers read, "Now is the Time to Invest in Skills." It was authored by executives such as the chairmen of British Telecom and Marks and Spencer. It used compelling data to prove its point: Firms that don't invest heavily in training are 2.5 times more likely to fail than firms that do invest heavily.

History shows that in the last sixteen years, the international community has seen the ratio of intangible to tangible assets grow from 0.6 to 1 in 1992 to 4 to 1 in 2008. This intangible value is not on the books of organizations, but it proves that the "right" people, if managed properly and if human capital processes are measured properly, will grow the firm. Further, during the same period, a 66 percent productivity gain occurred as firms found more efficient and effective ways to create and sustain high-performing workforces.[1]

Further historic data, published by Bassi Investments Research, show that firms investing heavily in human capital development outperformed the S&P 500 by 5.6 percent between December 1996 and September 2001.[2] Of even greater significance is the finding from joint research by KnowledgeAdvisors and Bassi Investments that firms that measured human capital so as to manage it better outperformed the S&P 500 by nearly triple that—15.18 percent between January 2006 and December 2008.

Identifying Human Capital Processes

So, what are the human capital processes that should be measured in today's grim economy, and, going forward for that matter, as a routine process? There are six core processes that need to be measured and they are recruiting, learning and development, performance, talent, leadership, and engagement. Each has subprocesses that allow for more micro measurement. They are as follows:

Recruiting

> Forecasting workforce requirements
> Recruitment, selection, and hiring
> International assignment
> Mobile workforce
> Employee turnover

Learning and Development

> Onboarding
> L&D
> Coaching
> Knowledge management

Performance Management

> Performance appraisal

Talent

> Competencies assessment

Leadership

> Succession planning
> Leadership development

Engagement

> Compensation and benefits
> Employee satisfaction

Employee engagement
Work-life balance
Workforce diversity

Measuring Human Capital Makes a Difference

Merely identifying and managing human capital is important, but it is
not sufficient. We know that we manage only what we measure. So how
can measurement make a difference? Here are some brief examples:

* On average, learning and development programs improve workforce performance by 4.8 percent, which translates to $2,820 per
  employee in improved workforce outcomes (based on 600,000
  evaluations taken two months after training over a three-year
  period).

* A major health-care insurer retained 93 percent of its top talent,
  people who were flight risks, after their participation in a leadership development initiative.

* A telecom equipment company attributed a 12 percent reduction
  in call-center support calls and a 10 percent reduction in errors
  owing to a skills-based program to ensure engineers who
  purchased their equipment could self-diagnose network problems.

* A major tele-floral company saved 15,000 hours of lost productivity with technology training of tele-floral agents, resulting in a
  $276,000 cost savings to bottom-line profits.

* A leading ERP company returned 18.2 percent in productivity
  gains by training end-users in its software and how to better
  use it.

* A consumer packaged-goods company attributed $74,000 in
  increased sales per person directly to a sales force effectiveness
  investment of $5,000 per person.

Based on over 500 million data points, KnowledgeAdvisors' benchmark database indicates that approximately 55 percent of learning does
not significantly impact job performance. This is referred to as "scrap"
learning, or unrealized value. According to ASTD, the average spent on
training and development is 2 to 3 percent of revenues. Conservatively,
even if training expenditures across an organization with $10 billion in
revenue were 0.5 percent, that would equal an annual investment of more
than $50 million, revealing waste of approximately $27.5 million of unre-

alized value. A rigorous measurement program can conservatively reduce 10 percent of the waste, or a $2.75 million reduction in cost.

But human capital measurement isn't just about outcome gains. It is also about efficiencies. For instance:

* A health-care organization used measurement technology to gauge a leadership program. It reduced the administrative burden of measurement (collecting, storing, processing, and reporting data) by 70 percent to 80 percent over prior measurement efforts.

* A payroll outsource provider measured learning effectiveness with reports generated from scalable learning evaluation technology that take fifteen seconds to generate, whereas the prior process required fifteen hours of manual work to produce the same analysis.

* A major accounting firm outsourced complex conferences with over 200 sessions in each to effectively measure all sessions and the overall conference in less than seven days' lead time.

* Corporate universities typically collect over 30,000 evaluations per month automatically with learning measurement tools and run over 5,000 unique reports on the data per month, using automated technology designed for L&D professionals to analyze learning data.

* A professional services firm leveraged smart-sheet evaluation questions consistently across the operation for two years, and a recent statistical analysis concluded that the smart-sheet scalable process offers more timely and consistently correlated conclusions on the data than onetime impact analysis. The company will forgo the onetime analysis and gain $400,000 in cost efficiencies by doing so.

Performance Management Is the Outcome of Measurement

Measurement of human capital doesn't matter if it is not part of a process. Like any metric, it must be used to stimulate change and drive people to take action. The best practices that ensure human capital metrics are used to inform decision making, and they start with reasonable metrics and transform them into useful catalysts of change.

"Roughly reasonable data" means that the information isn't perfect, but it has face validity; it looks right. Take a crawl-walk-run approach. Leverage the power and ease of evaluation. In every process previously mentioned, the organization evaluates its employees, gathers real-time feedback, and forecasts change—not just analyzes history. For example, an L&D evaluation can predict impact and management support immediately, without having to wait months or years and without having to spend time and money engaging in highly precise quantitative methods. Although not precise, the data collected are roughly reasonable and can be used in a timely manner to influence decisions. In the absence of the data, the emotional individual who yells the loudest in the room gets his way. That's not how stakeholders would like to see decisions made.

Technology can gather evaluation data easily. Tools exist specifically for human capital professionals to allow them to author, administrate, and report. The burden of administration is reduced in collecting, storing, processing, and reporting evaluation results. Further, combining business outcomes with evaluation results gives a measure that can be tracked in articulate and concise ways through scorecards and dashboards. These results give a decision maker a real-time view of the operation and allow him or her to be agile in decision making.

Ultimately, the human capital analyst needs to do the following with data to make them a performance management process that informs decision making:

1. *Trend it*. Gather data consistently and comparably. Do trend line analysis on key performance indicators. Trended metrics can include productivity (revenue per employee), employee contribution margin (revenue-labor/revenue), general financial trends (revenue, profit, stock performance), realized value from training programs, quality of hire, competency gaps, voluntary turnover, performance review scores, and leadership ratings.

2. *Benchmark it*. Internal and external benchmarks of both actual results and evaluation data allow an analyst, and others who use the data, to have a point of reference to better interpret the information being analyzed. For example, a telecom company had a job-impact rating from an L&D program report score of 68 percent, and managers thought it was poor performance, comparing it to a child's D+ in school. However, the benchmark data from other organizations conducting similar training were 43 percent. Once provided the reference, the managers had a different view of the impact of the program.

3. *Set goals against it*. Any measure worth managing needs to have goals set against it. The key is to have challenging yet attainable goals. Use historic trends and benchmarks to baseline the data when setting goals. But, use the goals as a worthwhile target. Goals can be inspirational and motivational if set appropriately and legitimately.

4. *Dashboard it*. A dashboard is a convenient place to store summary data that are visual and concise. Having a dashboard for senior executives with drill-down capabilities is a great way to emphasize the governance associated with metrics, but it is also a communication and change-management vehicle that informs stakeholders of decision making. Dashboards with four to six indicators for each of the six human capital processes referenced previously should be sufficient.

5. *Compare it to actual results*. Evaluation data are great and can be tapped to review the past and forecast the future. Then, correlate the data with actual results. For example, if you are measuring a Six Sigma program, track the error rates and see if they are trending down. Is that result correlating to the job-impact percentages that participants and managers feel the program obtained? Actual results may not always be available, but we must make every effort to use reasonable assumptions and gather the data to put alongside benchmarks, goals, and trends, and in dashboards.

Summary

In today's economic uncertainty, human capital measurement is a must-have for informed decision making. Using reasonable approaches and turning data into a performance management process will mean that your measurements are not a one-off but part of existing processes necessary to manage appropriately. Leveraging technology, standards, and benchmarks enriches the process and makes for easier and more meaningful data from which to draw meaningful conclusions.

Notes

1. KnowledgeAdvisors, "Business Case for Measurement in Economic Uncertainty," 2008.
2. KnowledgeAdvisors, "Human Capital Measurement and Its Impact on Stock Performance," 2008.

USING HR METRICS TO MAKE A DIFFERENCE

Lee Elliott, Daniel Elliott, and Louis R. Forbringer

By now, everyone who works in human resources is well aware that HR is one component of a mega-system—an organization—that somehow operates to do whatever the organization is intended to do. All work gets done in systems. That is not a point of debate.

What is not so widely known is that the natural state of a system is chaos. Wheeler has eloquently argued that once a system is working effectively, that effectiveness is undermined by adding new employees who don't know their jobs well, by changes in policy and equipment, by new managers who do not understand how the work is done, and so on. In fact, those attempting to keep systems performing at optimal levels are constantly battling these forces of entropy. If the battle is lost, the place falls apart—the system returns to its natural state of chaos and the organization fails.[1]

A key way to maintain high levels of performance in the organization is to monitor the subsystems, or processes, that drive the system. Unfortunately, processes are mute. They do not have an inherent way to let someone know that things are not going well until the problems become apparent and the damage is done. Obviously, the best option is to avoid the problems, but how does that happen? How does one "hear" what a process is saying about its condition before damage is done?

Again, Wheeler has provided a most useful answer. It is necessary to provide the process with a "voice." That is, the process has to be given a way to produce a fairly continuous stream of information about its well-being. The way to communicate with a process is to develop a truly meaningful and useful measurement, or metric, that captures the primary operating characteristics of the process. As the process operates, the metrics provide the needed information and do so with a frequency that will permit careful tracking of the state of the process. As such, once there are early indications that the process is deteriorating, then action can be taken to make the needed corrections so that the process continues to operate at desired levels of performance.[2]

An early pioneer in developing metrics for HR was Jac Fitz-enz. He was among the first to say that there is a strong need for HR to find a way to communicate with those processes in an organization that drive turnover, effectiveness, and efficiency of recruiting, appropriateness of various costs related to employees, and so on. Others have taken up the effort (e.g., Huselid, Becker, and Beatty[3]) and have developed even more HR metrics and have recommended ways to optimize organization performance. The questions for those in the HR trenches are: What metrics should we use? And, once we get the metrics: What should we do with them? Unfortunately, the answers are not simple. Moreover, appropriate metrics for one organization may not be appropriate for another.

Choosing the Most Appropriate Metric

To begin the process of selecting HR metrics, consider why the HR department in your organization exists. For most, the two primary reasons for having HR is to bring in enough well-qualified people to replace those who leave and to ensure those who are brought in stay long enough that there is at least the potential for substantial ROI. As such, two metrics that certainly would be useful are *job vacancy* and *turnover*.

These two can, in some circumstances, effectively "tell the story" of recruiting and retention. That is, by monitoring these two metrics, HR can have a fairly clear picture of what is happening relative to recruitment and retention. Of course, there is a multitude of additional metrics that could be used and, in some situations, other metrics—such as time to fill—might be better. However, for ease of demonstration, the discussion here focuses on these two metrics.

Next, ensure that the metric used is constructed in a manner so that it provides unambiguous information. A common approach to calculating job vacancy is as follows:

$$\frac{\text{Total number of positions open as of today}}{\text{Total number of positions filled as of today}} \times 100$$

Unfortunately, this calculation is not at all unambiguous. It is something of a mess. Consider a company that has 1,000 positions when all positions that are budgeted are filled. Now, look at how job vacancy, as calculated with this equation, can become very confusing:

Scenario 1: 100 positions open today, job vacancy is 11 percent
Scenario 2: 500 open positions today, job vacancy is 100 percent
Scenario 3: 750 open positions, job vacancy is ?

The problem is that with this calculation, turnover results in both the numerator and the denominator changing—the numerator increases *and* the denominator decreases; that is, nothing in the equation remains constant. An alternative calculation that would remove the confusion is:

$$\frac{\text{Total number of positions open as of today}}{\text{Total number of positions budgeted (for some period of time)}} \times 100$$

Using this equation, the scenarios noted above would change to:

Scenario 1: job vacancy is 10 percent
Scenario 2: job vacancy is 50 percent
Scenario 3: job vacancy is 75 percent

The latter calculation yields a metric that provides a greater understanding of the state of job vacancy. The lesson to be learned here is that you should not blindly accept that a given equation will yield the needed information to determine the well-being of the processes involved.

Plan for How the Data Will Be Used

Once the metrics to be monitored are chosen, it is important to have a plan in place to provide some detail on how the data will be used. That is, how will HR work with managers to gain an understanding of why the metric is moving as it is? For example, it's not enough to say to managers, "Turnover is up; what are you going to do about it?" Managers can become quite resentful in these situations. They might have some idea of why turnover is occurring, but often don't have a complete understanding. If a plan is in place to gain greater understanding of the metric before data are gathered, and both HR and management agree to the plan in advance, it becomes fairly simple to enact the plan once the metric begins to drift in a direction that suggests the process is being impacted by entropy.

Continuing with the example of turnover, HR could conduct an analysis of exit interviews to collect additional information on reasons the turnover is occurring. Unfortunately, the validity of exit interview information is certainly questionable in many situations. It is not uncommon for employees to be hesitant to tell the complete truth, for fear of burning bridges. Others just aren't willing to spend the time to provide an understanding of why they are leaving. Moreover, the numbers of people who leave in a given area may be too small to provide more than a glimpse of what is happening in the department that is experiencing turnover. In short, exit interviews can provide some useful information, but it would be helpful if there were a better way to gain an understanding of the metric.

Fortunately, there is a better way. Within the realm of research, there are quantitative research designs (e.g., analysis of variance) and there are also qualitative designs (e.g., case studies). The former use statistical analysis to produce conclusions about the data; the latter involve intensive studies of events that may or may not involve data at all. For turnover, a highly effective approach to understanding what is happening in the organization that not only has produced turnover in the past but also provides ample evidence of what turnover is likely to occur in the future is a qualitative research design known as *grounded theory*.[4]

Grounded theory does not yield some abstract theory about why turnover is occurring. Rather, a theory of why turnover has occurred and is likely to occur in the future is developed and is "grounded" in information. In general, you begin by searching broadly for what might be causing turnover. As you gather information, the focus narrows dramatically and the effort concludes with testing and verification to ensure that what is believed to be the causes of turnover are accurate. The result is a well-considered explanation of why turnover happened in the past, as well as a basis of understanding turnover that will occur in the future. Of course, knowing what is coming provides the opportunity to do something to prevent it. As Fitz-enz has argued, using HR metrics to predict what is coming for the organization is the next evolution in our use of such metrics.[5]

Fortunately, with some slight modifications to make the grounded theory process move more quickly than is typically seen in a qualitative research study, this approach can be used to develop a substantial understanding about turnover in an area of the organization.

The steps to take are as follows:

1. Preparation

* Describe the process to the managers that will be impacted.
* Respond fully to any questions they have.
* Assure them that there will be no secrets—and keep the promise.
* Provide a list of others who have gone through the process.
* Show the managers the list of questions that will be used to start the study and ask for their input.
* Modify the questions appropriately.

2. Initiate the study

* Select those who will be interviewed in the first group.
* Meet individually with each person selected; ask the planned questions and any additional questions needed for clarification.
* Carefully document the answers.
* Review the answers and look for patterns.
* Create a second set of questions based on the information that was derived from the first round of interviews.

3. Continue the study

* Select a second group—choose those most likely to provide the needed information.

* Use the second set of questions and any additional questions needed for clarification.
* Carefully document the answers.
* Review the answers and look for patterns.
* Continue this process until all concepts are "saturated" (i.e., there does not appear to be any additional useful information to be obtained).

Throughout the process, there are some analytic tools that are helpful to get to the underlying causes of past and future turnover as quickly as possible. Here are some suggested tools:

* *Use conceptual ordering.* Organize the information into discrete categories or concepts (e.g., turnover is occurring due to ineffective conflict). Develop a written description for each concept (e.g., ineffective conflict—leaves participants with substantial residual frustration after the conflict episode is concluded).

* *Dig deeper.* Watch for words or phrases that strike you as significant. Use "flip-flop" technique (i.e., look for opposites or extremes to make the information more meaningful). Keep the focus—don't get lost on a tangent. Obtain multiple points of view (e.g., ask people from another area in the organization about turnover in the area of focus). Gather information from multiple sources (e.g., bring in information from exit interviews).

* *Check the concepts.* Ask the participants about what appear to be the causes of turnover; this is done in an effort to check the validity of the concepts with those involved in the study. That is, the people who are providing the information about why turnover is occurring also are those who confirm that apparent causes of turnover are, indeed, the true causes.

* *Break the concepts into subconcepts.* When it makes sense, pull apart a potential cause of turnover. Consider "change strain" as a cause of turnover. Make special note of comments such as:

"We don't get a chance to learn new things before something else starts. We never get a sense of mastery."
"We are changing so much. I don't know where we're going. I'm beginning to worry about my future here."
"Stress here is just too much."

Upon careful examination, while all of these pertain to change strain, each suggests a slightly different component of change strain is creating turnover.

* *Insert memos.* As analysis of the documentation progresses, insert memos that include a list of the concepts and definitions. Be sure the memos fit together logically. Jot down breakthrough ideas immediately (i.e., once a cause for turnover becomes clear, write it down as a memo within the documentation).

* *Provide ideas for how turnover might be reduced.* Once the information gathering and analysis is complete, spend considerable time developing ideas that the managers might use to reduce turnover. Make the list long so the managers have choices—and the ideas in the list might lead to the managers developing other useful ideas. Get others who are knowledgeable to review the ideas.

Now the information is gathered, the causes of turnover are understood, and ideas have been generated for reducing turnover. At this point the information needs to be provided to the managers. Here are some suggestions for doing that:

1. Schedule a meeting and prepare the managers by giving some initial information intended to reduce the managers' anxiety. (It's common for managers to believe the reasons for turnover all have to do with them.)

2. At the meeting, go over the highlights of the report. Give the managers the report to read during the meeting. Answer all questions. Schedule a second meeting.

3. At the second meeting, address all concerns and the action plan with the managers to implement ways to reduce turnover.

This process ends when the managers do something credible to reduce turnover—and turnover decreases to acceptable levels. Once that happens, it's often beneficial to have a follow-up meeting with managers to review what was learned and to plan to enhance retention based on what was learned.

For example, what are some common causes of turnover that have been revealed using this approach?

* Ineffective conflict

* Dramatic increases in the cost of gas

* Strain of having to make changes
* Uncontrolled stress
* Cliques at work
* Feelings of rejection by co-workers
* Manager too busy, not available
* Too much grief (in a hospital setting)
* Bullies at work
* Ineffective management

This simplified version of the qualitative approach to information analysis—grounded theory—has been successful most times it has been used as the way to find why an HR metric is behaving as it is. Do note that this approach is not limited to an investigation of turnover. While it is not appropriate for all HR metrics, it is useful to understand the causes of variations of many of the HR metrics.

Bring It All Together—What Does It All Mean?

Once the HR practitioner has selected the optimal metrics to use to monitor key HR processes, and plans are in place for how to interpret and understand why the metrics are behaving as they are, then it is important to bring it all together. As Heather Cullen, HR performance consultant of The Hartford Company, has argued, it is necessary to use all the metrics together to "tell a story."[6] That is, you need to bring all the HR metrics together in a single document that can be used to understand what is happening to the primary HR processes in an organization.

The introduction of such a document will be an HR scorecard, such as shown in Table 6.1. In this scorecard, the HR metrics are clearly labeled and separated into categories that correspond to HR operations. Each operation can be relatively well understood by looking at the metrics. However, it becomes truly comprehended when this information is supported by intensive studies of any substantive changes in the HR metric that will tell why the changes occurred and what is to be expected in the future. Moreover, providing plans that have been developed—and are supported by managers—to address expected future changes in HR metrics that might adversely impact the organization will certainly take HR to a new level of usefulness to the organization.

Table 6.1. HR scorecard.

Category	Metric	Frequency
Attracting Talent	Job vacancy rate	Monthly
Attracting Talent	Number of hires	Monthly
Attracting Talent	Time-to-hire	Monthly
Attracting Talent	Type of hire—add vs. replace	Monthly
Attracting Talent	Source of hire	Biannually
Engage	Number of grievances	Annually
Engage	Employee referral	Biannually
Engage	Employee satisfaction scores on surveys	Biannually
Operations	RN FTE per patient	Annually
Operations	Salaries, wages, and benefits as a percentage of budget	Annually
Operations	Salaries, wages, and benefits per case-mix adjusted admission	Annually
Operations	Defects—issues, malpractice suits, etc.	Monthly
Operations	Cycle time—actual patient stay vs. planned stay	Monthly
Operations	Revenue per employee	Biannually
Retention	Total and voluntary turnover	Monthly
Retention	180-day turnover rate	Annually
Retention	RN ages—% eligible for retirement in 5 or fewer years	Annually
Retention	Top voluntary turnover reasons	Biannually
Retention	Retention rate for top performers by dept. or job code	Biannually
Workforce Demographics	Headcount vs. budget	Monthly
Workforce Demographics	Active FTEs	Monthly
Workforce Demographics	Contract employee use by job code	Monthly
Workforce Demographics	Count of staff by diversity category	Biannually
Workforce Demographics	Count of staff by gender	Biannually
Develop	Training type	Biannually
Develop	Training spend	Annually
Develop	Promotions	Biannually

Notes

1. D. Wheeler and S. Chambers, *Understanding Statistical Process Control,* 2nd ed. (Knoxville, Tenn.: PSC Press, 1992).
2. Ibid.
3. M. Huselid, B. Becker, and R. Beatty, *The Workforce Scorecard* (Boston: Harvard Business School Press, 2005).
4. B. Glaser and A. Strauss, *The Discovery of Grounded Theory: Strategies for Qualitative Research* (Chicago: Aldine de Gruyter, 1967).
5. J. Fitz-enz, *Building an Integrated and Predictive HCM System.* Presented to the Talent Summit, sponsored by the International Quality and Productivity Center, October 2007, Tucson, Ariz.
6. Heather Cullen, personal communication, 2009.

PART 3

The Model in Practice

CHAPTER SEVEN

Impacting Productivity and the Bottom Line: Ingram Content Group

Wayne M. Keegan, Chief Human Resources Officer

The Ingram Content Group (ICG) is part of a long tradition of successful companies built by the Ingram family. Dedicated to helping content reach its designation by providing a broad range of physical and digital services, Ingram has been a partner to publishers, booksellers, and libraries for more than four decades. ICG leads the industry in physical distribution, supply chain management, and fulfillment services with access to all markets both domestic and international. On average, ICG ships 2.4 million units each week to over 85,000 customers from four distribution centers.

Employee turnover had been a chronic problem for Ingram's distribution and fulfillment division for years, rising steadily until it hit a rate of 81.7 percent enterprise-wide at the end of 2002, and 102 percent in our flagship distribution center in La Vergne, Tennessee. For Operations/ Logistics leadership, the revolving door of talent was disruptive in its efforts to operate at best-of-industry standards. For the rest of the C-staff, the attitude was one of resignation—after all, these were tough, entry-level, blue-collar jobs in a warehouse/distribution environment with production standards. In essence, high turnover in the Operations groups was viewed as a fact of life.

Getting the Attention of Leadership

For Operations/Logistics leadership, excessive turnover was a disruptive factor in its efforts to effectively manage its facilities. Intuitively, we all knew that there was a significant human capital expense negatively impacting the bottom line. We were tracking the turnover data and benchmarking that against the data provided by the Department of Labor for Wholesale Trade. However, this practice alone was not capturing the financial impact of excessive turnover in terms that would allow management to make a cost/benefit determination of whether to focus the attention, resources, and efforts of the organization on this matter.

Initially, we explored two highly accepted methods for determining the cost of turnover: (1) capturing the individual expense items impacted by a separation event, and (2) using the more simple calculation of six months of base pay plus benefits for each nonexempt separation and one year for each exempt separation. However, while these are valid and widely used methodologies for calculating the cost of turnover, the expense numbers reported from these methods were such that they failed to pass the "reasonableness" test.

When outlining the expense implications to executive management of any human capital issue, the human resources leader needs to be aware that even C-staff or board leaders have a tipping point for reality, or reasonableness. Presenting a number that reaches a level where the sheer size, no matter how well laid out, simply shuts down the audience's willingness to accept the number as valid will significantly reduce the chances of influencing that executive leadership on the need to take action. For example, in our case, the total number of nonexempt/hourly separations for 2002 in the Operations/Logistics group alone was 1,821. However, even if we adjusted to include only those separations that exceed the DOL's Wholesale Trade benchmark, bringing the total down to 1,155, using the simple standard calculation at a rate of $26,000 per separation (base pay + benefits), we would be reporting a cost of excessive turnover for just this group of a little north of $30 million. Even for a company with top line sales of over $1 billion at the time, making a pitch that reducing turnover to the level of the benchmark would add $30 million to the bottom line would *not* pass the reasonableness test. Furthermore, we would have lost our audience and, more important, lost an opportunity to address a serious issue that was costing the company significant pretax dollars.

We knew that excessive turnover was disruptive to any efforts to maintain best-in-industry standards in the Operations/Logistics group, and we knew that this expense was a human capital loss significantly impacting the bottom line. The challenge we faced was to construct a formula that would capture the expense analytics used by the Operations and Finance groups in measuring operational performance. Therefore, we sought a formula that would establish a model for human capital value that could accurately identify the cost of excessive turnover, but also pass the reasonableness test in order to get the attention of senior leadership and to take action.

Crafting the Right Formula to Gain Leadership Support

Partnering with our Operations/Logistics colleagues, we analyzed the key operational and financial metric for their divisions: cost per unit, or CPU. Production standards had been established for the majority of the positions, so we evaluated the labor costs in relation to unit/line production standards.

From our collective experience, we knew that there was a significant gap between a tenured departing associate and a newly hired replacement regarding production output versus production standard. As a rule of thumb, we had accepted a thirty-day ramping-up period for the average new hire to perform at standard. However, this assumption had never been validated through a scientific production analysis. An analysis of the average production rates for new hires in 2002 revealed that the ramping-up time in achieving the production standard was greater than assumed.

For every replacement of an associate with six months or more of service, who was averaging 106 percent of production standard, the newly hired replacement initially performed at an average of only 50 percent of standard, 83 percent at three months of service. 95 percent for the months three to six months, and finally achieving the production standard after six months of employment. Clearly, there was a dramatic drop in productivity for each separation incident, and the challenge was to craft a metric that would capture that financial impact. We came up with the following metric for our human capital value model:

Average production standard	−	Average new hire production 0–6 mos. service	×	Unit/line labor costs	=	Separation expense

Applying this formula, we found that the average cost of lost productivity was $3,652 per separation incident.

The Causes, the Metrics, and the Intervention Strategies

Knowing the expense of excessive turnover was half the battle. We needed to identify what factors were driving it, establish the metrics to measure the impact in order to determine which factors warranted our attention, then craft the intervention strategies and track the effectiveness of the strategies once they were implemented. All of these metrics were listed on the HR dashboard and communicated to leadership as follows.

A. *Staffing*

1. We established quality-of-hire metrics measuring turnover at ninety days and one year; we benchmarked this against data provided by the Human Capital Report from the Saratoga Institute.

2. Utilizing the Activity Vector Analysis (AVA) assessment tool, we identified the behaviors required for each of the roles that would enhance the potential for retention. We administered the instrument to all applicants, correlating their results against the role profile.

3. We implemented a robust screening process for all hourly positions, subjecting these applicants to the same level of scrutiny as we would middle-management positions in the company. In our flagship distribution center in La Vergne, Tennessee, in 2006, we screened 3,875 applicants and hired only 282, or 7 percent; in 2007, we screened 6,869 applicants and hired only 200, or 3 percent.

B. *Leadership Development*

1. Partnering with a local college, we delivered a tailored ongoing development program for all levels of management in the Operations/Logistics group, but with a series of programs specially focused on Team Leads and Supervisors, the critical links between the company and our associates, to ensure the effectiveness of the leadership team.

2. In partnership with the ICG Legal team, we delivered a series of learning events to enhance communication and to educate leadership on key issues that impact associates.

3. We assessed effectiveness of learning initiatives through follow-up evaluations measuring learning and on-the-job application of newly acquired knowledge, skills, and abilities, as well as continued management inventory assessments. Return on investment was evaluated through turnover reduction, increase in leadership skills as measured through continued management inventories, and internal ascendance.

4. We redesigned performance management to include a focus on turnover. A turnover reduction goal was added to every member of the

Operations/Logistics management team, as well as the HR team, as part of their annual performance management reviews.

5. We established cross-functional turnover teams to create strategies, implement action items, and measure effectiveness as a means of achieving turnover goals.

C. *Rewards*

1. We ensured that base pay was competitive with local market conditions.

2. We implemented a pay-for-performance program system for the hourly team that was based on production and quality standards.

3. We secured their futures through education and communication of the importance of the 401k program. For the Operations/Logistics group during this five-year period, participation rose from 25 to 84 percent, surpassing the Wholesale Trade benchmark of 72 percent.[1]

D. *Associate Relations*

1. We established quarterly roundtables chaired by the executive for each department; notes were published, along with specific action items to be addressed.

2. We implemented a retraining program to assist associates who were struggling with production standards. Instead of treating associates who fell short of production standards as a disciplinary problem, we gave them an opportunity to improve through additional training.

3. Management and HR were trained to identify personal issues that may drive associates to leave, and to intervene as appropriate.

4. We increased employee engagement opportunities through inclusion on teams such as the Safety Committee and process improvement/LEAN teams.

Achieving Our ROI

Within five years of implementing the strategies to address excessive turnover, turnover for the Operations/Logistics groups dropped from 81.7 to 25.5 percent, thereby achieving a cost savings tied to added productivity of $13.4 million over the five-year period. See Figure 7.1.

In our flagship distribution center in La Vergne, turnover dropped during the same period from 102 to 28.8 percent. See Figure 7.2.

In 2006, for the first time in the company's history since 1999, when turnover had begun to be tracked, the Operations/Logistics group's total turnover was less than the DOL/Wholesale Trade benchmark and, thus, reported the first year of no expense tied to excessive turnover. That accomplishment was repeated in 2007.

Figure 7.1. Operations turnover.

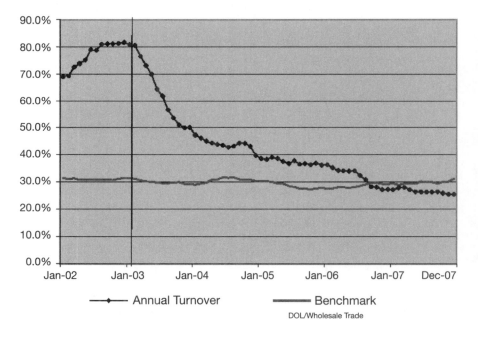

Figure 7.2. La Vergne distribution center turnover.

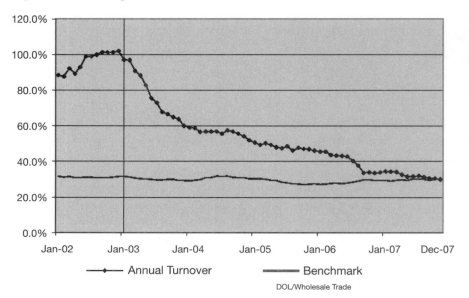

Productivity increases tied to the reduction in turnover and to the improvement in quality of hires during the five years of this study also allowed staffing levels to be reduced in the Operations/Logistics groups by 39.9 percent, or 913 associates, while volume in the distribution networks remained steady.

At the start of this study in 2003, new hires reached production standards on average at 180 days of hire; by the end of 2007, that number was reduced to 88 days. Additionally, the volume of staffing dropped 55.7 percent, from 1,799 hires in 2002 to 796 by 2007.

Final Thoughts

While the issue of excessive turnover has been addressed, we continue to focus on the quality of our hires in the Operations/Logistics groups in order to attract the best talent. We also continue our efforts to retain that talent by enhancing our onboarding process, ensuring that our rewards system and benefits are competitive, and through a robust communication program, ensuring that Ingram management never loses touch with its associates. In addition we continue to ensure that those who have the most direct contact with the associates—our Team Leads and Supervisors—are provided with effective ongoing leadership development.

In the twenty-first century, maximizing a company's human capital is a key competitive factor for success. If human resources leadership is to be effective and add value in support of this effort, they must operate as business leaders who happen to concentrate in the field of HR. The language of the C-staff and the boardroom is numbers. Analytics applied to human capital issues are essential in providing the predictive data that will allow leadership to manage this valuable asset more effectively.

Note

1. Profit Sharing/401k Council of America.

CHAPTER EIGHT

Leveraging Human Capital Analytics for Site Selection: Monster and Enterprise Rent-A-Car

Jesse Harriott, Jeffrey Quinn, and Marie Artim

Enterprise Rent-A-Car, owned and operated by Enterprise Holdings since 2009, approached Monster Worldwide in 2007 to help in the decision-making process of where to locate a new customer contact center. Enterprise had considered dozens of various locations, and the company believed that Monster's real-time labor market information could help it determine the most effective city to locate the new center. The following reviews Enterprise's business situation, as well as Monster's analytical framework that was used to inform Enterprise's decision. This led ultimately to the selection of the site (here referred to as "Market A"). The performance outcomes of Enterprise's Market A contact center are also discussed.

Enterprise Holdings

Enterprise Holdings, through its subsidiaries, owns and operates more than 1 million cars and trucks, including the largest fleet of passenger vehicles in the world today, under the Alamo Rent A Car, Enterprise Rent-A-Car, and National Car Rental brands. As North America's largest and most comprehensive car rental company, Enterprise Holdings also operates a network of more than 8,000 car rental locations in neighborhoods and at airports worldwide, and leads the industry with more than a third of all airport business in the United States and Canada.

Enterprise Holdings is headquartered in St. Louis, Missouri. Ranked no. 21 on the Forbes Top 500 Private Companies in America list, Enterprise Holdings is the only investment-grade company in the car rental industry. In addition, Enterprise Holdings is part of a global strategic alliance with Europcar, creating the world's largest car rental network. Other Enterprise business lines include Enterprise Fleet Management, Enterprise Commercial Trucks, Enterprise Car Sales, and WeCar car sharing.

The company is run by chairman and CEO Andrew Taylor, whose father, Jack Taylor, founded Enterprise Rent-A-Car in 1957, based on the simple philosophy: "Take care of your customers and employees *first*, and profits will follow." Enterprise's business model today is a direct result of Jack Taylor's simple but powerful belief, and especially how that belief relates to customer satisfaction, employee development, fleet growth, and profitability.

Enterprise Rent-A-Car has been recognized for its well-developed management training program. *BusinessWeek* has ranked Enterprise as a "Best Place to Launch a Career" for four consecutive years. And College Grad.com and *Black Collegian* magazine have consistently named Enterprise as a top college recruiter. Additionally, Enterprise believes almost exclusively in promoting from within—another attribute that has contributed to its good reputation among recent college graduates. Management trainees typically receive one or more promotions during their first year, then become an assistant branch manager and eventually a branch manager in their first few years.

A cornerstone to Enterprise's continued success has been its commitment to superior customer service. This commitment includes its contact center operations, and therefore much effort and research went into the decision to locate Enterprise's new facility.

Monster's Analytical Framework

Monster has a global footprint that reaches over sixty countries and over 80 million people each month. In the United States, visitors to Monster.com perform over 150 million job searches in a month and upload over 40,000 resumes per day. The profile of talent using the Monster site runs the gamut, with everybody from scientists to blue-collar workers searching for local jobs around the globe. Enterprise had worked with Monster for many years as a recruiting partner, and had recently started working with Monster as a source of human capital analytics. Therefore, when Enterprise was evaluating sites for the contact center, it contacted Monster for assistance.

Because of the vast amount of activity on Monster, much valuable insight can be gained from the data Monster collects on its site. Therefore, Monster created a separate division, Monster Intelligence, to analyze this information for customers. One of the products of this initiative is the Monster Employment Index, a monthly snapshot of online recruitment activity across a large representative selection of online career outlets, reflecting millions of employer job opportunities each month. The Monster Employment Index has data going back to 2003 in the United States and 2005 in Europe and Canada. The first such index of its kind, it is now used by many economists, companies, and major government agencies to track online recruiting trends by local market and occupation.

Monster also helps government leaders, business executives, and the economic and workforce development communities make fact-based decisions through its Monster Intelligence offerings. Monster customers use Monster's Real-Time Labor Intelligence services to make fact-based human capital decisions, attract and develop new industries, leverage regional skill sets to put dislocated workers back to work faster, and anticipate emerging jobs and industry trends. Monster Intelligence does this through its research reports, data subscriptions, and custom engagements. Figure 8.1 is an example of Monster data.

In order to assist Enterprise with its site selection, Monster proposed a multipronged analytical framework that included the following steps. These steps, however, can be applied to any business situation that involves staff site selection. The analytical framework is discussed first, and then Enterprise's specific situation is detailed.

The Business Need and the Capabilities Required

The initial step in any workforce planning–related exercise is to identify the business need being addressed and the capabilities and/or occupations that will help satisfy that business need. This step can take many forms, but at the most basic level it involves specifying the types of occupations likely to have the skills required to build the needed capabilities in the organization. Once those occupations have been identified, then a broad occupational overview for each is provided that includes:

Figure 8.1. Sample latent availability chart.

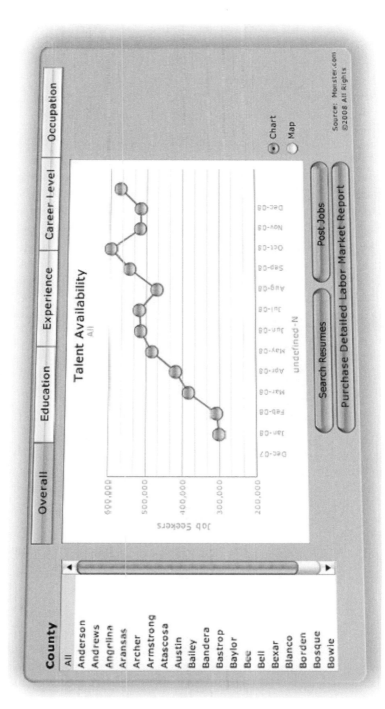

* Projected occupational growth

* Typical candidate profiles for this occupation

* Sector-specific information that impacts hiring (e.g., increased outsourcing, technology advances, generational makeup of the workforce)

A Short List of Possible Site Locations

In order to analyze options efficiently, it is recommended that an organization identify three to six locations that will then be analyzed in detail to make a site recommendation. This is best done with a mix of qualitative and quantitative factors. *Qualitative* factors include things such as:

* The location of current company facilities and offices

* Locations that provide the company with a competitive or business-development advantage

* Ease and/or cost of site location

* A company culture that fits with a location

* Infrastructure (e.g., universities, public transportation, commercial real estate, airports)

* Local business and economic development incentives

A short list of locations can also be created by identifying quantitative factors for each location and then sorting through them on the basis of those factors. *Quantitative* factors that can be used to rank locations in order of priority include:

* Unemployment rate

* Payroll change

* Rate of economic growth

* Concentration of desired occupations in each market

* Typical annual salary of desired occupation

This type of location sorting should be used only as a preliminary step to focus in on markets that might be of interest for the organization. A much deeper analysis of each market will be needed in order to ascertain whether it represents an ideal location for the recruitment of talent.

Available Talent

After three to six locations have been selected for consideration, the next step is to evaluate and compare the talent pool across the locations. This is done in several ways.

* Calculate the talent density for each critical occupation. *Talent density* is defined as the total number of people working in an occupation in a location, divided by the total workforce for that location, then multiplied by 100. This figure is used to understand, all other things being equal, how difficult it would be for a company to recruit talent in one location compared to another location. The time series trend of this metric should also be examined to understand whether market conditions are changing for the better or for the worse.

* Compare a national job search index for each critical occupation to a local job search index for each occupation. The job search index is calculated by taking the total number of job searches by occupation and by location, divided by the total for that location, then multiplied by 100. This metric is a direct measure of job-seeking activity and is an indicator of how likely a person with a particular occupation in a specific location is to apply for a job opening.

* Prepare a talent profile for each critical occupation. In the course of evaluating a local market, it is important to understand the profile of the people your company would potentially be recruiting. In some cases, it is advisable to do a quick survey with talent in the local market to understand matters important to your company or to the recruitment processes. Factors to profile include:

* Mobility of talent (e.g., willingness to relocate)
* Full-time versus part-time or contract workers
* Career level
* Education level
* Media habits and job-seeking behavior of talent
* Salary requirements

The Demand for Talent

In the same way that it is important to evaluate the supply of talent, it is equally important to evaluate the demand for talent. The demand for talent represents the amount of competition your company will experience should it choose to enter the local market. Therefore, knowing the demand trend is critical to understanding how successful a major recruiting initiative will be in each market. To do this:

* Evaluate posting trends over time for each critical occupation in order to understand whether demand for talent is slowing or intensifying.

* Calculate the talent demand index for each occupation. The talent demand index is a calculation of the number of job postings over the total number in the occupation workforce, multiplied by 100. This metric should be compared to the national average, in existing corporate locations, as well as evaluated over time to understand whether the local market is in a state of transition.

* Consider supply versus demand. Look at the labor conditions for each of the markets by plotting the markets in a graph similar to that shown in Figure 8.2, showing a simple talent-market plot. This will help you identify the relative competition for talent in each market.

The Economic Situation

It is helpful to summarize the economic conditions for each market as an aid in understanding the economic backdrop for each proposed site. Include the following in each market summary:

* Unemployment and payroll trends
* Major industries and employers of the region
* Rate of economic growth or decline in the market
* Basic demographics of the workforce
* Economic incentives for companies to locate in the region
* Cost of facilities/office space in the market

The Competition

An important step is to evaluate the potential competitors for talent in each market. This should be done in several ways.

* Use job-posting trends to identify your close competitors' presence and recruitment activities in each location being considered.

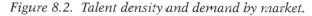

Figure 8.2. Talent density and demand by market.

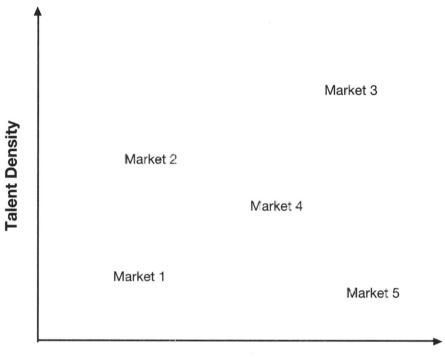

* Identify which industries hire the most for the occupations your company will recruit to fill. Identify and profile top companies in each location being considered.

The Enterprise Analysis

Monster followed the analytical framework just outlined to provide actionable insight using real-time and historical data to support Enterprise's decision on where to locate its contact center. The first step was to identify the business need and capabilities required. That is, the new contact center would need to handle more than 10,000 reservations and customer-service calls per day. The services provided from this new center would include reservations assistance and customer support. Working with the Enterprise team Monster identified the most critical occupa-

tions, including various career levels (e.g., entry-level, managers, directors) of customer-service representatives.

As the next step, Enterprise selected a short list of four possible site
locations. For purposes of the case study, we call them Markets A, B, C,
and D. Although Enterprise had narrowed the locations under consideration internally, the Enterprise team requested that Monster take an
external view and compare these locations to other markets across the
United States to ensure that all possibilities were evaluated and that no
favorable location was overlooked.

When evaluating locations, it is important to understand the supply
of talent to ensure that there is reasonable availability of people with
the skills your company needs. As outlined in the analytical framework,
Monster considered many metrics when reviewing the talent pool in each
location. At the time of the analysis, Monster analyzed millions of candidates who would help fill Enterprise's needs and uncovered the following:

* There were more than 3.5 million customer-service resumes in
  the Monster database, with an average of over 99,000 new
  resumes being added each month. This equated to about 177
  customer-service resumes for each job posting on Monster.

* On average, there were over 4.3 million customer-service job
  searches each month, and there were over 2 million job-search
  agents sent to candidates looking for similar jobs. Over 84
  percent of these job-search agents were received daily via e-mail.

Although Enterprise had identified four target locations, Monster
provided information on other markets that had the most talent to support Enterprise's hiring needs. That is, Monster reviewed the top locations with customer-service candidates listed on Monster and also the
top locations with the largest year-over-year growth in customer-service
resumes (see Figure 8.3). Monster also evaluated growth metrics for over
200 locations, allowing for market-to-market comparisons.

At the time of the analysis, there were nearly 3,000 customer-service
resumes registered on Monster in Market A. But new resumes posted on
Monster in Market A had slowed at the time of the analysis, dipping 10
percent compared to the same period the year prior (see Figure 8.4). Yet,
on average, there were over 290 resumes per job posting in Market A,
creating a solid supply opportunity for Enterprise. When compared to
the national benchmark, Market A's ratio of resumes per posting was very
favorable, which led to further consideration of Market A as Enterprise's
new contact center.

In many cases, Monster evaluates additional talent-related metrics to

Figure 8.3. Top five customer-service resume locations, percentage change.

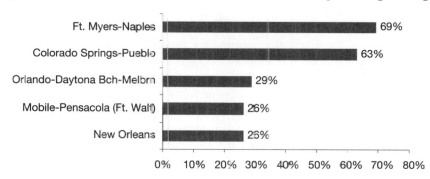

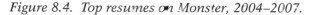

Source: Monster internal data.

assess a market for clients. Some of these additional talent-related factors include:

* *Desired Salary.* For example, if a key occupation in one market has a median salary of $27,000 and an alternative market has a median salary of $44,500, the company could use this information to forecast its operating expenses.

* *Flexibility in Scheduling.* The percentage of workers who desire a temporary, part-time, or full-time opportunity may differ significantly from market to market. If a company wishes to leverage a flexible workforce as part of its staffing strategy, this may be an important factor.

Figure 8.4. Top resumes on Monster, 2004–2007.

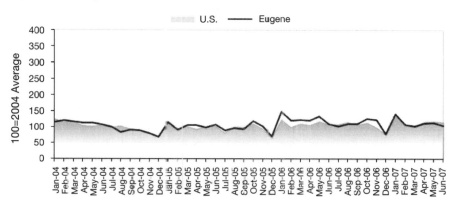

Source: Monster internal data.

Monster assessed the demand for talent in each potential market. For example, it ranked over 200 markets based on the number of resumes per job posting and conducted additional analyses of the top twenty locations for 2007 with the highest resumes per job posting within the area of customer service and call centers (see Figure 8.5). The resumes per posting ratio is a critical metric to aid in understanding the demand for customer-service workers in different markets compared to a national benchmark. A high number of resumes per job posting indicates an abundant labor supply, thus a surplus of interested candidates.

Although the four markets on Enterprise's short list did not fall within the top twenty markets nationally, Market A was ranked in the top 25 percent of the over 200 markets in terms of resumes per posting. Overall job postings on Monster in Market A had grown 12 percent over the

Figure 8.5. Locations with highest resumes per posting, customer service and call center.

Top 20 U.S. Markets	Rank
Waco-Temple-Bryan, TX	1
Flint-Saginaw-Bay City, MI	2
Toledo, OH	3
Detroit, MI	4
Tallahassee-Thomasville, FL	5
South Bend-Elkhart, IN	6
Huntsville-Decatur (Florence), AL	7
Wichita-Hutchinson Plus, KS	8
Atlanta, GA	9
Shreveport, LA	10
Greenville-N.Bern-Washngtn, NC	11
Columbia, SC	12
Jackson, MS	13
Colorado Springs-Pueblo, CO	14
Charlotte, NC	15
Augusta, GA	16
Florence-Myrtle Beach, SC	17
Evansville, IN	18
Savannah, GA	19
Omaha, NE	20

Source: Monster internal data. 2007.

same period a year earlier (see Figure 8.6). However, customer-service job postings in Market A grew at an even greater 27 percent over the same period the year before (see Figure 8.7). While 27 percent growth might be cause for alarm, the rate of job postings to labor supply was low compared to other markets. This lower level of demand for customer-service representatives, along with other talent-related factors, reinforced the standing of Market A as a top consideration.

Figure 8.6. Job postings on Monster, 2004–2007.

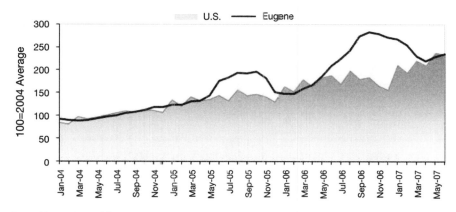

Source: Monster internal data.

Figure 8.7. Customer service and call center job postings on Monster, 2004–2007.

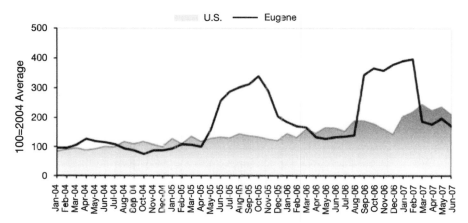

Source: Monster internal data.

Monster also analyzed the current economic trends related to customer-service and call-center occupations that could impact hiring for these critical occupations. Below are some key takeaways from the analysis at a national level, as well as for the key markets that were under consideration:

* As an industry, dedicated call centers had experienced a dip in employment over the past ten years. The last recession (2000–2002) hastened the automation and offshoring of traditional call-center services by a large contingent of American companies.

* By the end of 2004, there were approximately 2.1 million customer-service representatives employed in the United States, which was 1.5 percent of the overall workforce.

* Projected employment growth between 2004 and 2014 for the customer-service occupation was 23 percent greater than the average of all occupations (see Figure 8.8).

* The state of Arizona had the highest concentration of customer-service representatives—2.7 percent of total state employment.

* Market D had the highest job growth, indicating a strong local economy where new job opportunities were being created at a rapid pace.

* Market A's metropolitan area jobless rate had decreased to 4.7 percent in May 2007, down from 5.1 percent a year earlier (see Figure

Figure 8.8. Call center employment, 1997–2007.

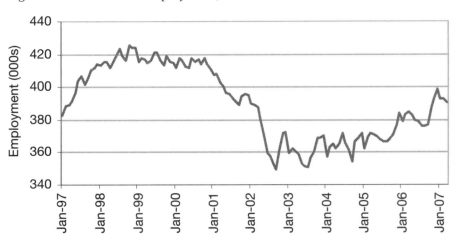

Source: Bureau of Labor Statistics, BLS.gov.

8.9). These numbers were considerably more favorable for recruiting compared to other markets under consideration. For example, at the time of the analysis, the Market D metropolitan area jobless rate was 3.0 percent.

* Market A was the weakest of the four markets short-listed by Enterprise in terms of job creation. Payroll in Market A grew 1.1 percent year over year in May 2007, which was slower than the U.S. rate as a whole (see Figure 8.10).

Monster also looked at the competition for customer-service talent. It identified companies that had existing call centers or were in the process of opening up such facilities in the considered markets. For example, Market E and Market F (which were within fifty miles of Market D) had become home to over 200 new customer-service centers. The competition and cost for talent in these markets were much higher than in other markets, and this would be a key influencer in Enterprise's decision. The favorable competitive situation in Market A, combined with many other factors, provided support for the recommendation that Enterprise select Market A as the location for its new customer contact center.

The Outcome

As a result of the thoughtful consideration of many factors, Enterprise selected Market A for its contact center. Enterprise chose that market

Figure 8.9. Unemployment rate, U.S. vs. Eugene-Springfield, Oregon.

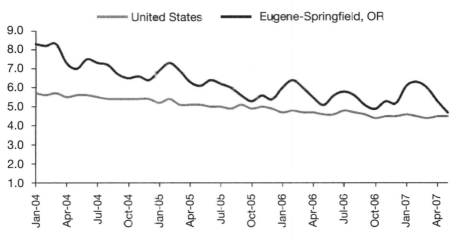

Source: Bureau of Labor Statistics, BLS.gov.

Figure 8.10. Growth in payroll employment, U.S. vs. Eugene-Springfield, Oregon.

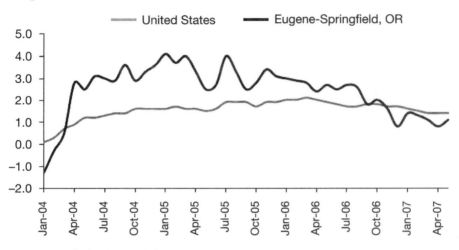

Source: Bureau of Labor Statistics, BLS.gov.

for several reasons, including a strong labor supply relative to demand. Enterprise also found Market A to be a good site because of its proximity to a university, which provides a consistent source of educated and skilled employees who have flexible schedules and need part-time opportunities. "The workforce here is great," said a local contact center director. "We're so lucky to be in a city where we have access to a skilled, educated work-force."

Enterprise chose a downtown location because of its business-friendly environment, great building, and accessibility to public transpor-tation. The contact center brings hundreds of people to work downtown, which means that more people are spending money in the downtown area and encouraging further development in the process.

As far as the recruitment strategy to staff this new branch, Enterprise focused on a workforce with a slightly different profile from its other call centers. To supplement its primarily full-time team, Enterprise worked with the university to make opportunities available that were flexible and appealing to the students. Having access to an educated, flexible work-force allows Enterprise to maintain balanced coverage at the contact center without having to outsource—a practice that is typical in this industry.

The contact center began taking calls for Enterprise in April 2008. Employees at the new center now handle more than 10,000 reservations and customer-service calls a day for Enterprise, National, and Alamo. The performance of the contact center has been outstanding, with high customer-resolution rates and high employee and customer satisfaction. The care and diligence that Enterprise exercised in analyzing all of the factors in selecting a site led to a successful site implementation and resulted in a desirable business outcome.

9

Predictive Management at Descon Engineering

Umair Majid and Ahmed Tahir

Descon Engineering Limited (DEL), a recognized multidimensional project management company operating in Pakistan and the Middle East, aims to become a world-class organization providing its customers with reliable and high-quality, yet economically viable, turnkey engineering and construction (E&C) solutions. DEL is part of the conglomerate named Descon, an association of legally independent companies integrated in a management relationship that operates under a common corporate identity, financial control, and ownership philosophy that is manifested in a distinct corporate culture. Descon, in its entirety, operates in engineering, chemical, trading, and power as its core businesses.

The service portfolio of DEL covers engineering, procurement, construction, maintenance, and manufacturing of process equipment for various sectors, including oil and gas, chemical, petrochemical, power, fertilizer, cement, and infrastructure. There are currently 5,000 management employees working with the company worldwide, and the company has seen exponential business growth in the last five years.

DEL is still moving up the value chain under the charismatic leadership of Abdul Razak Dawood, its founder. Once the managing director, he is now chairman of the conglomerate and is leading the company on its way to becoming world class.

Learning from the Past to Predict the Future

DEL now has a history that spans over thirty years, and during these years the company underwent various changes in strategy, structure, size, technology, workforce diversity, geographical locations, and business portfolio. Some of these changes were due to environmental factors and others were provoked by internal forces. The company also went through restructuring on various occasions. Major changes in the degree of centralization and decentralization were implemented three times. Each time, the organization learned new things, especially the ability to make proactive decisions and to achieve a balance between centralization and decentralization.

1986 Decentralization: The First Time

In 1986, DEL was a middle-size organization with a management staff of 300 and was operating in the domestic market. In fact, DEL was the leading Pakistani company in engineering and construction business. It had two major lines of business: construction (civil, mechanical, and electrical) and manufacturing. Each line had an executive director, and there was a managing director at the top. All staff functions, including human resources, finance, procurement, and store, were centralized. Though it was in the business of construction and manufacturing, the company did not have formal departments for handling quality assurance; quality control; or health, safety, and environment (HSE). Keeping his view of growing the business and foreseeing new projects, Dawood decided to delegate control.

Initially, the two functions of store and procurement were decentralized—that is, Construction would have its own Store and Procurement and Manufacturing would have its own. Much decision-making authority was passed down the line, aimed at increasing the efficiency of operations. It took just a couple of months to implement the decentralization because the change was made without a comprehensive environmental scan or a decentralization strategy. The resulting organization is shown in Figure 9.1.

However, within six months, Dawood realized that the change had been a mistake and that the time was not right for decentralization. The company began losing money, and the satisfaction level of its clients

Figure 9.1. Store and Procurement as decentralized functions.

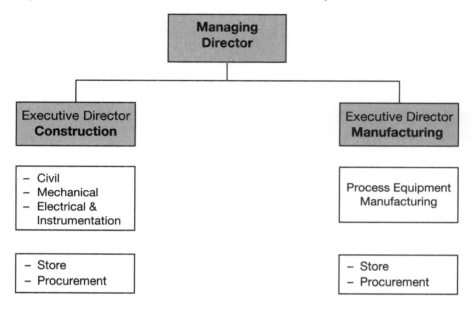

declined because of late completion of projects—a taboo in the project management industry. Dawood brought the centralized control back into place.

The reasons that the first decentralization failed were many. First, the decision regarding decentralization was based more on intuition and on perceptions of DEL's management rather than coming from an objective analysis of prevailing business conditions and company strengths and weaknesses. Second, the managers at the top of both business lines were not competent enough to deal with the dynamics of delegation and empowerment. Third, proper systems and procedures were not in place, causing widespread manipulation of authority, and were left uncorrected because of unclear control mechanisms. Fourth, people who were in decision-making roles were not properly trained to handle such a change in structure.

Although the first attempt at decentralization was not a success, lessons learned would be applied to future planning. For instance, the company would need to be more predictive and analytical in any transformation, instead of just fixing current problems and acting in response to immediate events. Processes would have to be improved and written rules needed to clearly outline the limits of authority and the division of responsibilities. Most important, the company would have to develop leaders who could manage the expected future growth.

The company worked with the same centralized structure for more than a decade. However, during this time capable people were sought for senior positions. This planning enabled the organization to manage its growth and prepare for decentralization when the time would be right.

1997–1999 Decentralization: The Second Time

Because of favorable business conditions especially for the construction sector, and because the company had a strong reputation in the region, DEL grew at a rapid rate in terms of business volume, profitability, size of the organization, market penetration, and geographical presence. A second attempt at decentralization was initiated in 1997, but this time the process was to be slow and careful.

In November 1999, Abdul Razak Dawood joined the government of Pakistan as Minister of Commerce, Industries and Production, and so he handed over control of DEL to Mazhar Ud Din Ansari, who would serve as the new managing director. Dawood became chairman of the company. Additionally, DEL had lately established an overseas business unit in Abu Dhabi, so as to enter the Middle East market. The second decentralization involved six areas: Civil, Mechanical, Electrical and Instrumentation, Plant Services, Manufacturing, and Abu Dhabi, as shown in Figure 9.2.

Decentralization was more successful this time because of management's more predictive and proactive approach. Many of the lessons from 1986's change effort were applied, which mitigated certain risks and avoided potential problems. The decentralization plan was put into operation only after a fair analysis of past problems, company capabilities, and environmental opportunities and threats There were now experienced and capable people in senior positions to assume responsibilities.

In the early 2000s, management decided to diversify the business portfolio, a plan that laid the foundation for today's Descon conglomerate. As part of this plan, the company established separate business areas in relation to the types of projects. For instance, a new business area named Infrastructure Projects Business Area (IPBA) was established to capture a share of Pakistan's growing market for large-scale civil infrastructure projects. The Plant Construction and Services Business Area (PC&SBA) was established to acquire and execute plant construction and plant maintenance (shutdown) projects. The Manufacturing Business Area, which dated to the 1980s, was revitalized as the leading supplier of process equipment to operating companies, global EPC contractors,

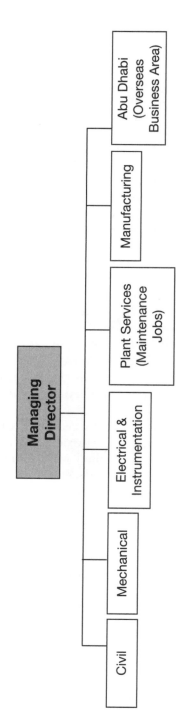

Figure 9.2. Six decentralized areas with one overseas business unit.

and original equipment manufacturers (OEMs) worldwide. (For definitions of *business area* and other relevant terms, see the following sidebar.)

Business Area

A business area (BA) in Descon Engineering Limited (DEL) is a significant organizational segment or division within the overall corporate identity, and is distinguishable from other business areas in the company because it serves a defined external market where management can conduct strategic planning in relation to its projects. BAs are managed as self-contained units for which discrete business strategies (in line with the company's overall strategy) are developed. BAs perform the line functions, are involved in core business processes of the company, and are aimed at generating revenue.

For example, at DEL, the Infrastructure Projects Business Area (IPBA) manages the mega civil-infrastructure projects like dams, barrages, and highways in the domestic market. The Plant Construction and Services Business Area (PC&S BA) covers a wide range of local plant construction and plant service projects. To cover plant construction and service projects in the Middle East, there are two major business areas: the Qatar Business Area (QBA) and the Abu Dhabi Business Area (UAE BA). The Descon Manufacturing Business Area (DMBA) provides project management services to its local and international clients in the area of process equipment manufacturing. To take care of turnkey projects, the Engineering Procurement Construction Business Area (EPC BA) has been established.

Business Support Department

A business support department (BSD) in DEL provides relevant support to the business areas—the line functions involved in core business processes of the company—to achieve their business goals. The nature of BSD work is advisory and supports the business organization, helping it work more efficiently and effectively. BSDs do not generate revenue; instead they are cost centers.

BSDs include Human Resource Development, Administration, Finance, Commercial, Business Development, Proposals Management, Information and Communication Technology, Quality Assurance/Quality Control, HSE (Health, Safety, Environment), and Contracts Management.

Joint Venture

A joint venture (JV) is an entity formed between Descon Engineering Limited and another company or organization to undertake business together in certain areas by capitalizing on the strengths of each other. Descon has, in total, four joint ventures: ODICO; JDC-Descon; Presson Descon International Limited (PDIL); and a training joint venture, TWI-Descon.

The company also expanded geographically at this time. After establishing its Abu Dhabi Business Area, it set up a new business area in Qatar. To complement its organizational expertise and facilitate its geographical presence in the world, the company entered joint ventures with three major organizations: Presson Enerflex (Canada), Olayan (Saudi Arabia), and JGC (Japan).

By virtue of its nature, a joint venture (JV) was operating as an autonomous body. The business areas were also autonomous to a great extent, though not fully independent of the head office. To support the core functions performed by these business areas, several staff functions (HR, Finance, Business Development, Proposals Management, and HSE) were formalized. Departments responsible for the staff functions were called BSDs (Business Support Departments)—Corporate. Looking at the business volume handled by each business area, management decided to decentralize the staff functions, too.

All did not go smoothly, however. Proper systems and procedures remained to be developed and people in leadership roles needed training to handle the affairs of this fast-growing organization. Also, future leaders needed to be identified and groomed from within the organization, as well as acquired from the job market, if the business were to continue to run efficiently and effectively.

In Abu Dhabi, business growth was too fast. DEL was awarded three major contracts, but the company lost a great deal of money on two of them and could only break even on the third one. The reason for this, according to the chairman, was that "the Finance and HR had weak control and that was because we did not have proper systems and procedures in place there. If you go for decentralization without having proper systems, you pay a price. And we paid a price."

2007 Onward: Creating a Balance Between Centralization and Decentralization

When there were some major incidents in 2005–2006, the warning indicators started blinking and DEL's management realized that something had gone wrong during the last decade that could prove to be fatal for the company.

In April 2007, when Shaikh Azhar Ali replaced Mazhar Ud Din Ansari as managing director of DEL, management started analyzing the situation. It didn't take long to realize that it had overdecentralized. Corporate had lost the string with which to tie the centralized control to the decentralized units. That is, it had given too much decision-making freedom to the business area heads, which had created a huge power imbalance. In the head office, the right hand did not know what the left hand was doing. For example, the Abu Dhabi Business Area had built a fabulous state-of-the-art process equipment manufacturing facility with the name ADWORK, incurring a huge capital expenditure without the head office's awareness. Even Corporate Finance, located at the head office, was unaware of it. There had been no approval from the head office and hence no approved budget. Corporate Finance didn't have monthly or quarterly financial reports. Things were going from bad to worse.

When the situation was analyzed in detail, management discovered several gray areas of control. For example, there was no established Division of Responsibilities (DOR) to support the functionality of a decentralized structure. Each business area was operating primarily within its own silo, at its own pace, resulting in nonintegrated outcomes. Corporate did not have control over business areas, and there were no proper checks and balances. The senior management in the business areas and business support departments had never been trained to manage business in a decentralized structure. There was a leadership drought at the business area level. Although there was a system for succession planning, namely the Executive Vitality Dash Board (later named the Management Evaluation Scheme, or MES), it was not implemented across the company. There were also a number of flaws in the succession system, and hence it was not producing the desired results. Also, Finance and HR had no control because they lacked proper systems and procedures. Like the business areas, HR was operating in a silo, under pressure to perform and concentrate on daily HR operations, with little attention to future scenarios.

Predictive Management Is Instituted at DEL

The stage was set for another restructuring. There were many lessons learned from the past two attempts, and management was willing to go the extra mile to get everything right this time. Primary here, management would become far more predictive. As Chairman Abdul Razak Dawood said, "I want this company to be in the category of 'built to last.'"

In July 2007, at a two-day forum for heads of Descon's business areas, business support departments, and joint ventures, there was discussion of the future direction for the company. Shaikh Azhar outlined the plans to a group that included business heads he had appointed after he had taken the reins. A large number of these heads had been promoted from within, which was a positive sign for the future.

In October 2007, at another forum, Azhar detailed the road-map for Descon:

> Organization design is to match organizational challenges. The management has decided to strengthen the business area organizations with the delegation of operational issues to operations managers. Business area heads are to focus on strategic planning, business development, HR, financial management, and systems implementations.
>
> As we move on to a higher level [in the value chain], we need to restructure our organization accordingly in order to meet the challenges. The structure of the organization has been a challenge for us. This time the degree of centralization versus decentralization is being finalized with clear divisions of responsibilities for providing the proper interface between BAs and BSDs—that is, Corporate.
>
> All policies are to be structured and developed at corporate level. All BAs have to follow corporate policies. No policy is to be developed at BA level. Corporate will audit BAs for compliance and implementation of corporate policies.
>
> BSDs' personnel seconded in the BAs are the extension of BSDs in the head office. Their selection, placement, and transfers are to be expedited by the BSD heads in consultation with the BA heads. Project Management Systems [a BSD for development and maintenance of the IT and project management systems across the company] will develop systems at corporate level and this process will be centralized. Policies at the BA level need to be

standardized. Currently, every BA follows its own practices and policies. Each BSD will define its vision, mission, objectives, and Division of Responsibilities.

In the past, all financial limits and powers were vested in Corporate Finance. We shifted this authority and transferred all financial powers from Corporate Finance to BAs, without defining any financial control and system. It was a big mistake and we have borne its consequences. We thus need to maintain equilibrium between BAs and Corporate Finance. A financial manual will be developed and finalized that will outline the guidelines on financial limits and the degree of decision making.

"Descon" in the years to come is to be promoted as a brand in our entire group of companies. Historically, the word refers to Descon Engineering, but now the time has come to project "Descon" first, rather than "Descon Engineering." There shall be more focus on transforming the company from an undisciplined organization to a disciplined and well-integrated one, working under one philosophy outlined by the head office.

At this point (in February 2008), Dr. Jac Fitz-enz—a pioneer and leading authority in the field of human capital measurement and predictability—was invited to assist the transformation by introducing the predictive management model and principles to DEL's senior management staff. A two-day training session, attended by the leading members of management at DEL, provided a platform for diagnosing the organization's strategic requirements and determining how predictability and human capital management initiatives could position the company on the way to becoming world class.

The session started with an analysis of external environmental forces (markets, competition, economy, business opportunities, globalization, technology, customers, suppliers, etc.) and internal factors (vision, brand, culture, systems, competencies, etc.). Responses on pre-training strategy questionnaires distributed to training participants, results of the environmental analyses, and the year's workforce intelligence report (WIR) provided the basis for an organizational review to identify areas where DEL needed realignment to sustain its competitive edge. Various approaches for workforce planning and evaluation of HR processes were discussed. Participants identified the missing links among functions of HR, establishing these missing as the major reason HR services had not been properly integrated. Finally, through predictive analysis, the group pinpointed various areas for improvement, named the major development initiatives, and formulated a customized strategic framework to implement the new model, HCM:21.

The Implementation of HCM:21

The Human Resources Development (HRD) function in the company was considered to be a weak BSD. To strengthen this function and transform its role from an operational department to a strategic business partner, Tahir Malik had earlier become head of HRD. Now, following the session with Dr. Fitz-enz, he realized he faced many challenges:

*   HR costs were rising, owing to a boom in construction and a burgeoning real estate sector in the Middle East.
*   Many other players were coming into the market, paying employees unsustainably high salaries, which DEL could not offer at the moment. Indeed, DEL was finding it difficult to attract star employees.
*   No career-growth paths and promotion criteria were defined, and as a result retention of key performers was proving to be a big challenge. There was no proper succession-planning process. Although a management evaluation scheme (MES) was available, it had never been implemented across the company and also had some flaws.
*   As most of the heads were new in their roles, they needed to acquire necessary general management skills in the shortest possible time. Yet, Descon hadn't focused on management training, and as a result it had incompetent people in top positions.
*   There was a drought in leadership at the middle level.
*   A proper employee training and development system was lacking.
*   Employee remuneration and benefits were not competitive, and they were inconsistent and not equally applied.
*   Perceptions in the organization about Descon's brand were inconsistent with those in the marketplace; a proper strategy for brand imaging and its communication was not available.

It was time to take a big leap forward—to implement HCM:21 in its true spirit. This model would transform HR from an administrative role to a strategic business partner. To begin, Tahir Malik started strengthening his team. The subfunctions of Corporate HRD were reorganized into Recruitment and Selection (R&S), Training and Development (T&D), Compensation and Benefits (C&B), and the newly incorporated function of Organizational Development. To carry out the change process in an appropriate and timely manner, Malik assigned responsibilities and ownership to relevant HR functional teams. Also, he established a DOR for defining the work relationship between Corporate HRD and the individual BAs' HR (called HRM, owing to its operational role) to ensure delivery of HR services efficiently and effectively.

With the vision of becoming the employer of choice, Malik instituted a number of initiatives to implement HCM:21.

Hiring Strategy Revitalization

In the past, the hiring strategy was reactive, and people were hired without linking the closure (demobilization) of existing projects with the initiation (mobilization) of new ones—that is, there was no comprehensive workforce induction planning in relation to future business requirements. The new and revitalized hiring strategy aimed at ensuring the preparation of a workforce induction plan so that hiring would be done only to match well-planned and approved organization charts.

Although promoting staff from within to fill higher and mission-critical positions was the priority, management also decided to hire "the best and the brightest" from the job market for positions that could not be filled from within; this would introduce best practices and bring new ideas into the company, hence challenging the status quo.

To cope with the shortage of talent, the Recruitment and Selection team explored new markets, including Southeastern Asian countries (Malaysia, Philippines, Korea, Indonesia and Vietnam), Eastern European countries (Romania, Czech Republic, Poland, and Ukraine), Central Asian states (Azerbaijan, Uzbekistan, Turkmenistan), and South Africa.

The range of appropriate recruitment sources was also widened, to include career Web portals, local and international headhunters, job advertisements in local and international magazines and newspapers, liaisons with top-notch universities and institutions for on-campus hiring, internal manpower data banks, employee referrals, and coordination with Descon's associated companies for cross-placement of human resources.

Establishment of a Training and Development System

The Training and Development function had not been carried out in any true sense of the term. Trainings were conducted in a haphazard way, usually on the recommendations of line managers. There was no system in place for identifying and analyzing the training needs of employees. As part of HCM:21's implementation, a proper Training and Development system was set up. Ten training processes were established, detailing roles and responsibilities, entry criteria, inputs, tasks, outputs, exit criteria, integration, and general guidelines. These processes included a training needs analysis, development of a training plan, trainers'/training institutes' assessment (pre-training) and selection, curriculum design and course customization, creation of or acquisition of training products, training program administration and logistical operations, informal training and other modes of employee learning and development, training effectiveness measurement, training material and data management, and training process improvement.

The Employee Development Programs

In relation to training and development needs, two comprehensive management development programs (MDPs) were designed. The first, MDP-1, was for junior managers, with the goal of enhancing their general management and administrative skills. The second, MDP-2, was for middle and senior managers, with the aim of enhancing their capacity of team-building, leadership, delegation, and change management.

For heads and top executives, an executive development program (EDP) consisting of various strategic courses was developed.

The Hire, Train, Develop, and Retain Program

An attempt at HR integration, the Hire, Train, Develop, and Retain Program (HTDRP), was developed with the aim of identifying top talent from a diverse group of quality universities and institutes (both local and international), then orienting and training these individuals in the company's business processes and systems, developing and updating a competitive remuneration package, and making and implementing a viable retention strategy for retaining this talent. The program was an integrated framework that combined the efforts of all functional areas of HRD.

As a result, well-planned batches of fresh graduates were hired and trained, both at the company level and at the BA level. Major training programs administered under HTDRP included the Graduate Engineers Training Program (company level), Certified QA/QC Engineers (company level), Certified HSE Engineers (company level), and Project Engineers Leadership Program (BA level, for strengthening the EPC business area).

The In-House Faculty Development Program

This corporate-level program was designed to build the organizational capacity for administering in-house training programs designed and delivered by in-house trainers—that is, Descon employees. There were certain training programs that could only be designed (or customized), delivered, and evaluated by in-house trainers—for instance, programs based on Descon's business processes, project management systems trainings, and in-house knowledge-sharing sessions. Also, for a large organization like Descon Engineering Limited, conducting trainings in-house, by internal trainers, was usually cost-effective. The in-house trainers covered topics ranging from project management, general management, and interpersonal skills, to application area trainings and project environmental issues. The train-the-trainer programs were conducted to identify and groom potential in-house trainers.

Analysis of Organizational Climate, Culture, and Attitudes

To study employees' opinions on the quality of their work climate, and for identifying areas for improvement, the Organizational Development function designed a climate survey. The results were compiled and presented to management, and various recommendations that ensued included revising HR policies and procedures. Also, a number of employee motivation and engagement initiatives were taken—for example, the Descon family gala, Descon annual dinner, employee sports programs, Outward Bound team-building programs, and the *Descon Lounge* (a monthly in-house publication for employee participation).

Salary Surveys and Pay Restructuring

Because of a highly diversified business portfolio and an overdecentralized business past, there was inconsistency in pay structures across the company. To bring internal equity and justice in compensation and benefits, the company hired a third party to distribute salary surveys and conduct informal salary reviews. The existing pay structure was revised, with careful consideration of internal and external factors. Indeed, this was one of the biggest HR achievements, as it provided the baseline for employee retention.

Branding Communications

Any communications problems concerning branding had long been ignored. To correct this situation, a proper strategy for both brand imaging and its communication was developed. Some salient features of DEL's branding communication strategy included:

* Centralization of brand management, and establishment of one consistent policy across the company.

* Standardization of the company's positioning statements, logos, taglines, etc. For example, the company's positioning statement with respect to customer services was "Partners in Progress"; with respect to HR, the tagline was "Becoming the Employer of Choice."

* Preparation of a Descon Brand Book for providing standard branding communication guidelines in the company.

* In-house brand awareness sessions held to bring consistency to brand perceptions both inside and outside the organization.

* New employees onboarded regarding branding—making Descon brand awareness an essential part of their orientation.

* Encouraging continual thought for future branding opportunities.

Use of HR Metrics

Although HR metrics related to all the functional areas had been developed in the past, they were never implemented with a result-oriented approach. The training session on Descon human capital management, however, proved helpful in revamping and implementing HR metrics. These metrics included:

HR expense percentage
External cost per hire
Internal cost per hire
External time to fill
Internal time to fill
Cost per trainee
Employee trained percentage
Training cost per hour
Internal training hours percentage
External training hours percentage
Compensation expense percentage
Compensation factor
Separation rate

Most important, impact data against these and other HR metrics were collected and analyzed on a regular basis, and reports were generated. The implications and patterns identified in the reports helped HR revise and develop new HR strategies and policies.

Implementation of Enterprise Resource Planning

To manage the growth of the company and provide a centralized control mechanism, management conducted a preliminary investigation (an initial feasibility study) for implementation of an enterprise resource plan (ERP). Then, management contracted one of the most reputable ERP solution providers to integrate the systems, not only within HR but also to connect HR with other functions and systems in the company.

The Management Evaluation Scheme

The biggest challenge for Tahir Malik was to give the company a proper succession-planning process. He decided to improve on the existing management evaluation scheme (MES) and implement it throughout the company.

The main objective of the MES is to enable the company to maintain the team that can lead it and its BAs to superior performance, in terms of both quality and quantity, by providing an effective and continuous supply of human resources. Company chairman Abdul Razak Dawood, during his address to the Descon HR Forum 2008, highlighted the importance of MES for the company:

> Why is MES important? [The real question is] Do we have leaders who will take the corporation to a much higher level than where it is today and who will take care of the company? MES is the only hope. That is why it is important. We must have a hundred people we can look to in order to choose leaders for tomorrow who will be leading our engineering, power, and chemical businesses.
>
> The matter is worrisome. It is top management's responsibility to identify the future leaders for the company and groom them. HRD will have to play a key role. For example, have you [HR people] evaluated a person properly before selecting him? Suppose we have to choose a horse to send to the Derby race in England. We will properly assess and evaluate the horse. Now,

that's only a horse. But [in our case] it's the human being—God's creation with all the complexities. If you include a person in the bench strength [for MES] who shouldn't be there, or miss a person from bench strength who should be included, you are not being fair to the company. It's not easy to evaluate people, HR! It's your *job* to evaluate. Similarly, what you hear throughout the year about your employee—his strengths and weaknesses—[you should] note it down and put it in his file, so that when the evaluation time comes, this information can help.

The whole process of MES was revised and standardized. A career anchor questionnaire, level identification criteria, and succession-planning criteria were developed. A benchmark was set to categorize employees in five different levels according to their performance and potential for growth:

* *Level I:* High Potential–High Performance. Ready now to take the higher position.
* *Level II:* High Potential–High Performance. Shall be ready in two to three years to take the higher position.
* *Level III:* Fit for Purpose. Understands and performs his or her job very well, but can't take the higher responsibility.
* *Level IV:* Concerns. Performance seldom meets expectations; appropriate training and guidance are required.
* *Level V:* Exit. Lack of commitment, no potential for improvement, and therefore notice of intent to separate would be required.

The objectives in categorizing the employees in these levels were to let the employees know where they stood vis-à-vis other employees and how the company ranked them; to develop career paths for Level I and II employees, which would develop them into future leaders; to enable the company to determine appropriate programs for employee development, with special focus on successor development; and to ensure focus on succession planning at all the levels.

After putting everything in place, in July 2008, the MES was implemented organization-wide. Management was clear about its taking some time to mature and produce what Descon needed. And after this successful implementation, management had the names of individuals who were the High Potentials and a means for developing their talent so they could assume leadership roles in the future. Every BA and BSD had its succession plan for mission-critical positions along with the bench strength. By integrating all the BA and BSD succession plans, corporate management had a company-wide succession plan. The gray areas—where there was a leadership drought—were identified and strategies were formulated to water those areas.

When MES 2009 was initiated, the last year's MES review was conducted. The review revealed that 30 percent of the career moves (planned in 2008) were successfully implemented. About 80 percent of the MES-based training needs had been addressed. Most of the mission-critical positions, like project managers, construction managers, planning managers, and process engineers, had been filled with the successors identified through MES.

MES 2009 was an improved version of the original scheme, and it was also implemented in two of Descon's joint ventures: JGC-Descon and Presson Descon International Limited. More important, the MES for BSD staff residing in the BAs was consolidated and presented to the managing director by the respective BSD heads. This was an encouraging example of process ownership and the BSD heads' onboarding with an HR process.

The Way Forward

Implementation of the HCM:21 model has helped DEL position itself on the track toward world-class engineering, manufacturing, and construction. However, the journey has just started, and the desired outcomes of these initiatives are only just emerging. According to Chairman Abdul Razak Dawood:

> Things are getting better now. [For instance] MES is better than what it was last year. In 2010, it will be much better than what it is today. Rotation policy is about to be fully implemented. To me, the most important thing is "to put the company in a position where it can become world class." We need to go further; we need to improve the systems; and for that, we don't want our people to become complacent, because the road to success is always under repair.
>
> If the next chairman, managing director, and BA and BSD heads are no better than the existing ones, we have not done our

job. A few days back, I sent an e-mail to my executives that, in Vietnam, a wonderful business opportunity was emerging. But I asked them to forget about it because I didn't think we were ready to take it on. The good news is, we are not growing too fast. So we have time to get ready.

CHAPTER TEN

Working a Mission-Critical Problem in a Federal Agency

Jac Fitz-enz

A federal agency that I will identify as Research Economic Services (RES) has been chartered by the U.S. Congress to conduct what industry would call "competitor intelligence." This phrase implies that the agency should gather data on foreign countries that include economic, military, political, cultural, and other factors. The data are then formatted for a variety of purposes and distributed to many federal departments and agencies.

RES has been criticized in recent years for the quality, timeliness, and cost of its services. It has undergone studies by the General Accounting Office, Inspector General, House Select Committees, and outside consultancies, all of which were looking for solutions to these problems. In the fall of 2008, Human Capital Source (HCS) met with representatives of RES to discuss how the principles of predictive management (our HCM:21 model) might be applied to this situation.

The Human Resources Systems

RES is staffed by a combination of civilian and military personnel. It also contracts with outside research service providers. Civilian and military systems of RES personnel are dissimilar in several ways that make performance measurement a crippling problem. For instance, pay plans are different for the civilian and military personnel. Personnel development operates on two different principles, in that military personnel receive a great deal of formal training whereas civilian personnel more likely grow through on-the-job experience, or what some call "scar tissue." They do receive technical training.

In addition, there is no objective measure of organizational success or failure. The absence of a dependent variable makes standard statistical analysis extremely difficult, if not impossible. During our background research for this assignment, we were told that some RES projects succeeded or failed for reasons outside of its personnel's control. This was not a face-saving excuse; it turned out to be true in a number of cases. The bottom line was that the problems could not be solved solely through changes in HR systems or even management's behavior. The history of RES's formation had saddled it with inherent structural inhibitors that could be cured only through political means. Nevertheless, we believed that some improvements were possible if we could find a way to set a quasi-dependent variable and correlate the behaviors and processes with it.

Project Manager as Mission Critical

The most mission-critical position in RES is that of project manager (PM). Typically, projects are multiyear in length and involve use of advanced technology, some of which must be developed along the way. To make matters worse, PMs do not always see a project through from beginning to end. This is particularly true of the military cadre, whose assignments usually are no more than four years before they return to their service parent.

Owing to the complexity of a project's communication, employee commitment, ongoing engagement, personnel development, and retention are all conundrums. One of the previous studies identified organizational structure as an inhibitor. The HR function was charged with improving its systems to offset at least some of the organizational restraints.

The challenge was to find specific actions—that is, policy changes, training and development, interventions, performance management systems—that could be linked to project improvements. Absent quantitative objectives, we had to specify some visible, measurable antecedents, which hypothetically would drive improvements.

Creating a Target

Analytic work normally requires a goal or target, or a dependent variable against which one can relate many interactive variables. For example, it is expected that successful performance is measureable in terms of individual or group actions. When there are no past or current quantitative performance targets, it is difficult, if not impossible, to link action to result at the project level. Lacking that target, what can be done to assess success?

As a starting point, our HCS team decided to create a surrogate dependent variable that we labeled "organizational effectiveness" (OE). It was hypothesized that if we were able to link the interactive variables to certain objective points within OE we could at least move forward with concrete recommendations. The OE target was defined as follows: A successful project (SP) is a function of organizational effectiveness. In turn, OE results from the interaction of facilitating (F) and inhibiting (I) organizational, technological, and human (individual) variables.

Specifically, the key terms were:

* *Organization* (Org): Processes, systems, policies, and structures related to project manager talent management
* *Technology* (Tech): Project manager knowledge and ability to manage state-of-the-art investigative technology
* *Human* (Hum): Attraction, deployment, compensation, development, and retention of talent

Expressed as an equation, we had:

$$SP = f\,(OE)$$
$$OE = f\,[(OrgF + OrgI) + (TechF + TechI) + (HumF + HumI)]$$

The Analytic Process

The HCS staff met first with the HR managers to be briefed in detail. From these meetings in early 2009 a study plan was designed. It was to consist of a data-gathering phase that started with personal interviews of all key management personnel, including the director and deputy director and outside individuals who had past personal experience with RES. This entailed nearly thirty initial contacts, with some follow-up clarifying discussions.

Based on the data from the interviews, HCS designed a survey instrument that would be given to and responded by approximately 250 management personnel in the agency. Also, a document review was done of studies and reports on RES from the past ten years, and this review included forty-two documents of considerable length. When stacked one upon another, the pile was nearly a foot high. After all data collection was completed, we applied statistical procedures to discern the meanings and relationships between interview and survey data. These results were compared to data gleaned from the document review.

The lack of a dependent variable made it impossible to carry out normal quantitative predictive analysis at the individual level. Using standard statistical programs, we could not tie independent variables such as training, tenure, parent organization, education, performance management, or several other factors to a successful project. Nevertheless, we were able to find strong correlations between the beliefs of various knowledgeable groups on personal characteristics, training, and on-the-job experiences of those judged to be successful PMs. We cross-correlated the views from military and civilian personnel and from individuals at three levels of management, as shown in Figure 10.1.

Survey results showed a high level of belief that success as a PM depended on three competencies:

* Leadership
* Integrity
* Decisiveness

On the matter of work experience, on-the-job experience—working up from small to large projects—was deemed to be the best predictor of success. Formal organizational training was viewed as useful but not critical. This could be, in part, because there is no discernable career path to PM. Mentoring was also seen as useful but, for the same reason, not as critical. Responses were consistent also across gender, age, education, and total experience (inside and outside RES). When we ran a three-cluster solution across the categories of organization, supervisory level, and RES experience, the results were the same.

What this told us was that the opinions across groups were similar. This was a surprise to management, however. Because of the outside criticism that RES had received, there was a feeling that the organization was breaking apart. Yet while there were certainly differences on some topics in various groups, we found more similarity than difference.

In total, the process took six months. A report was submitted, and subsequently a briefing was delivered to top management.

Figure 10.1. Agency and supervisory-level comparisons.

	Agency		Supervisory Status		
	Military	**Civilian**	**Non-Supervisors and Team Leaders**	**Supervisors**	**Managers and Executives**
Attributes	Leadership	Leadership	Leadership	Leadership	Leadership
	Integrity	Integrity	Integrity	Integrity	Integrity
	Decisiveness	Decisiveness	Decisiveness	Decisiveness	Decisiveness
	Delegation	Coordination	Coordination	Coordination	Courage
	Coordination			Courage	Delegation
Training and Experience	Experience in Acquisitions	Experience in Project Management	Experience in Project Management	Experience in Project Management	Experience in Project Management
	Experience in Project Management	Experience in Acquisitions	Experience in Acquisitions	Experience in Acquisitions	Experience in Acquisitions
			Acquisitions Training		

Findings and Recommendations

In order to predict with precision what makes a successful PM, any HR operation needs dependent variables at the individual, group, and organizational level, as mentioned earlier. This means that RES needed to develop a measurement system that functions at three levels: strategic, operational, and future focused. Specifically, it must:

* Clearly articulate strategic imperatives, link operating objects to those strategic imperatives, and develop a set of leading indicators to keep the organization focused on emerging trends and requirements.

* Allow for quantitative analysis of individual performance.

The outcome measures to accomplish this needed to be both short- and long-term. Short-term measures would require a dedicated effort to determine the conditions, goals, and dependencies of success in selected projects. The measures would identify fundamental processes, stages, and outcomes. Long-term measures would create a composite variable for a successful project: ratings of on-time, on-budget, and on-spec. Each rating would be weighted and combined to form a successful project state. A composite variable would then be assigned to each individual working on a project.

Conclusions and Lessons Learned

At the point of this writing, the RES management has not decided what to do with the findings. As mentioned, politics play a major role in this case. Persons in superior positions have not determined the long-term fate, design, or role of the agency.

As for HR situations in which dependent variables do not exist and there are apparent differences of opinion, there is, nonetheless, no need to concede that improvements cannot be identified and implemented. As General George Patton said, "A good plan today is better than a perfect plan tomorrow." "Analysis paralysis" has killed many a good idea. There are seldom as many valid data as one would like for making decisions. Nevertheless, as the saying goes, when confronted with lemons, make lemonade. That is, surrogate dependent variables can be constructed and tested. Where there is a will to change and improve, analytic techniques— some standard and some innovative—can be applied to advantage. The goal is not extreme precision but, rather, improved operations.

CHAPTER ELEVEN

UnitedHealth Group Leverages Predictive Analytics for Enhanced Staffing and Retention

Judy Sweeney

Within the health-care industry, it's safe to say that the human resources (HR) challenges can be as complex as they are numerous. While health-care organizations share many of the same staffing concerns as other types of industries, certain variables are unique to this sector. Indeed, the issue of hiring and retention in the health-care industry is a major concern because of a shortage of qualified medical personnel such as nurses. In addition, the 24/7, year-round nature of the industry creates unique full-time and part-time employment problems that need to be solved.

In addition, the high-stress nature of the profession means that the HR department needs to be particularly prepared when creating retention strategies. Many HR departments, however, still operate in silos, separated and largely disengaged from other corporate functions. This situation, combined with the challenges of staffing shortages, aging staff populations, and increasing demands for services, often leaves health-care organizations plagued with turnover, performance, and budgetary issues.

Health-Care HR for the Twenty-First Century

The challenge facing the health-care industry is to streamline and optimize its HR management while maintaining high-quality patient care. A solid human capital management strategy is needed to emphasize staffing, recruitment, and retention. This includes monitoring and tracking the requisite metrics to tackle staffing shortages, tighter government regulations, and intense competition for top professional talent. To meet these HR needs, successful firms in the health-care sector are looking to dramatically improve their technology processes. This search includes ways to leverage the benefits of predictive metrics so as to prioritize goals and align current actions with future objectives.

What Is Predictive Analytics?

Predictive analytics is a method for leveraging business intelligence (BI) tools such as data mining and statistics to make predictions of future events. The predictive analytical model enables HR departments to be more proactive and agile in identifying unexpected staffing and performance opportunities and to anticipate problems before they happen. In effect, by using the predictive analytics model in day-to-day HR operations, health-care companies can be more effective in running the business of talent.

As a leading health-care organization, UnitedHealth Group (UHG) is one such company using predictive analytics to improve care and HR concerns in an increasingly challenging environment. Today, UHG is one of the largest health-care operators in the United States, with access to more than 340,000 physicians and 3,200 hospitals, and whose policyholders submit tens of thousands of health claims and related documents daily. UHG's mandate is to combine outstanding clinical insight with consumer-friendly services and advanced technology to help people achieve optimal health.

To this end, the company consists of five distinct business segments and offers services ranging from network-based health-care coverage for small, medium, and large companies; to global drug development and marketing services for the pharmaceutical and biotech industries; to investment capital for start-up and early stage companies that operate in the areas of health and well-being.

According to Michelle Fernando, Manager, International Recruitment Operations, the company faces many human capital management challenges in today's health-care environment. These include improving the quality of care and patient satisfaction while decreasing costs in an environment where hiring is an ongoing concern.

Workforce performance management, or recruiting, hiring, and retaining top talent, can significantly enhance health-care financial and operational performance. Therefore, UHG determined that migrating to a talent-management software solution that leveraged predictive metrics would be the best solution for its HR—and company performance—requirements. For example, across its international locations and businesses, HR managers were all reporting recruitment metrics differently, leading to a need for greater data consistency. Not only was there an overlap of work being done, but there was also an excess number of reports trying to capture the needs of each business partner.

In UHG's example, the company sought to improve its internal hiring processes on a global scale. This includes increasing international focus on employee hires. In the case of the company's India offices, the firm needed to increase its internal hiring percentages.

"The recruiting culture in India is very volatile; career opportunities and turnover rates are very high in a highly specialized health-care industry. It's a unique business with specific skill sets. It was a challenge for us to engage the employees, keep them happy, and give them reasons to stay," says Fernando. "In these offices in particular, we were looking for innovative ways to boost internal hiring percentages to improve overall staff retention. Using analytics helped us get a handle on the issues and gave us clear ways to measure and improve our processes."

UHG as a fast-growing organization must continuously recruit large numbers of candidates. UHG needed to come up with a consistent approach to measure the quality of hires. How were the qualifications, skills, knowledge, and experience of new hires meeting expectations as compared to initial requirements, as well as assessing time to productivity, department and organizational fit, staff turnover rates, and overall quality of hire? Simply put, the organization needed a more effective way to identify and diagnose its situation and in turn to make improvements in these areas. "HR reports were also done manually and requests were taking too long to fulfill. This was translating into increasing costs, inconsistent business information, and reduced productivity," says Fernando.

Developing a Talent Management Strategy

Wanting to quickly address its business challenges and streamline its HR and workforce performance processes, UHG worked with talent-management solution provider Taleo to develop and deploy a new technology environment that leverages metrics to help companies be more predictive, thus making better business decisions and creating stronger career-pathing solutions for new and existing staff.

Specifically, UHG is using the Taleo Enterprise Edition to enhance its talent management processes for HR managers and employment candidates. Taleo is an on-demand, Software as a Service (SaaS) solution that is ideal for complex global companies like UHG. "The goal was to leverage technology to provide data-driven information on our staffing processes to identify opportunity areas and make improvements. The Taleo-based talent-management platform has helped us to streamline HR processes and analytics to better identify qualified candidates and improve the overall quality of hire," says Fernando.

UHG used the Taleo platform to develop its International Recruitment Operations Dashboard, a self-service interactive Web 2.0 portal that allows staff at UHG to easily view and download relevant HR information. In order to ensure that the right resources and skills are available to execute a successful hiring and retention strategy, UHG is using a technology platform that helps capture the desired job knowledge metrics and requirements and match them to the skills, competencies, and knowledge of the candidates—all from a centralized global database. This is accomplished using four key metrics or measurements: quality of hire, source of hire, percentage of internal hires, and system utilization. These metrics enable them to ensure competent, qualified staff and high staff-retention rates.

For example, the "quality of hire" measurement is crucial for United-Health Group to determine that the employees hired are the right people and a good fit from a cultural, productivity, and experience perspective. This system also helps the company reduce the number of "quick quits" and improve employee retention—helping to keep staff engaged because they are a better fit in the first place. Thus, new hires are more prone to develop high-quality relationships with their peers, and UHG has seen a reduction in first-year attrition rates.

In terms of "source of hire," having a centralized database allows the company to more easily streamline its global hiring practices by being able to trace back to the original source to weed out poor recruitment practices and firms. For example, the system now allows the organization to track and monitor data such as the specific career fairs or organizations that have provided a successful candidate in the past.

"Using a predictive analytical model, we can better analyze the employers that people came from and the sources we hired from. As a result, we can determine if there's a specific company that has a high percentage of quality of hires and we then know that that's a company we may want to target. In terms of sourcing and recruitment, this is useful information for us, as it may lead to better hires in the future," says Fernando.

The Measure of HR Success

By using predictive analytics and having metrics available on a global scale, UHG is now better equipped to improve the quality of hire and staff retention worldwide. "Quality of hire is important for us. Having access to this data allows us to predict workers who are a better fit for the organization and become more productive quicker. We are now able to leverage our data and make stronger business decisions," says Fernando.

To improve HR staffing processes, HR developed a central reporting portal for all international reports. This enables staff to leverage predictive metrics and access a single set of global reports that can be filtered as necessary to allow for a consistent set of data from one region or organization to another.

Users, for instance, can access the International Recruitment Operations Dashboard directly through an online interface that features detailed report information, including location, organization, business segment, and job function. The dashboard is refreshed on a daily basis, allowing users to have access to the most up-to-date HR data across the organization. This means that recruitment metrics are now more accurate and consistent across the organization. As the solution is hosted online, the new reporting model requires minimal maintenance from UnitedHealth Group's International Recruitment Operations team. In addition, with the improved reporting and analytics tools, UnitedHealth Group can better target areas for improvement throughout the staffing process.

For dashboard reports, each metric has a description and a benchmark goal, and all metrics have a link to the detailed report where the measure originated. This enables management to better determine staffing costs, staffing cycle times, and overall productivity. For example, the organization now has a more detailed skills-based candidate relationship database. It allows for better capture skills, ability, and experience in a central database for both active and passive candidates with self-service profiles. In fact, the organization conducted a user survey in its Asia Pacific region, where 93 percent responded that the dashboard was easy to navigate and 86 percent said that the detailed reports were easy to understand.

Ultimately, the talent-management platform in place at UnitedHealth Group is helping the organization to significantly improve its recruitment and retention processes in order to boost its financial and operational performance. Technology tools help organizations like UHG to break down silos, streamline operations, and allow workers to have centralized, real-time access for mission-critical information and transactional data. "We really needed to be more methodical and analytical about our use of HR technology," says Fernando. "The enhancements we have made help UnitedHealth Group to better analyze employee turnover trends and the effects of this turnover throughout our entire organization."

PART 4

IV

Looking Forward

CHAPTER TWELVE

Look What's Coming Tomorrow

> "Success is to be measured not so much by the position that one has
> reached in life as by the obstacles which he has overcome."

—BOOKER T. WASHINGTON

The theme from the start of this book has been that of managing tomorrow today. More explicitly, this book is about human capital management for the twenty-first century, as developed in our model, HCM:21. I've shown how this model of predictive management is built around the tools of human capital analytics. Several practitioners and thought leaders have shared their experience with you, as well. By now you should have a clear idea of what human capital analytics is and how you can use it to build a more effective human resources function or business unit in your organization. In every organization, regardless of function, it is people who produce its product or service. By applying these principles and tools, you will be helping build the competitive position of your company or, in the case of nonprofits, contribute to its organizational effectiveness.

What We Know About Tomorrow

Without attempting to be a fortune-teller, I can state with a high degree of confidence that the *new normal* will be notable for:

* A market of intense competition
* A workforce quite different from that of the last quarter of the twentieth century

* Technological advances that hit at a speed you will find difficult to assimilate
* Political upheavals that will affect business in many parts of the world
* A continuation of terrorism threats that raise the general level of tension
* Structural changes in the way corporations are organized

All this will make managing a large organization an extremely difficult task. It will be a challenge that will demand not only better data collection and information management but also a quantum leap into business intelligence founded on hard evidence and statistical analysis. Organizations that aspire to market leadership will have no choice but to manage predictively. The days of buying vendor packages without doing a thorough analysis of both internal and external conditions are rapidly coming to a close. That's because when managers aren't good communicators, a new performance management software package won't make them better, especially if they don't want to or know how to talk to people. Packages cannot give you competitive advantage, for a very simple reason: Whatever you can buy anyone else can buy also. And management is still a person-to-person phenomenon.

What Analytics Can Deliver for Your Organization

High-risk decisions have to be made under circumstances that are seldom crystal clear. For example, what actions are necessary to retain mission-critical talent under certain market conditions? Would you select incentive compensation, challenging assignments, work-life balance, or rapid promotions? What data do you have to support such a critical future decision? If the mission-critical population is large and geographically dispersed, and the technology or customers are changing, who can say which action will have the highest success rate? And can you afford to be wrong? Certainly, relying on the past to predict the future is the summit of stupidity.

Software vendor SPSS points out the advantages of predictive analytics:

1. *Get a higher return on your data investment.* Predictive analytics combines information on what has happened in the past, what is happening now, and what's likely to happen in the future to give you a complete picture of your situation.

2. *Find hidden meaning in your data.* Predictive analytics enables you to uncover hidden patterns, trends, and relationships and transform these into action

3. *Look forward, not backward.* Use the data you already have to help you anticipate future events, and be predictive rather than reactive.

4. *Deliver intelligence in real time.* With predictive analytics, you can automatically deploy analytical results and act as changes occur.

5. *See your assumptions in action.* Advanced analytics tools help you develop hypotheses, test them, and choose the scenario most likely to give you the desired results.

6. *Mitigate risk.* Predictive analytics helps you evaluate risk using a combination of business rules, predictive models, and past employee actions, thus minimizing exposure to unforeseen events.

7. *Discover unexpected opportunities.* You can use predictive analytics to respond with greater speed and certainty to emerging challenges and opportunities.

8. *Guarantee your organization's competitive advantage.* With predictive analytics, you drive improved performance in all operational areas. When your organization runs more efficiently, you have what it takes to outthink and outperform your competitors.

Thought Drives Action

The companies that have leapfrogged the market have done so not by buying "packaged solutions" but by gaining insights into opportunities that others either did not see or did not have the courage to realize. Amazon, Avon, Federal Express, McDonald's, Nucor, Sony, Swatch, Volkswagen, and other trailblazers capitalized on disruptive technologies to change their markets. In doing so, they set the pace for others, forcing the laggards to scramble and try to catch up.

Thomas Alva Edison allegedly had a sign in his office that said: "It is remarkable how far some people will go to avoid thought." And that says it all about the potential for your organization. *Thought drives action.* Buying prepackaged HR programs will keep you in the back of the pack. Our predictive management model, HCM:21, vaults you over your talent-war competitors, who are busy putting patching on their old organizational models. HCM:21 will lead your organization into a new realization of human capital management.

Still Evolving

Over the past thirty-plus years we have evolved human capital measurement from transactional metrics through benchmarking and descriptive analytics to predictability. But we are not finished. The next stage, soon to be written, is data integration.

The leading practitioners of human capital metrics tie HR services to some organizational outcome. They may link it to changes, positive or negative, in operating processes, customer behavior, or financials. This is how they show value added. It is the goal toward which we have been striving over these last three decades.

Once this is completed, never again will people be seen as an expense. Human resources services and programs will be viewed and managed as investments. In the best of cases accounting will be able to capitalize at least some HR services as future value-building investments. This will profoundly shift the perception of employees in the direction of being assets and of human resources services as essential business tools. It will be up to HR professionals to demonstrate that they can operate accordingly. If they cannot, I foresee the department's being split into governance services reporting to the CFO and business services reporting to the COO, with IT taking over HR data management.

Now we are engaged in expanding those admirable one-off efforts into a data-integration methodology. Just as we did with the Predictive Initiative, we have organized a consortium to apply data mining and advanced statistics to build a tool that will support organizations' attempts to make connections between human capital and the functional outcomes of the enterprise on a regular basis. Figure 12.1 shows this new vision.

VIEWS OF THE FUTURE: HUMAN CAPITAL ANALYTICS

I've asked a number of bright people with whom I have had the pleasure to work over the years to share their insights into the future of human capital analytics—good *and* bad. These people have not been afraid to think. Pay attention to them.

◆ ◆ ◆ ◆

Figure 12.1. *Data integration: linkages and feedback.*

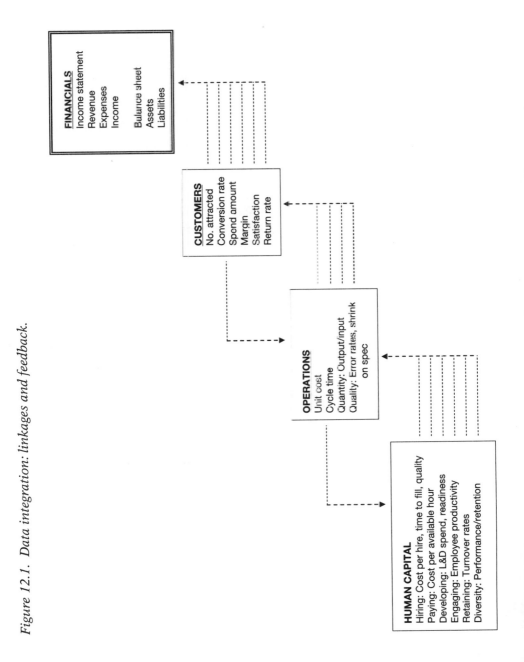

FINANCIALS
Income statement
Revenue
Expenses
Income

Balance sheet
Assets
Liabilities

CUSTOMERS
No. attracted
Conversion rate
Spend amount
Margin
Satisfaction
Return rate

OPERATIONS
Unit cost
Cycle time
Quantity: Output/input
Quality: Error rates, shrink on spec

HUMAN CAPITAL
Hiring: Cost per hire, time to fill, quality
Paying: Cost per available hour
Developing: L&D spend, readiness
Engaging: Employee productivity
Retaining: Turnover rates
Diversity: Performance/retention

TIM MACK
President, World Future Society

Out of this group of prognosticators, I am probably the one with the least HR experience. However, it is clear that Jac Fitz-enz and the colleagues who have contributed to this book are thinking seriously about where HR and human resources analysis should be heading.

More reliable and relevant qualitative metrics will assist in bridging the gap between the HR professional and senior management. The most critical element here is *relevance*. Reliability can be easily demonstrated, but it is the ability to cross the disconnect in emphasis and experience that is critical—that is, to *translate* the metrics concerning human capital into a management frame that resonates with the stakeholders—and that top managers must effectively integrate to keep "their doors open." In this instance, combining overview with storytelling by practitioners lends authenticity and reality to observations about new directions. Interfacing quantitative and qualitative thinking is critical, and this is the direction that the field needs to move in—to speak to both the head and the heart. Finally, "collapsing the silos" is a necessary goal, but a challenging one. The barriers between functions are often seen as beneficial and protective, and are usually well defended. Nevertheless, it is essential that organizations speak with one voice.

DAVID ULRICH
Professor, University of Michigan

Decisions based on evidence are more accurate, sustainable, and trustworthy. Often in the "soft" field of individual and organization capabilities, we rely on instinct rather than evidence. While leaders with many years of cumulative experience may have great instincts, too often novices or new leaders have instincts that are not grounded in experience. Evidence-based management is basically the manifestation of accumulated experience. By translating many unique experiences into databases, leaders can begin to see patterns that drive informed decisions. Most leaders would not make product decisions based on feelings alone; rather, they use data based on how different product features meet or do not meet customer expectations. We should expect no less from people analytics.

First, to produce better people analytics, we need to do a more rigorous job describing what is done. The field of psychology has developed standards for what characterizes soft psychological states in its *Diagnostic and Statistical Manual* (DSM)—for example, states of depression, anxiety, or obsessive compulsive are defined in behavioral and operational terms. Similarly, HR needs to create generally accepted and more rigorous descriptions of HR practices.

Second, with clear definitions, HR can identify the antecedents and consequences of HR practices. Antecedents might include the factors that shape how HR investments are made; consequences detail the outcomes of HR efforts—namely, individual abilities and organization capabilities.

As HR analytics become more accepted, the intuition that derives from experience can be transferred to those new to the profession. In baseball, the book *Moneyball*, by Michael M. Lewis, changed leadership thinking by bringing discipline to intuitive thinking. Likewise, HR professionals who become comfortable with analytics will have another tool for delivering the value they have to offer the organization.

CHARLES GRANTHAM
Executive Producer, Working Design Collaborative

As the old adage says, "If you can't measure it, you can't manage it." Looking into the future, we see an increasing emphasis on the so-called triple bottom line, which extends corporate performance monitoring into new areas of environmental impact and "social factors." Although many of these concepts are still only loosely defined, the metrics that relate to building greater capability in human resources development will take center stage within the next five years. Investors will shun companies that don't invest in human resources development for the long term. Workforce development will become a corporate responsibility, and hence we are going to need good measurements to gauge progress in that field.

STEPHEN WEHRENBERG
Director, Future Force, U.S. Coast Guard

The future of analysis in HR lies in developing a simple model of learning. The learning cycle begins with events—something happens. We observe those events and reflect on what we have observed. We compare what we have observed to our existing model of reality, and when it doesn't fit, we either adjust our model or create a new one to explain what we have observed. Based on the model, we predict what outcome a certain action might have. We test our prediction by acting in such a way as to intentionally create a desired or predicted result. We then compare the result (event) to the prediction, reflect on those observations (the gap), and so on.

For far too long, those of us in HR have failed to complete this cycle. We have created policies that are prima facie good, without a clear understanding of what we are trying to achieve. And once the policy is in place, we rarely assess our success in the years that follow. In other words, the learning loop is broken. The application of analytic methods that helps us understand how much of benefit A leads to how much of the desired result B—or how much A is needed to achieve result B—will enable us to better predict our policy results, connecting the loop so that we have "organizational learning." It's as simple as stating what we are trying to achieve and measuring the degree to which we have achieved it.

KEVIN WILDE

Vice President, Organizational Learning and
Chief Learning Officer, General Mills, Inc.

My speculation is that analytics for human capital will become much more useful in the near future for successful organizations. The enablers of this brighter future will be:

* Continued investments in technology, making it easier to access the right information and gain insight

* More critical thinking about what matters and what drives performance

* Advancements in how business HR leaders manage the function to add value

JESSE HARRIOTT

Chief Knowledge Officer, Senior Vice President,
Monster Worldwide

The future use of analytics in human capital management is unfolding rapidly. Demands from senior management to show an ROI from HR, as well as the proliferation of technology in this field, are enabling this change. But these factors cannot be expected to drive the change. Leaders in the adoption and utilization of human capital metrics need to be the human resources professionals. Only they understand how HR can really add value to the organization and, therefore, are in the best position to predict and find causal relationships between HR initiatives and business outcomes.

In order for HR to lead the adoption of human capital metrics, HR professionals across the field will need to learn these analytic methods. Training and certification programs will certainly help, but this effort will also require a secular shift in what it means to be an HR professional. Formal analytic disciplines related to human capital metrics will certainly emerge as they have in other departments, such as marketing (marketing research), finance (accounting), and sales (sales operations). The future world-class HR department will track and understand the workforce, applicants, and alumni as vigorously as marketing tracks an organization's customers.

In the future, HR-related metrics will be accessible to everyone in an organization, not just the HR department. To be data-driven will be an expectation, not a way for top HR staff to stand out. The real challenge will be learning how to deal with the overwhelming amount of data. Therefore, the successful HR professional will add value by focusing the organization on the most important HR metrics and by acting on HR initiatives that measurably impact the business.

DAVID SCARBOROUGH
Scientist at Large, Kronos, Inc.

There are several important trends in employee selection and HR analytics that can be reasonably extrapolated forward. Identity theft (now the most common white-collar crime) is likely to become so pervasive that personal-identity scanning technology will be necessary for Internet commerce. Technical solutions are likely to lead legislative and enforcement responses to this crime wave. Biometric and other personal-identity authentication devices will become routine at the consumer level.

In this regard, employers will incorporate identity authentication into online employment application processing, partially resolving one of the biggest constraints to pre-employment testing over the unproctored Internet. The role of machine intelligence in HR information systems is likely to continue to expand on several other fronts as well. Expert systems are likely to find new uses in data acquisition, data warehousing, and decision support. Other types of artificial intelligence (neural networks, genetic algorithms) will increasingly be used to extract practical information from online data flow. Blended AI technologies, which combine different types of intelligent processing, will result in better tools for behavioral prediction, training delivery, performance monitoring, compensation management, career development, and succession planning.

Computer gaming technology will be adopted by employers seeking to improve employee training efficiency and effectiveness. Advances in speech recognition, virtual reality simulation, and visual and sensory display technologies will permit surprising advances in the machine–human interface. Some scientists anticipate job-related machine implants to improve human performance and expand human potential.

New technology has a way of migrating across disciplines. Unfortunately, our ability to merge advances from genetics, robotics, material science, nanotechnology, and other domains with the applied behavioral sciences and management is limited. Perhaps the only thing we can reliably anticipate is surprise.

NICK BONTIS

Director, Institute for Intellectual Capital Research; Associate Professor, McMaster University

Unfortunately, HR departments have generally been given the negative moniker of "hard to empirically defend their existence." No one can argue against the fact that human capital is the most critical asset of any organization. What we really need is the analytical and empirical capability that other organizational functions (e.g., marketing, finance, operations) have enjoyed for decades. Future respect for HR will come only if the profession adopts sophisticated modeling and measurement processes.

LEE ELLIOTT

Vice President, Human Resources, St. Francis Medical Center, Grand Island, Nebraska

There certainly has been dramatic progress made in the area of human capital management, principally by Jac Fitz-enz and Wayne Cascio, but as Dick Beatty has said, it is possible to become "overmeasured and underinformed." The question now is: What is coming in the future for HR metrics? Fortunately, that answer has already begun to appear.

There is a critical need for HR metrics to be included in annual reports. Not just one or two numbers, but enough numbers to truly show what is happening to the people in an organization. Some discussions have been held on this; however, more work is needed.

Another need is for higher-order numbers crunching to better understand the HR dynamics of an organization. A laundry list of HR metrics included on some dashboards is certainly informative. Unfortunately, the knowledge gained from these metrics is a long way from understanding what is truly going on. Discovering that will require advanced statistics.

Fortunately, there are people working with such advanced statistical tools, such as David Scarborough, who has shown how neural networks can be used to enhance understanding. At Saint Francis Medical Center, we've been using qualitative research tools from fields such as anthropology to predict HR metrics.

The last idea to be mentioned—and certainly the most exciting—is using HR metrics to predict the future. Dr. Fitz-enz is leading the pack in this effort. He is using advanced statistical tools to show what human capital will look like in the future. In all, huge progress has been made, and the path ahead to the future is clear. Now, it's time to make it happen.

DAVID CREELMAN

CEO, Creelman Research

In the future, HR leaders will have access to skilled analysts who can do the HR analytics. They won't necessarily be in the HR department; they could be part of a central analytics group or be consultants, but the point is that they will be readily available. Access to this expertise will make analytics much more of a normal activity for HR. Data should be available, too, although I expect that in the future getting the data from different systems will still feel like a lot of work.

Access to HR analytics should be a great thing for HR, bringing useful insights and more rigor to the function. My only concern is that we will end up with analytics snobs at war with HR traditionalists. Analytics have their place, but they are still only part of the answer. Just as a business leader needs to know enough about IT not to get snowed, so too HR leaders need to know enough about analytics to use it wisely.

ROW HENSON

Oracle Fellow

I believe the future of analytics for human capital management is quite bright, as compared to the dim efforts of the past several decades. Of course, we've all been talking for many years about the value of measuring human capital, but after many talks and many books, we find that few organizations have really been able to analyze HCM information effectively.

So, why do I think the future is bright? Technology for analytics is more easily used to collect, analyze, and even predict future trends. Instead of analysis being an afterthought that gets tossed to the "number cruncher," we are now seeing analytics embedded in the business process instead of as an after-the-fact report. For example, as a recruiter goes to fill an open requisition, the recruiting process can automatically present an analysis of where the last best fit for that position came from, what it cost, and what the average time is in the position. With Web 2.0 technologies, analytical information from both inside and outside the organization can be presented in myriad ways—charts, graphs, text—as a part of the process and not separate from it. In addition, powerful tools are available to look at predictive trends, based on which organizations can take action before there is a problem—for example, in turnover, which is the most costly loss for many organizations.

The industry is seeing proof that investment in human capital is a leading indicator of financial results, not a lagging indicator, as often thought in the past. Industry leaders such as Dr. Jac, Dave Ulrich, Robert Kaplan, and Laurie Bassi have been preaching this gospel for many years, and finally the numbers show without a doubt that people, indeed, are our greatest asset!

In the past, human resources organizations were not typically known for their analytical skills. But the next generation of human resources leaders are being introduced to "analytical thinking" as a key competency for the effective management of people. Colleges and universities now include this topic as standard in their curriculum. Thus, I continue to be optimistic. As the benefits of good analytics prevail, there will be no turning back! Better tools. Better decisions. Better organizations.

STEPHEN GATES AND PASCAL LANGEVIN
Respectively, Professor of Strategy, Audencia Nantes School of Management, France, and Professor of Management Accounting and Control Systems, EM LYON Business School, France

Since the beginning of the twentieth century, when financial performance measures such as ROI were developed, there have been warnings of the dangers in allowing dominance over all business activity. Critics have insisted that these measures led to management by the "rearview" mirror.

After all, financial measures only report the effects of decisions taken in the past, and they do not provide information about future performance. In addition, they encourage managers to maximize short-term results to the detriment of long-term performance. The dominance of financial measures, and more broadly, the search for profit maximization and shareholder wealth, can and has led to disasters just as the one we are currently experiencing.

Nevertheless, the role played by men and women, and their competencies, knowledge, and motivation, in value creation has long been recognized. Various tools have been proposed to try to measure a company's human capital. Among those, the balanced scorecard tries to link indicators of human capital to financial performance. However, there is still a long way to go. On the one hand, human capital indicators that are truly linked with strategy remain to be developed. On the other hand, companies tend to give responsibility for implementing performance measures to their financial department, which reinforces the link between these nonfinancial and financial measures.

Companies should step back and adopt a more cross-functional approach. In particular, they should strengthen the collaboration among HR managers, management accounting experts, and business unit managers to implement HC measures. HR managers have knowledge of various aspects of human capital, management accounting experts have experience in designing and implementing performance measurement systems, and business unit managers can identify the means necessary to attain strategic objectives.

With a little time and experience, companies will be able to develop performance measurement systems that can help them not only create more value but also share this value more equitably.

KIRK SMITH
Performance Consultant

I see this field expanding into measuring the patterns of relationships in the organization. Organizational network analysis (ONA) and the entire field of network science is fertile with possibilities for measuring the value of the "shadow system" of relationships in an organization. In their groundbreaking book of the 1990s, *Improving Performance: How to Manage the White Space in the Organization Chart,* Rummler and Brache touched on this idea without realizing that an entirely new branch of science would emerge based on the "white space."

White space is the area between boxes on an organization's chart and it represents the "interstellar" space of communication (or lack thereof) between cross-functional processes—in short, how work gets done. If we would measure and manipulate the patterns of relationships that are most productive in facilitating cross-functional processes, we could take human capital management to a new level.

Rob Cross and Robert Thomas have broken new ground in this field, as discussed in their book, *Driving Results Through Social Networks: How Top Organizations Leverage Networks for Performance and Growth*. They are not talking about social media—those are just tools. It is the patterns of relationships optimum for specific situations that are more important. The authors give real-life examples of how charting patterns of relationships in an organization has helped with strategy execution, culture change, onboarding, project success, and process improvement. As the saying goes, if you can measure it, you can manage it. Organizational network structures can now be measured and the potential for improving results by manipulating (managing) those structures is virtually unlimited.

The flow of information in social networks, or organizational networks, is an important form of communication, and leaders in organizations often say one of their biggest problems is a lack of communication. Maybe more attention should be paid to the structure of the networks in organizations. This is where the real informal learning takes place. Indeed, informal learning is a large part of human capital, and this type of measurement can take us far in quantifying human capital.

MICHAEL BOYD
Professor, Bentley University

Without being prepared for the expected future, it is impossible to move beyond the present. In the arena of managing and leading human organizations, the search for the best formula has become a key concern across all areas of human activity—business, government, athletics, religion, politics, and so on. There really are no exceptions to the need for finding the "best" methods, practices, activities, perspectives, science, or social interface capability in how human beings create value in an organized endeavor.

The absolute truth is that one cannot prepare for a future without first knowing the starting point. A key insight of the industrial age was the realization that work and activity could and should be measured in order to understand and improve processes and outcomes. Only through full understanding of how the present has been accomplished can we intelligently plan a path to the desired future.

While establishing that plan is critical to organizational success, the impact of human free will (including competition) often creates the need to react to the present in nonpredicted ways. That unplanned activity then changes the data used for measurement and analysis of organizational activity. So any analysis used for decision making must be sufficiently sophisticated and scientific to account for abnormal or unexpected considerations. Sometimes the data may impact the future; other times they simply reflect an anomaly that should be discarded. The skill, of course, is in determining the difference.

The strategic aspects of a business that are human centric are normally managed within the science and art of human resources management. The knowledge and skill necessary to determine how to accomplish objectives through human organizations is extensive and complex. Without the ability to analytically design, measure, and improve the processes used to accomplish work, the results, at best, will be only as good as the past. The questions for us all to focus on are: What should we measure? How do we measure it? and What does it mean? Those who have spent decades creating the science used to answer these questions, such as Dr. Jac Fitz-enz, can offer guidance and tools to help organizations move ahead in a world requiring infinitely more complex and impactful human resources management analytics. Everything keeps moving faster. There is less time for decisions. Analytics will become the means for competitive advantage.

LAURIE BASSI

CEO, McBassi & Company

A well-designed employee survey is a powerful tool for systematically tapping the wisdom of your workforce, and hence, it is the foundation for human capital analytics. Unfortunately, traditional one-size-fits-all employee engagement/satisfaction surveys are inadequate to the task, and they are impeding progress on human capital analytics in far too many organizations.

Employee engagement, while necessary for driving business results, is not sufficient. Stated another way, employee engagement and business results are not synonymous. Many executives and HR professionals, however, have become far too focused on employee engagement. In this environment, I have seen employee engagement come to be viewed as an end, rather than a means to an end.

I'm not suggesting that you throw out your employee surveys. Rather,

I'm suggesting that you demand more of them—that they begin to produce actionable business intelligence. The way to get there is to use employee surveys, along with human capital analytics techniques, to systematically identify the true human drivers of your business results.

NOEL HANNON
Hannon Associates; Retired HR Director, Motorola

Predicting the future of anything is risky business. (How many times will the Chicago Cubs be picked to become champions of Major League Baseball?) In this case, though, the answer may be self-contained: The future of analytics is "the future." It is time we move beyond looking behind us and reporting what has happened and, instead, understand where we are headed and how we will get there. This being said, the past will play an important role in the future. Pattern recognition will be important to building the analytics that will ensure we remain on track, moving toward the achievement of business and financial goals.

For example, just reporting overtime and absence data is not very compelling. But analyzing them with data on shrinkage (in retail) or accident rates (in manufacturing) may give the insights, such as when multiple weeks of more than 10 percent overtime in a department appear to coincide with increased absenteeism and an increase in shrinkage or accident rates. And these insights can be used to build the early warning system that will allow the business to make necessary adjustments before problems occur.

We need to begin working hand in hand with the businesses in an organization to define the role of human capital in the achievement of short- and long-term objectives. Then, we need to construct the analytics that will allow us to monitor, manage, and optimize that human capital to ensure it is fulfilling its role.

As human capital analytics grows in its importance, there are also likely to be organizational impacts. Those who have worked in the areas of HR technology and measurement recognize that we now have more data about the workforce than at any time before. The problem is that we have not been good at turning the data into information that makes a difference in meeting business (not HR) objectives.

What causes this? Is it limited depth of knowledge of the business strategy and operation? Is it lack of analytic skills and an inability to see the links between data and business objectives? Or, is it simply that these two important traits seldom exist in the same individuals or organizations—that is, the individuals who are "at the table" lack the analytic skills to envision how workforce data could be used, while those who know the data and have the necessary skills do not understand the relationships among the workforce, HR strategy, and business strategy?

Whatever the cause, there is a sense among my colleagues in consulting and technology development that the HR organization may not be the place to begin a dialogue on the importance of human capital analytics. There is growing concern that HR may never completely understand the power that exists in the data it has traditionally "owned." It appears that the responsibility of applying the science of human capital analytics will reside outside of HR, either in a different part of the organization (perhaps the strategy office or finance) or in a totally new organization carved out of HR—one that would focus on the management of the workforce drivers of today and the talent that will define the workforce of tomorrow.

REX GALE

Principal, Buck Consultants

Predicting the future is somewhat akin to programming your GPS. Once you know your destination, and even the pathway to get there, human action is still required to reach your goal.

Predictive cognition is the next frontier in improving business performance. Business has largely ignored the fifty years of research on the predictability of human behavior and the impact on business performance. Humans predictably err, and mountains of research on cognitive biases, decision biases, and other heuristics that predict human behavior and performance are the next data-mining frontier. Many companies use psychological assessments for selection and succession, yet they are not mining the most critical data: predictive cognitive data.

Instead of the "war for talent," companies should be fighting the "war for high performers." What are the predictive factors that cause top performers to deliver better results? What are their specific behaviors? What are their specific skills? What are their specific traits? Understanding what drives high performance, by role, then systematically embedding these high-performance insights and selection standards in your sourcing, screening, selection, and promotion processes will drive individual and organizational performance.

Predictive analytics peels back the onion skin of the enterprise to uncover the insights within that will predictably improve business performance. Similarly, predictive cognition peels back the onion skin of the mind to uncover the insights of the high performers who not only know what needs to be done but know how to get it done.

WAYNE CASCIO
Professor, University of Colorado, Denver

A 2008 survey on human capital management technology by the Institute for Corporate Productivity found that satisfaction with current human capital management technology is mediocre at best, that larger companies are most likely to use it, and that recruitment is the one function for which companies are most likely to use a vendor. Conversely, performance management, compensation, and succession planning are areas that companies are most likely to customize and for which they develop internal solutions. The same survey also found that integration with other systems and products is clearly lagging.

I expect that this situation will change dramatically in the next decade or so. This will happen as broad frameworks that capture more than just measurement per se begin to catch on, and as Web-based software that provides a "road map" to identify key cost and productivity elements will be used more widely to assess the costs and benefits of investments in people.

One such framework is LAMP: logic, analytics, measures, and process. After all, analytics and measures are just tools to improve decisions about talent. They are likely to have maximum impact when they are presented as part of a broader logic designed to influence decisions about talent, and rolled out using a process designed to bring about genuine organizational change. As users begin to appreciate how different HR activities and important outcomes like absenteeism, turnover, and productivity are interrelated, human capital analytics will play a central role in driving strategic business decisions.

KAREN BEAMAN
CEO and Founder, Jeitosa Group International

One critical direction for the future of human capital analytics is to bring the "human" aspect into our efforts. Today's metrics cover a broad spectrum of counting (e.g., heads, positions, terminations), measuring (e.g., time to hire, performance, turnover), evaluating (e.g., FTE ratios, average salaries), comparing (e.g., actual versus budget, top performers versus average performers, industry benchmarks), and assessing (e.g., productivity of new hires, business impact of talent development). Yet there is little or no regard for the relevance of the metrics we use within a global context.

The languages we speak, the cultures we live in, the experiences we have, and, yes, the metrics we use all shape our perceptions of reality and influence what we value. We know that different cultures in the world have different customs and values; thus, it follows that they naturally interpret metrics differently in their own cultural context. For example, what an American might rate a 5 (on a five-point scale), the German might rate a 4 and the Frenchman a 3—even though they are all rating the same thing. Their perceptions of the world are different because of their different cultures.

Personalities (optimists versus pessimists), cultures (independent versus interdependent), nations (democratic versus socialist), and historical/political events (aggressive, passive, isolationist) are just some of the factors influencing how we perceive things and how we take action in the world. The concept of cultural relativity must be applied to human capital analytics if we want to be relevant to the business on a global basis.

MICHAEL KELLY

Survey Consultation, Former Saratoga
Institute Survey Director

The dreaded response to any data is also the most common: "So what?" Human capital data just sit inert unless they can be arrayed in patterns of tenure, trends in turnover, influences on innovation, and other movements that extend fast forward into the future. Enter human capital analytics.

The manager's question, "What should we do next year?" can be answered with "Take steps to curb turnover by 5 percent and net income will soar by 8 percent." HR analytics shift the focus forward in ways that will be taken seriously by anyone who understands a balance sheet, especially those who follow sales forecasts.

An organization's greatest need today is for clarity in what is going on in the workplace and what the market holds for the future. HC analytics are the future for those who learn to read the messages hidden in the number piles. HR finally has the power to turn a new understanding into profit.

JAY JAMROG AND MARY ANN DOWNEY

Respectively, Senior Vice President, Research, and Talent Pillar Director, i4cp

What will HR metrics look like ten years from today? Over the past twenty-five years, many calls have been made for the HR profession to install better ways to measure not only the efficiency but also the effectiveness of various HR functions and, even more important, the impact that HR is having on the organization. The theory is this would lead to more enlightened strategies for managing human capital and give HR the long-lost respect that the profession craves.

So, how far have we come? The results of i4cp's 2009 survey show that while almost three-quarters of the respondents said that they had HR measurements, most were only measuring the efficiency of HR functions. Less than a quarter were attempting to develop effectiveness metrics, and very few were measuring the impact on the organization.

No board or CEO would ever accept this paucity of data from any other department. If marketing were measuring only efficiency, they would be reporting something like, "Last year marketing placed more ads in more magazines at less costs." The board would demand that marketing give data on increases in sales or market share.

So, what can HR do? A thriving human capital management metrics process takes four ingredients: good people information, a culture that makes decisions based on data, effective tools, and dedicated resources. Most organizations are not willing to devote much time and effort to this process. As a result, we believe that, for most organizations, the measurement of human capital management will look only incrementally better ten years from now.

Still, organizations willing to devote the resources over time will have predictive models that can help determine which roles, skills, and knowledge give the organization a competitive advantage. They will represent real-world versions of a modern managerial ideal: the organization that is so excellent in so many areas that it consistently outperforms most of its competitors.

PATTI PHILLIPS

President and CEO, ROI Institute

With increasing interest by the chief financial officer in human capital investment, effective human capital analytics will become an increasingly sought-after process in tomorrow's organizations. Robust quantitative methods will be applied to derive meaning from various levels of results, providing usable information to decision makers. Attention will be paid to indicators of commonly reported constructs such as reaction, learning, and application. The benefit-cost ratio and ROI metrics will continue to be critical measures of economic feasibility and program success. Utility will be the focus of measurement processes as data will be used to improve workforce productivity, plan for future resource needs, and minimize investment risks. Human capital analytics will become the linchpin between an organization's largest investment and its overall success.

KEVIN MARTIN
Vice President, Enterprise Research, Aberdeen Group

As organizations seek to gain visibility in key business processes and to eliminate the "gut feel" that has dominated in years past, data-driven decisions pertaining to the future state of the organization will become essential. This is why human capital analytics is a prerequisite to successful long-term workforce planning. And, it is also why workforce planning at best-in-class organizations will be tightly integrated with the organization's overall strategic planning.

The multiyear HR transformations pursued by organizations over the past decade must include and go beyond the ability to centralize disparate HR data into a single source. They must include the integration of that data with other functional data to enable gap analysis or the modeling of future scenarios. However, all will be minimized unless HR and line-of-business managers are trained to use the reporting and analytics to make employee-related decisions that correlate to business objectives.

ERIK BERGGREN
Director of Customer Solutions, SuccessFactors

The best way to predict the future is to invent it. With the lion's share of your operating expense in labor, there is no other area of your business that could yield better return from better decisions made. At the same time as people constitute the biggest expense, they are the only active ingredient for executing your strategy. With that said, it's remarkable to see how much companies invest in order to manage everything else in relation to what is invested in managing the human capital.

With increased understanding of your workforce comes better knowledge of managing it. This is knowledge that, if adequately presented to managers, can and will be used to make better decisions. The reality is that those companies that manage data on human capital are doing much better than their competitors.

To get that strategic knowledge, you have to collect strategic data in your transactions. People's potential, performance, skills, and so on are all examples of strategic data. Ignoring the data means missing a huge opportunity. Start tracking it and analyze the meaning of trends in a business context so that all the HR-related data answer questions on how to help the company grow, reduce costs, and improve productivity, margin, and market share. Smart use of strategic HCM data is today's answer to the problems of tomorrow.

ALEXIS FINK
People Insight Research Manager, Microsoft Corporation

Scientific reasoning and numerical understanding have been giving humanity the power to understand, predict, and improve since the time of Copernicus. Our challenge in HR is to finally move beyond superstition and conjecture in our approach to the assets that, in the end, truly drive our businesses. Specialty subdisciplines like industrial-organizational psychology have successfully applied research and analytics to human capital problems for decades, but they have largely done so within a limited set of topic areas and organizations. Infusing HR as a discipline with the rigor and expertise to truly solve problems rather than making guesses is the next great opportunity in business.

Capitalizing on this opportunity, however, presents a system challenge. HR leaders, business leaders, and HR professionals must all reconceptualize the management of human capital and also have the skills and capabilities to ask new questions and deliver different answers. Those organizations that can make this transition most effectively and most efficiently will bring a significant advantage to the marketplace.

RUGENIA POMI
Sextante Brasil

The economic crises of September 2008 have affected society worldwide. In Brazil, in our culture, September always brought the springtime, the blossoming of the beauty and colors and the anticipation of the new fruit! And suddenly in 2001, September 11 brought a sign of rupture—a collective alert of danger. Then, seven years later (again in September, from the same powerful country), and unexpectedly for most academics and experts in all fields, a world economic crisis impacted all segments of our society.

* What of our dreams and what will they become now?
* Our conflicts, our problems, and our challenges—where have they gone?
* Where do we want to go?
* Can we dream? Do we have a new vision capable of replacing the old one?
* Who were the ones we used to trust and whom do we want to establish alliances with for tomorrow?

From my perspective, I see a paradigm shift in the economic, social, and political model. Departing from the philosophical vision and landing on the operational one, I see these most immediate facts regarding people management in our organizations.

First, companies have drastically cut their expenses and have become even more selective when making investments—where absolute prudence is now the rule for new ventures. Second, there will be space and opportunity for those professionals who seek self-knowledge and who understand how to contribute creative solutions in a spirit of network collaboration. Third, we need to reduce everything that does not generate positive financial and social values, and discourage behaviors and attitudes that bring organizational disease: gossip, intrigue, suspicion, disparaging the competition, insecurity, low morale, threats, and fears.

At the same time, it's necessary to organize the house, to clean, maintain, and repair. After that, it is necessary to rethink the employment contract and remuneration process itself. It is time to create more flexible work relationships—to give some time off, negotiate periods of unpaid leave, offer part-time work, and so on.

Ideally, future companies will make their decisions about their human assets based on objective methodologies, intelligent planning, and evaluation tools for the production of goods and services. Cultural assessment of the organization's DNA, with performance metrics and frequent benchmarking, will become even more essential. It's time to understand the current context as a tremendous opportunity to analyze, review, adjust, redirect, and rewrite the definition of talent

JOHN BOUDREAU
Professor, University of Southern California

The future of human capital analytics lies more in the minds of leaders and employees than in human capital analysis systems. Of course, the future will bring ever greater and more accessible amounts of data about people in and beyond the organization. Of course, leaders must advance their competencies for human capital analysis and data-based decisions.

Yet, these points have been true for decades, and research at the Center for Effective Organizations suggests that progress has been all too slow. Indeed, one of the lowest-scored questions in our research is: "Do HR systems educate leaders about the quality of their human capital decisions?" The future may hinge more on the implied mental models that underlie our analytics and whether our constituents understand or even believe them. The ultimate measure of human capital analytics is not their elegance, predictive power, and reliability but, rather, whether leaders and employees improve their decisions when they use those analytics.

JOHN GIBBONS
Evidence-Based Practice Leader, The Conference Board

Just when we got the proverbial "seat at the table" somebody moved the chairs again. Ensuring that the HR function is *aligned* with the strategies of the business just won't cut it in the business environment of the future.

Simply put, the word *alignment* means to ensure that something is in line with or in agreement with something else. In the case of HR, alignment has come to commonly refer to building HR programs and interventions that support the strategies of the business. And aligning an organization's people strategies with its business strategies has become the goal of nearly every HR practitioner in the twenty-first century.

Consider the evidence. Work systems that foster innovation and management styles that actively engage employees' intellects and passions have been shown to have a direct link to business performance, whether at the individual, group, or enterprise level. The question, then, becomes: Why should HR leaders settle for a role that is simply "in agreement with" the goals of the business? The answer is that they shouldn't, and they won't in the future. Alignment will be a given, while *impact* will emerge as the goal of people who manage the human component of the business equation.

HR metrics (and human capital analytics, in general) will become the means by which HR will make this transition. Analytics that are evidence-based and that demonstrate a causal link between the variables in the human dimension and the variables in the financial and operational dimensions of business will become the basis for decision makers across the entire enterprise, not just HR. HR leaders will also be different. A new generation of HR practitioners is already emerging who are well grounded in the underpinnings of driving a business; have a mastery of the information systems; and, most of all, employ an analytic frame of reference that allows them to make decisions based on cause-and-effect arguments and evidence of impact.

And for those of us who may find this future a bit cold compared to our relatively warm, mostly intuitive HR world of today, simply consider this: When you can speak with authority, your arguments for doing the right thing will never again fall on deaf ears. In fact, for many, that seat at the table may very well be the one at the *head* of the table.

ED GUBMAN

Founder and Principal, Strategic Talent Solutions;
Executive Editor, *People & Strategy*

Our field has been pursuing better human capital metrics for a long time now, but despite some real creativity, we are hampered by lack of agreement on the big-outcome measures. We have trouble getting metrics to capture mind share and popular usage because we have nothing comparable to finance's ROI, net income, and the like. And, without accepted outcome measures, deep-dive HR analytics leads us further into the trees without knowing where the forest is.

What to do? As a profession, we need to take ownership and responsibility for a few key aspects of human capital that measure and drive business success, particularly productivity, engagement, and the leadership talent pool. In particular, HR people rarely want to own the productivity measure in their organizations, claiming that there are too many things outside their control. So what? People productivity is the biggest value driver in most companies. If we would own it, we could elevate our profession and our metrics to become vital to our businesses. Until we do these things, we will have sequoia-size measurement aspirations and sapling-size realities.

MARK HUSELID

Professor of HR Strategy, Rutgers University

As the markets for products and services become increasingly globalized, uncertain, and risky, the temptation for many managers is to abandon the conventional analytical tools (e.g., headcount projections, regression analyses, Markov Chains, ROI analyses) in favor of ad hoc planning and analyses (or no planning at all).

I think that this is a mistake. The solution, I believe, is not to attempt to develop overall models of labor supply and demand and then translate them into estimates of return on investment of various HR management practices (selection, development, etc.). Rather, more focused analytical procedures designed to ensure that top talent is placed in critical positions are much more likely to prove useful. Developing such procedures means that we have to be very clear about:

* *Our strategy*—how we will grow, where we will play, how we will win

* *Our strategic capabilities*—the bundle of information, technology, and people that will differentiate us from our peers

* *Our strategic positions*—those roles that have a disproportionate impact on our future success

* *Our inventory of strategic talent*—the extent to which we can consistently place top talent in strategic positions

* *Our HR action plan*—how we will redesign our HR management system to support the process of strategy execution

Once we've developed this level of clarity and focus, we're in a strong position to be able to understand those situations where improved levels of talent do, and do not, make a difference for business success. Then, we're able to bring not only traditional workforce planning tools to bear on the problem but also new and more promising tools developed by social scientists, such as network analyses, structural equation models, and a wide variety of new approaches using artificial intelligence. The goal of such models is to help managers focus less on average performance levels and more on performance variability as predictors of employee performance, and ultimately, strategic success.

LIBBY SARTAIN
Former CHRO, Yahoo HR Adviser

Predictive workforce analytics have long been the Holy Grail for HR. If we can better predict our future workforce needs based on long-term strategic planning, we can deliver the right workers ready to do the right work at the right time. But, the world of work is changing. In the past few years, the marketplace for talent has churned like never before. Organizations' need for top talent has intensified while the supply and demand of essential workers ebbs and flows. Conditions are uncertain. Past variables no longer predict future outcomes. Perhaps the secret lies in the current workforce: What can we do to get them ready to be our future workforce?

The HCM:21® Model:
Summary and Samples

In today's unpredictable market, the CEO mandate is to grab competitive advantage. The focus has shifted from cost reduction to top line growth, excellence in execution, and acquiring top talent. To accomplish this goal, executives are looking for new paths and new resources to exploit the next cycle's growth opportunities. Clearly, the asset with the greatest value potential is human capital.

Despite ongoing market transformations, very little has changed in the "people game." Organizations still operate in silos distinct from and largely disconnected from each other. Although computer technology has made human capital management more efficient, it has not delivered strategic value because we have not changed our management model. In essence, there has been no seminal shift in the way we manage people. We desperately need to revitalize human capital management.

Now, for the first time, you have an opportunity to make a quantum leap in human capital management. Presented here is the model we call HCM:21, or human capital management for the twenty-first century. This breakthrough model was developed over a period of eighteen months by the Predictive Initiative, a consortium of major corporations, vendors, and management associations committed to transforming HR into a strategic function. HCM:21 is not a human resources program. It is both a management model and an operating system. The model identifies mission-critical organizational issues and entities. Then it operationalizes how they align, are interdependent, and need to be integrated. An outline of the model is shown in Figure A.1.

Following are the steps essential to this model:

A. The Strategic Scan
B. Capability Planning
C. Process Optimization
D. Integrated Delivery
E. Predictive Measurement
F. Analytics

Included here are sample forms corresponding to these steps that should make your realization of the model clear.

A. The Strategic Scan

Human capital management typically starts with workforce planning. Planning compares business plan staffing requirements with internal and

Figure A.1. The HCM:21® model.

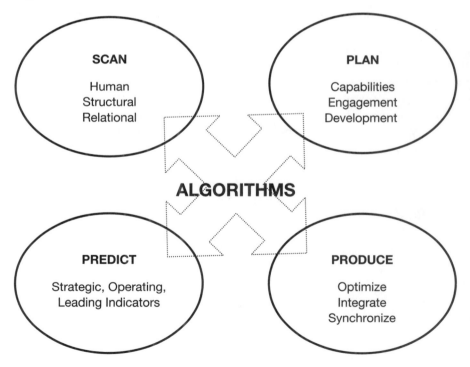

SCAN

Human
Structural
Relational

PLAN

Capabilities
Engagement
Development

ALGORITHMS

PREDICT

Strategic, Operating,
Leading Indicators

PRODUCE

Optimize
Integrate
Synchronize

external labor pools. From there a strategy is developed for filling gaps in the workforce. Although the marketplace is continually undergoing radical change, quite often there is no change from past practices. Before you can plan future human capital investments, you need to understand all aspects of the market. This includes competition, technology advancements, and regulations, as well as economic, political, and human capital trends. This is why the external and internal scan is essential. HCM:21 is launched with a strategic scan of external forces and internal factors that might affect the three fundamentals of the organization: human, relational, and structural capital, shown in Figure A.2.

Samples of how and where these forces and factors might affect your organization follow as Forms A-1 through A-6. Most important, they remind you that problems in one of the sectors of the organization usually affect the other sectors. Technology investments usually require training of operators. Economic downturns and upturns change the interactions between human and relational capital and often demand structural investments. The English metaphysical poet John Donne said, "No man is an island, entire of itself; every man is a piece of the continent, a part of the main." This is also true of organizational entities and

Figure A.2. Template for a strategic scan.

Organizational Capital	Human	Structural	Relational
External Forces			
Labor supply	Acquire and retain	Remodel workspaces	Find new contacts
Economy	Incent service	Sell off real estate	Retain customers
Globalization	Find new people	Reorganize	Expand suppliers
Regulations	Modify benefits	Go green	Lobby government
New technology	Train staff	Invest in equipment	Update customers
Competitors	Research new knowledge	Design new products	Speed to market
Internal Factors			
CEO's vision	Translate for employees	Make new signs/forms	Advertise in market
Culture	Employee branding	Protocol review	Talk to customers
Brand	Describe to employees	Design facilities	Marketing materials
Capabilities	Facilitate/support	Upgrade processes	Sell competence
Leadership	Survey employees	Review span of control	Visit customers
Finances	Control new hires	Manage expenses	Curtail travel

functions. Here is your first encounter with the inherent integration of organizational activities.

The Strategic Scanner

The Strategic Scanner is a series of six forms or templates to use in completing the strategic scan. There are basically four types: (1) a detailed corporate-wide survey and identification of external and internal factors; (2) an equivalent survey and identification performed on a function or department level and covering both external and internal factors; (3) an identification and review of the corporate vision, mission, and values; and (4) an analysis of corporate objectives and initiatives.

Instructions and Comments: External Forces (A-1)

External Forces are elements outside your company that you believe will have a present or future effect on your organization. This template sample has a general starter set of External Forces, and you may delete these and/or add others as you see fit.

First, identify issues that will arise as a result of External Forces. Describe them in a few key words or phrases and enter onto the spreadsheet templates provided here. All key issues should be clearly identified, but not all impact cells have to be filled in. Consider primarily those significant issues or forces that will demand attention across the entire organization. Second, to give the scan consistent structure, link the issues to your organization's three forms of capital: human, structural, and relational:

* Human capital is your employees and active contingent workers.

* Structural capital is essentially things that you own, ranging from facilities and equipment to intellectual materials, codified processes, patents and copyrights, and IT software.

* Relational capital is working knowledge of and relationships with outsiders including customers, suppliers, competitors, regulators, and communities in which you do business.

This corporate-level scan forms the basis for subsequent forms at the departmental or functional levels to link consistent plans and objectives throughout the company. Each level must react to these forces and issues in ways that keep the organization aligned and internally integrated. See the sample response provided here.

A-1. STRATEGIC SCANNER—External Forces (Sample)

I. EXTERNAL FORCES

Change in	Issue	Impact on Organizational Capital		
		Human	Relational	Structural
Labor Supply	Reduced availability of programmer/analysts in key location markets.	Increase outreach and diversity efforts.	Both R&D and customer requirements are being delayed. Need to refocus development priorities and schedules.	Consider consolidation of resources or support locations to match availability.
	Difficulty in sourcing production and warehouse workers with requisite language and math skills.	Work with temporary agencies and local job boards to increase talent pool and improve basic skill levels.	Increased mandate to understand and communicate realistic customer shipment expectations.	Reduced ability to plan or meet peak production schedules.
Economy	Given current economic outlook, business growth projected as flat for next 2 to 3 years.	Find new ways to improve direct service operations.	Recognizing mutual concerns, retain and reinforce current supplier and customer relationships.	Sell unused real property and unneeded equipment.
	Higher costs of living and housing make recruiting and relocation to this area very difficult.	Increase college recruiting in and new hire relocation to lower-cost areas.	Join with other companies and industry groups to address affordable housing needs in this area.	Consolidate existing operations into lower-cost areas.
	State income tax structure increasing in several current manufacturing sites.	Audit payroll tax structure for employee pay and benefit tax savings, if possible.	Review sales tax structure for out-of-state customer revenue impact.	Reduce noncritical expansion plans.
Industry Trends	Mergers & acquisitions continue among key companies in our industry.	Reformulate management succession-planning process to accommodate unwanted M&A raiding of key senior employees.	Constant attention to stockholders, employees, customers, industry, and community leaders who would all have "a voice" in possible M&A activities.	Review corporate telecommunications, public relations, and security policies.

A-1. *STRATEGIC SCANNER—External Forces* (Continued)
(Sample)

I. EXTERNAL FORCES		Impact on Organizational Capital		
Change in	**Issue**	**Human**	**Relational**	**Structural**
Technology Advances	Third-generation products due to market no later than mid next year.	As new technologies are introduced, employee skills and competencies must concurrently be upgraded.	Customers must be better prepared to adopt and integrate new products into existing operations without interrupting current high service levels.	Review Operations' structure to better produce unique products to address changing market demands. Also review Service's ability to support both current and new products.
Globalization	Economic value and market opportunities of our overseas operations continue to increase annually.	Begin identification of labor market and educational and cultural sources to facilitate eventual local hiring needs.	Complete regional economic, political, and environmental scans now in progress.	Establish new offices in Central Europe and Middle East far in advance of our economic expansion plans.
Competition	Lack of differentiation among top three companies in domestic marketplace.	Identify, train, and develop new skills and competencies within workforce to handle reinvigorated design tasks.	Develop more competitive stance in sales and marketing without affecting current customer relationships.	Critically need unique products to address changing market demands.
Customers	Expanding international customers while maintaining domestic base.	Rotate and cross-train domestic and international sales teams to work in global customer presentations.	"Go green" to better position ourselves as a preferred supplier of high-tech products and services.	Redesign sales and service offices to have same branded "look and feel" in all locations globally.
Suppliers	Supplier base is currently steady, but new materials are always being added to procurement lists.	Develop new training program for added procurement team. Increase mutual on-site visits.	Continually review current relationships via Supplier Feedback & Improvement Cards.	No structural changes anticipated.

Instructions and Comments: Internal Forces (A-2)

This corporate-level scan of internal forces follows the same directions as those for the external scan. It is a general starter set of forces; you may delete some of these and/or add others as fits your situation. When this strategic scan is completed at the corporate level, it can be recreated at the divisional or department level as appropriate.

Organizational Analysis and Response

Instructions and Comments: External Forces (A-3)

To prepare this stage, copy the entries in the "Change in" and the "Issue" columns from the Strategic Scan to the "Change in" and "Issues" columns on the A-3 template. This ensures consistent consideration of all uses when multiple sheets are used by different functions or departments. Then, decide which functions or departments are primarily affected by these issues. You need to supply a "Needed Response" for each "Issue." The "Response to Excel" column is for listing "stretch factors" that are designed to achieve true excellence

Optional: This sheet can be duplicated, so that each function and/or department receives a copy for local completion. Responses are then merged for the corporate summary.

Instructions and Comments: Internal Factors (A-4)

Obtain current or revised corporate statements from the Vision, Mission, and Values sheet (Form A-5) and insert in Form A-4, as done for the external forces.

Corporate Vision, Mission, and Values

Instructions and Comments

Form A-5 should be completed by the chief executive officer or senior leadership team. Review these current vision, mission and values statements and amend or modify as needed. Determine what current or future actions may be taken at corporate level to better commit to, communicate, and implant these positions in the corporate culture.

When completed, provide copies to the functions or departments for their individual organizational analyses and responses

Corporate Objectives and Initiatives

Instructions and Comments

Form A-6 should be completed by the officer or senior leadership team. These are key initiatives described at the corporate level. More

A-2. *STRATEGIC SCANNER—Internal Forces*
(Sample)

II. INTERNAL FORCES			Impact on Organizational Capital	
Change in	Issue	Human	Relational	Structural
Vision	"By conducting ourselves ethically, humanely, safely, environmentally, and globally, we will become the #1 supplier of advanced technology components worldwide within the next decade."	Global expansion mandates translation of Vision, Mission, and Core Values statements into at least nine languages.	Need to ensure same Vision is included in external advertising, new product brochures, marketing materials, and publicity.	Long-stated Vision seems well included in corporate plans, employee goals, and most internal publications.
Mission	"Through our people, process, and technology, we develop and deliver leading-generation consumer products."	Focus on multiple programs to make employees into our company's real competitive advantage.	Consider advertising campaign to better position this public message.	Protocol review of all ongoing internal processes to ensure common direction.

Values	"Our company's core values are Leadership, Integrity, Commitment, and Excellence."	To better reflect current concerns, the concept of safety needs to be added to our Core Values statement.	Requires added communication to vendors, suppliers, and service providers on added safety awareness.	New signage and badges need to be published to reflect new Values statement.
Brand	Brand identification is not considered a key issue at this time.	Ensure "people" receive equal attention as process and technology in branding.	Not immediately required.	Not immediately required.
Culture	Redesign may be necessary to gain employee engagement and commitment.	Continually reinforce culture by recognizing and rewarding demonstration of Core Values by employees.	See Vision remarks for inclusion of cultural components in external publications and activities.	Redesign corporate facilities with new Values signage.
Strategy	Need to ensure strategic goals and tactical objectives are communicated through all levels of the organization.	Include more "strategic" corporate messages in ongoing town hall meetings with employee groups.	Confirm key customers' strategic plans are aligned with our goals for next 2–3 years' sales cycle.	Formalize this internal strategic review process to ensure structural goals alignment at corporate levels.
Finances	Given current economy, growth outlook is flat for next 2–3 years.	Institute headcount and position controls in low-impact operations.	Reduce travel and seminars without affecting customer relationships.	Tighten financial and accounting controls to achieve annual targets.

A-3. ORGANIZATIONAL ANALYSIS AND RESPONSE—External Forces (Sample)

	I. EXTERNAL FORCES		**Organizational Impact**		
Change in	**Issue**	**Functions Affected**	**Needed Response**	**Response to Excel**
Labor Supply	Reduced availability of programmer/analysts in key location markets.	Information Technology		
	Difficulty in sourcing production and warehouse workers with requisite language and math skills.	Operations; Human Resources		
Economy	Given current economic outlook, business growth projected as flat for next 2–3 years.	Sales; Marketing; Operations		
	Higher costs of living and housing make recruiting and relocation to this area very difficult.	Human Resources		
	State income tax structure increasing in several current manufacturing sites.	Finance; Operations		

Industry Trends	Mergers & acquisitions continue among key companies in our industry.	Marketing
Technology Advances	Third-generation products due to market no later than mid next year.	R&D
Globalization	Economic value and market opportunities of our overseas operations continue to increase annually.	Sales; Marketing; Operations
Competition	Lack of differentiation among top three companies in domestic marketplace.	R&D; Marketing
Customers	Expanding international customers while maintaining domestic base.	International Sales
Suppliers	Supplier base is currently steady.	Purchasing; Operations

A-4. ORGANIZATIONAL ANALYSIS AND RESPONSE—Internal Factors (Sample)

	II. INTERNAL FORCES		Organizational Impact		
Change in	Issue	Function Affected	Needed Response	Response to Excel	
Vision, Mission, Values	Review, reeducation, and reinforcement of these statements are required, especially in global expansion mode.	All functions			
Brand	Brand identification is not considered a key issue at this time.	Marketing			
Culture	Redesign may be necessary to gain employee engagement and commitment.	Corporate Management; Human Resources			
Strategy	Need to ensure strategic goals and tactical objectives are communicated through all levels of the organization.	All functions			
Finances	Given current economy, growth outlook is flat for next 2–3 years.	Corporate Management; Finance			

A-5. VISION, MISSION, AND VALUES
(Sample)

	Organizational Responses	
	Current	**Future**
I. VISION "By conducting ourselves ethically, humanely, safely, environmentally, and globally, we will become the #1 supplier of advanced technology components worldwide within the next decade."	Consider rebranding company image to more global presence while maintaining strong domestic-industry stance.	Develop new company slogan or "tagline" to publicize and emphasize this vision.
II. MISSION "Through our people, process, and technology, we develop and deliver leading-generation consumer products."	To meet current business objectives and customer commitments, must deliver new product offerings on time and within budget.	Need to better hire, develop, recognize, reward, and retain our best employees as this company's competitive advantage.
III. VALUES "Our company's core values are Leadership, Integrity, Commitment, Excellence, and Safety."	The concept of safety has been added to our Core Values statement. From product design, to component manufacturing, to costumer application, safety is integral to everything we do.	Continually reinforce these values by finding ways to recognize, reward, and celebrate employee demonstration of these values.

A-6. CORPORATE OBJECTIVES AND INITIATIVES
(Sample)

Corp. Goal #	Goal or Objective	Primary Responsibility	Timing
1.	Successfully execute 3-Year Strategic Plan for next-generation product launch, including multi-client solutions, according to announced systems schedule and QRS optimization document.	Operations; Sales & Marketing	First-year schedule and cost model measured and reported monthly to Board of Directors.
2.	Align the Sales/Acct. Mgt./Operations groups' customer-facing strategy to increase revenue by 12.5% year over year. Consider reevaluation of Sales structure based on limited available global resources.	Sales & Marketing; Account Management; Operations	Measured quarterly and achieved annually.
3.	Implement new business initiation process from sales to start-up for all International regions to achieve 8% net OI by year end.	International Operations	Design by end 1st qtr; implement within 2nd qtr; annualize results and audit end of 4th qtr.
4.	Achieve gross revenue, net margin, operating income, and cost containment targets as measured by approved department budgets.	All departments; Finance	Measured quarterly and achieved annually.
5.	Design and improve structured approach to key position skills and leadership competencies for current and 3-year future needs. Match with redesign of management development programs.	Senior Mgt. Team; Human Resources	Design by end 2nd qtr; pilot in 3rd qtr; implement by 4th qtr.

detailed goals and objectives are covered in the function- or department-level form. See B-1.

Review current corporate objectives and initiatives, and amend or modify as needed. It is recommended that you limit this to five key strategic objectives. After the form is completed, provide this review of corporate objectives to the function/department groups to obtain information that will be used in the delivery planner that follows in step D.

B. Capability Planning

Once the scan is completed, you have the foundation for an advanced workforce-planning process. Rather than continue to apply an industrial-era model, filling holes with interchangeable bodies, now you can think in terms of building capability for the intelligence age in which we function. The strategic scan told you who and what you have to compete with and where your internal process and structures might need recalibration. Now, you can start building capabilities across essential functions.

Capability Planning Worksheet

Instructions and Comments (B-1)

This section begins the workforce analysis process, both current and future. The first step is to divide the workforce into four categories in terms of their valued capabilities:

1. Mission critical—essential to survival
2. Unique—market differentiators
3. Important—operational necessities
4. Movable—outsource or eliminate

After reviewing the "Change in" entries on the Strategic Scanner sheets and the "Needed Response" listings on the Organizational Analysis and Response sheets, list the key 'Capabilities" required for organizational success on the Capability Planning sheet (see B-1). Designate the "Primary Function(s)" needing those skills, abilities, or expertise; or indicate the "Organizational Responses" to meet such needs. Then outline the responses that may be immediately taken (tactical measures) and those longer-range responses to be considered (strategic initiatives).

Optional: This B-1 form may be duplicated, then assigned to individual functions or departments for completion.

B-1. CAPABILITY PLANNING—Function- or Department-Level Responses (Sample)

Capability	Primary Function	Criticality*	Organizational Responses	
			Current	**Future**
1. Third-Level Statistical Methodology Analysis	Operations	MC	Required for next-generation product launch. Presently have two employees enrolled in college courses—expected graduation in June.	Expand college recruiting program for new hires. Consider internal training program for present employees.
2. MIS Database Administration Skills	Information Technology	SO	Presently using outside contractors for temporary assignments.	Need to reinstitute active market search, especially for expansion to international locations. Consider using search agencies for regular hires.
3				
4.				
5.				

* Criticality Codes: **MC** = Mission critical for competitive advantage. **DU** = Differentiating; uniquely valuable in marketplace. **SO** = Important for sustained efficient operations. **RR** = No longer critical skills; reassign, retrain, or release.

Succession Planning

Once the capability planning is completed, you follow with our advanced succession planning system. This system is built around five principles:

1. Assigning a senior line executive the primary responsibility of managing the system

2. Identifying high potential (Hi-Po) personnel as far down the organization as possible

3. Designing personal growth programs and reviewing and updating the Hi-Po list at least annually

4. Monitoring advancements and their effect on mission accomplishment and revenue growth

5. Ensuring the development plans are aligned with strategic business plan and corporate KPIs

When you have at least 75 percent of your Hi-Po candidates' development programs fully operational and their replacements ready, you should see a rise in revenue growth per FTE and mission fulfillment. The reason for this is that your Hi-Pos are the key people who drive overall performance.

C. Process Optimization

It is natural to fall into a routine, unquestioning way of running a process. That's why periodic process analyses can greatly increase both efficiency and effectiveness. This can be used in any process analysis, in any function. In human resources, it can be applied to hiring, compensation, development, or retention.

For example, one human capital management application is staffing. In any process there are inputs, throughputs, and outputs. In staffing, the *inputs* are job applicants who come through a variety of sources, such as advertising, job boards, agencies, and employee referrals; *throughputs* are the selection and orientation methods you use, such as individual and group interviews, testing, assessment, or onboarding; and *outputs* are new hires who can be evaluated in terms of performance (B), salary progression (C), growth potential (P), tenure (T), or other outcomes.

For example, a dozen people in a selected mission-critical job group were hired two years ago. The end goal was to learn which combination of sources and methods yielded the best hires for this job group. Findings of past experiences with hiring and retention were compared to the strategic scan and the planning data. This established a base upon which to build a staffing strategy for the future. The result of this work led to cuts in the cost of sourcing and improvements in the hit rate for exceptional hires. It clearly demonstrates the added value achieved by a solid staffing strategy and clear-cut methods. In Figure A.3, you can see which combination of source and method yielded the best results. From this it is possible to see which sources produced the high performers, as well as which attracted people who stayed. The figure also shows the correlation

Figure A.3. Process optimization.

	SOURCES						METHODS					RESULTS			
	N	**M**	**S**	**E**	**J**	**W**	**I**	**G**	**T**	**A**	**O**	**B**	**C**	**P**	**T**
Al		M					I		T			2	2	1	1
Bea					J		I	G	T		O	2	2	2	2
Cee				E			I	G		A	O	3	2	3	2
Didi	N						I		T		O	2	2	2	2
Earl					J		I				O	1	1	1	2
Frank					J		I		T			2	1	1	1
Gina						W	I	G		A	O	3	2	1	2
Hal		M							T		O	2	3	3	2
Isaac			S				I	G		A	O	3	3	2	2
Jon				E			I	G	T		O	2	3	2	2
Ken	N						I	G	T			1	2	2	1
Leo	N						I					2	1	1	1

N = Newspaper, M = Prof Magazine, S = Search, E = Referral, J = Job Board,

    W = Walk In

I = Personal Interview, G = Group Interview, T = Test, A = Assessment,

    O = Onboarding

B = Performance, C = Pay Increases, P = Potential Rating   Score: 1 = low, 3 = high

T = Tenure: 1 = leave, 2 = stay

between onboarding (O) and tenure (T). When you have a very large work population, you will need to apply the sample algorithm that is included in the HCM:21 package.

Process Optimizer: Staffing Process Analysis

Instructions and Comments (C-1)

Form C-1 helps you consider what may be the most effective recruiting methods you are currently using to source those key jobs or competencies identified by this survey. Under "Key Job," list each person hired during the relevant period. (Coded names and ID numbers may be used for privacy purposes) For each individual, consider his or her primary recruiting source and onboarding methods. The methods listed are suggestive and others may be added to better reflect your organization's programs. Then evaluate each person's performance, potential, progress, and tenure to date. For a job group, look for patterns that are most effective, cost-efficient, and performance consistent in finding suitable candidates and in retaining higher potential employees.

Optional: This sheet may be duplicated to allow each key job to be listed on a separate page.

Process Optimizer: Training Process Analysis

Instructions and Comments (C-2)

Form C-2 helps you consider what may be the most effective training methods you are currently using to develop employees in those key jobs or competencies identified by this survey. Under "Key Skill," list each person trained in the relevant period. (Coded names or ID numbers may be used for privacy purposes.) For each individual, consider whether internal or external training is used or programs are attended. The methods listed are suggestions; others may be added to better reflect your organization's programs. Then evaluate each person's performance prior to and after the training, and the impact of that training on the individual's potential and continued tenure. As a skill group, look for patterns that show effective, efficient, and consistent improvement in performance and potential of employees trained by different methods.

Optional: This sheet may be duplicated to allow each key skill to be listed on a separate page.

Process Optimizer: Turnover and Loss Analysis

Instructions and Comments (C-3)

Form C-3 helps you consider what may be the common causes of controllable and noncontrollable turnover and its impact on the perfor-

C-1. PROCESS OPTIMIZER—Staffing Process Analysis (Sample)

Employees Hired 2007 & 2008 YTD	Sources*						Methods†						Results**			
	N	M	J	E	S	W	I	G	T	A	O	P	P	F	S	R
KEY JOB 1: Programmer/Analyst																
Al White		M					I				O		2	2	2	Y
Bea Purple			J				I	G	T		O		2	2	2	Y
Cecile Turquoise				E			I		T		O		2	2	2	N
Didi Orange			J				I	G			O		2	1	2	Y
Earl Black	N						I					P	1	1	1	N
Frank Gray		M					I			A			2	3	3	Y
Gina Blue			J	E			I	G		A			3	3	3	Y
Hal Lavender					S		I	G			O		2	2	2	N
Isaac Silver	N						I		T		O	P	2	2	2	Y
Jon Pink						W	I				O	P	1	1	1	Y
Ken Green				E			I	G					2	2	2	Y
Leo Tangerine				E			I			A			3	2	2	Y
KEY JOB 2: Operations Director																
Alice Circles				E			I			A	O		3	3	3	Y
Leo Rectangles					S		I	G					3	2	2	N
Charles Rounders Jr.			J				I	G		A	O	P	3	2	2	Y
Bob Squares				E			I	G		A	O		2	3	2	Y
Marsha Triangles					S		I						2	2	1	Y

*Sources: N = Newspaper ads. M = Professional magazines. J = Internet job boards. E = Employee referrals. S = Search agencies. W = Walk-in applicants.
†Methods: I = Individual interviews. G = Group interviews. T = Skills testing. A = Assessment. O = Onboarding process. P = Probationary period.
**Results: P = Current performance (1 to 3). F = Future potential (1 to 3). S = Salary progression (1 to 3). R = Retention (still on-board? Y/N).
Note: P & F may also be weighted.

C-2. PROCESS OPTIMIZER—Training Process Analysis
(Sample)

Employees Trained 2007 & 2008 YTD	Internal*					External†					Impact**			
	I	F	M	X	C	O	E	S	T	U	P	C	F	T
KEY SKILL 1: Database Administrator														
Charlie Able	I			X			E			U	1	2	2	6
George Baker	I			X			E			U	2	2	2	5
Howle Fox	I		M	X			E	S			2	3	3	?
Juliet India	I		M	X			E		T	U	1	2	1	1
KEY SKILL 2: Operations Controller														
Michael November	I		M	X			E				2	?	2	2
Oscar Sierra	I		M				E				2	2	1	1
Papa Tango	I			X							2	2	2	4
Romeo Lima	I		M	X	C						3	3	3	3
KEY SKILL 3: Process Supervisor														
Victor Delta	I				C						1	2	2	1
Walter Easy	I	F	M		C			S			2	3	2	5
Xavier Bravo	I	F	M		C				T		2	2	?	6
Yogi Dog	I			X	C		E				3	3	3	4
Zeke Alpha	I			X						U	2	1	1	8

*Internal: I = Informal OJT training. F = Formal job training. M = Self-directed materials. X = Computer instructed. C = Corporate colleges.
†External: O = On-site programs. E = Off-site programs. S = Trade/business schools. U = University courses.
**Impact: P = Prior performance (1 to 3). C = Current performance (1 to 3). F = Future potential (1 to 3). T = Tenure (years service to date).
Note: C & F may also be weighted.

C-3. PROCESS OPTIMIZER—Turnover and Loss Analysis (Sample)

Employees Termed 2007 & 2008	Controllable*						Noncontrollable†						Impact**			
	J	S	C	T	D	O	F	R	S	L	IP	IB	P	F	R	T
KEY JOB 1: Programmer/Analyst																
Jane Smith	J												2	2	2	3
Isaac Smathers		S	C										2	3	2	2
Robert Smithers					D								1	1	2	1
Samuel L. Smythers		S											2	3	2	4
Riccardo Desoto					D								1	2	2	2
Mary Ann Dodge	J	S											2	3	3	1
Walter P. Chrysler										L			3	3	3	3
Henry Ford III											IP		2	1	1	47
KEY JOB 2: Process Supervisor																
Herman Elm			C	T									2	3	3	4
Big Tom Oakley									S				2	2	3	2
Sally Asher										L			2	1	3	2
Phillip Maplethorpe					D								2	3	3	4
Allen Greentree						O							2	3	3	4
Cherry Wood		S											3	3	3	5
Jim Birch	J		C										3	3	3	6
William Pine			C	T									1	2	3	2

*Controllable: J = Better job offer. S = Better salary offer. C = Lack of career options. T = Lack of training/development. D = Dissatisfied with supervisor. O = Voluntary other.
†Noncontrollable: F = Family status change. R = Relocation. S = Return to school. L = Leave of absence. IP = Involuntary performance. IB = Involuntary behavior.
**Impact: P = Current performance (1 to 3). F = Future potential (1 to 3). R = Replacement availability (1h to 3low). T = Tenure (years service to date).
Note: P & F may also be weighted.

mance of the organization or the key competencies identified by this survey. Under "Key Job," list each person who left the company during the survey period. (Coded names or ID numbers may be used for privacy purposes.) For each individual, consider his or her primary reason for employment termination. The reasons listed here are common and are used to differentiate between controllable and noncontrollable terminations. Then evaluate each person's performance, potential, ease of replacement, and tenure. As a skill group, look for patterns that may be effectively addressed, especially those considered controllable.

Optional: This sheet may be duplicated to allow each key skill to be listed on a separate page.

D. Integrated Delivery

This step has three sections.

Integrated Delivery Planner: Corporate Objectives, by Function or Department

Instructions and Comments (D-1)

This sample is for a human resources department. The sheet should be duplicated for separate completion by each major function or department in the organization. The corporate objectives have been developed by the officer or senior staff during the Corporate Objectives and Initiatives phase of this process. They should be copied directly from Form A-6 onto this form.

Integrated Delivery Planner: Key Goals for Function or Department

Instructions and Comments (D-2)

The function's or department's key goals are listed here and cross-referenced to the corporate goal number that they support.

Integrated Delivery Planner: Related Department Goals

Instructions and Comments (D-3)

Key related or support goals from other functions are listed here and cross-referenced to the corporate goal number.

D-1. INTEGRATED DELIVERY PLANNER: CORPORATE OBJECTIVES, BY FUNCTION OR DEPARTMENT (Sample)

Corp. Goal #	Function or Department		
	Goal or Objective	Responsibility	Timing
1.	Successfully execute 3-Year Strategic Plan for next-generation product launch, including multi-client solutions, according to announced systems schedule and QRS optimization document.	Operations; Sales & Marketing	First-year schedule and cost model measured quarterly.
2.	Align the Sales/Acct. Mgt./Operations groups' customer-facing strategy to increase revenue by 12.5% year over year. Consider reevaluation of Sales structure based on limited available global resources.	Sales & Marketing; Account Management; Operations	Measured quarterly and achieved annually.
3.	Implement new business initiation process from sales to start-up for all International regions to achieve 8% net OI by year end.	International Operations	Design by end 1st qtr; implement within 2nd qtr; annualize results and audit end of 4th qtr.
4.	Achieve gross revenue, net margin, operating income, and cost containment targets as measured by approved department budgets.	All Departments; Finance	Measured quarterly and achieved annually.
5.	Design and improve structured approach to key position skills and leadership competencies for current and 3-year future needs. Match with redesign of management development programs.	Senior Mgt. Team; Human Resources	Design by end 2nd qtr; pilot in 3rd qtr; implement by 4th qtr.

D-2. KEY GOALS FOR FUNCTION OR DEPARTMENT
(Sample)

Dept. Goal #	Corp. Goal #	Goal or Objective	Responsibility	Timing
1.	5.	Design and improve structured approach to key position skills and leadership competencies for current and 3-year future needs. Match with redesign of management development programs.	CHRO & Management Development Dept.	Design by end 2nd qtr; pilot in 3rd qtr; implement by 4th qtr.
2.	3.	Complete evaluation and reorganization of International HR organization to better support key global operations as measured by business component management.	International HR staff at each designated location	Design by end 1st qtr; implement within 2nd qtr; annualize results and audit end of 4th qtr.
3.	2	Develop more effective sales incentive plan and streamline compensation accounting practices to achieve 25% reduction in their administrative costs.	Compensation Dept.	Design by end 2nd qtr; implement by 4th qtr.
4.	5.	Activate new modules to HRIS system to support succession planning; competency planning, 360 reviews per HR & IT schedules.	Compensation, Training, and ER departments	Measured monthly against proposed IT schedule.
5.	4.	Meet all annual headcount and operating budget targets, including cost reduction plan targets for external ER activities.	CHRO	Measured monthly and achieved annually.

D-3. RELATED GOALS FROM OTHER FUNCTIONS OR DEPARTMENTS

Dept.	Corp. Goal #	Goal or Objective	Responsibility	Timing
Operations	1. & 5.	Implement new production skills evaluation and training process in all North American sites to support new product roll-out schedule.	Operations Training Dept.	Measured quarterly and achieved annually.
International	3.	Initiate formal performance of all personnel in new business initiation process across all International regions to measure readiness to achieve target net OI by year end.	International Operations	Design by end 1st qtr; implement within 2nd qtr; annualize results and audit end of 4th qtr.

E. Predictive Measurement

Today, many HR departments are engaged in some type of measurement. The problem is that most of them have not moved past measuring internal cost and quantity level. Typical metrics are cost, numbers hired and trained, ratios of HR staff to employees and HR budget benchmarks. These can be useful measures of HR efficiency; however, the numbers do not interest management because they focus on costly HR activities and not on value-adding business results.

Modern analytic tools and behavioral science methods support higher levels of analysis. For example, you can dig into your turnover rates and discover what is causing them to rise or fall. You can track the return on investment of many HR services from incentive pay plans and training offerings, to staffing, engagement, and retention strategies. These numbers address the issues that drive the current business operation. As such, they attract management's attention because they show value added.

The latest and most exciting measurements are the leading indicators and intangible metrics. These predict what is most likely to happen in important future events. With these data points, the C-level executives can strategize and invest with minimum risk. Given the volatile markets today and into the future, risk management is at the core of human capital investment. High degrees of success yesterday do not guarantee similar returns tomorrow.

Lagging and Leading Indicators

Most data generated by companies lag, reflecting past periods. Accounting, production, sales, customer service, and other factors including human resources regularly report on yesterday. While this information can be useful for review, it does not lead directly to the future, and extrapolating old data into the future is a risky business. To manage for tomorrow you need new metrics that are inherently predictive. We call these leading indicators.

A number of factors can be turned into leading indicators: Readiness, Capabilities, L&D Return on Investment, Loyalty, Culture, Leadership, Absenteeism, Innovation, Brand, Retention, Engagement, and Reputation. Note that most of these indicators are intangible. With experience, you learn to see patterns in data that are predictive of the future. Measures of management bench strength, or *readiness*, are certainly indications of the organization's ability to transition smoothly to new leadership tomorrow. This is why the HCM:21 model is referred to as

"Managing tomorrow, today." Likewise, employee opinions regarding their leaders have been shown to be valid signs of future retention or attrition. In addition, lagging indicators often can be reverse-engineered and turned into leading indicators. For example, metrics such as *absenteeism* and *retention* are predictive of future attrition and low productivity. Similarly, the practice of counting units of past performance is no longer sufficient; now you have to look over the horizon, using data that have predictive capability.

Metrics Evaluation

Instructions and Comments (E-1)

These are suggested topics for your development of relevant benchmarks, strategic initiatives, or corporate direction to facilitate predictive metrics. Evaluation should be made against SMART targets that clearly define proactive and positive movement from current status toward the

E-1. METRICS EVALUATION

	SMART TARGETS
A. Strategic-Level Metrics	
Revenue per FTE HCROI HCVA Brand Recognition Market Reputation R&D Spend	*Sample SMART Target:* "Achieve gross revenue of $250,000 per full-time equivalent employee (FTE) measured corporate-wide by year end 2008."
B. Operational Metrics	
Hiring Effectiveness Competitive Total Compensation Training & Development Retention & Commitment Management Tenure Key Worker Turnover	
C. Leading Indicators and Intangibles	
Leadership Culture Engagement Competency Readiness Succession Readiness Technology Innovation	

corporate future state outlined via this survey process. SMART targets are marked as S = Specific, M = Measurable, A = Actionable, R = Realistic, and T = Time-bounded.

F. Analytics

Business intelligence tools have been adopted by finance and marketing, but they are seldom applied to human capital management. With the HCM:21 model you can statistically analyze connections across various human capital functions and outcomes. In the past scanning, planning, processing, and measuring were distinct functions. Now, with alignment and integration as your foundation, you will find relationships hidden in the data. By applying various multivariate techniques you can see both inside and across functions.

In section C, Process Optimization, you saw the connections among sources, methods, and results. You can find similar connections between processes and the external/internal variables developed in the Strategic Scan (section A). For example, market factors such as a depressed economy focus management's concern on customer service so as to retain customers. Service incentives are developed (compensation), recruiting service-oriented people becomes an imperative (staffing), and training in customer service is required (development). When these responses are monitored, you are able to track the effects on customer retention, presumably leading to greater market share.

Likewise, across almost any human capital intervention, you should be able to find correlations with operational improvements (PIQS) in production, supply chain management, and customer service. Eventually, these correlations lead to cost reductions, shorter time to market, increased sales, higher gross margins, faster response time to customers, and quicker resolution of their problems.

Barriers to Achieving a New Human Capital Management Approach

The logic has always been there. Operationally, the barrier to HR change has been the weak alignment across functions—relationships that were either never truly established or quickly broke down. Also, within units, services have not been integrated well. Siloed subdivisions are inherently not only inefficient but also obscure natural connections and breed parochialism.

There is no longer any excuse for such operational failings. We have the knowledge of the behavioral sciences, as well as the statistical tools and computer power to link activities. With predictive management, you have a tested, practical, strategic model and operating system. Making connections, finding value, and calculating return on investment are simple operations with HCM:21. Figure A.4 illustrates the concept.

Changing the Game

Continually working on process improvements and making additional investments in disconnected software can only keep you far back in the pack. The only way to break out, take the lead, and drive top line growth

Figure A.4. Connections through statistical analysis.

is to come up with an entirely new way of managing human capital. You can change your pace and pass your competitors by adopting a new offensive strategy called HCM:21, a model and a strategy that have been adopted by companies around the world.

Index

About the Author

Jac Fitz-enz, Ph.D., is Founder and CEO of Human Capital Source. Dr. Jac is acknowledged worldwide as the father of human capital strategic analysis and measurement. He published the first human resources metrics in 1978, and he introduced benchmarking to HR in 1985. In 2007, he was cited as one of the top five "HR Management Gurus" by *HR World*, and the Society for Human Resource Management chose him as one of the fifty persons who, in the past fifty years, have "significantly changed what HR does and how it does it." In 2006, the International Association for Human Resources Information Management presented Dr. Jac with the Chairman's Award for Innovative Excellence in Information Management.

In June 2007, Jac Fitz-enz organized a group of twenty companies to build Predictive Management: HCM:21, a model that aligns, integrates, and predicts the effects of HR services on organizational performance, using human resources analytics to generate leading indicators and measures of intangibles.

Dr. Fitz-enz has published eleven books and nearly 300 articles, reports, and book chapters on measurement and strategic management. He has trained more than 85,000 managers in forty-five countries. His column "Leading Edge" appears monthly in the journal *Talent Management*.

E-mail: source@netgate.net, website: www.humancapitalsource.com

31901047153491